Debating Surrogacy

DEBATING ETHICS

General Editor
Christopher Heath Wellman
Washington University of St. Louis

Debating Ethics is a series of volumes in which leading scholars defend opposing views on timely ethical questions and core theoretical issues in contemporary moral, political, and legal philosophy.

Debating the Ethics of Immigration
Is There a Right to Exclude?
Christopher Heath Wellman and Philip Cole

Debating Brain Drain
May Governments Restrict Emigration?
Gillian Brock and Michael Blake

Debating Procreation
Is It Wrong to Reproduce?
David Benatar and David Wasserman

Debating Climate Ethics
Stephen Gardiner and David Weisbach

Debating Gun Control: How Much Regulation Do We Need?
David DeGrazia and Lester H. Hunt

Debating Humanitarian Intervention: Should We Try to Save Strangers?
Fernando R. Tesón and Bas van der Vossen

Debating Pornography
Andrew Altman and Lori Watson

Debating Sex Work
Lori Watson and Jessica Flanigan

Debating Surrogacy
Anca Gheaus and Christine Straehle

Debating Surrogacy

ANCA GHEAUS & CHRISTINE STRAEHLE

OXFORD
UNIVERSITY PRESS

OXFORD
UNIVERSITY PRESS

Oxford University Press is a department of the University of Oxford. It furthers
the University's objective of excellence in research, scholarship, and education
by publishing worldwide. Oxford is a registered trade mark of Oxford University
Press in the UK and certain other countries.

Published in the United States of America by Oxford University Press
198 Madison Avenue, New York, NY 10016, United States of America.

CIP data is on file at the Library of Congress

ISBN 978–0–19–007217–9 (pbk.)
ISBN 978–0–19–007216–2 (hbk.)

DOI: 10.1093/oso/9780190072162.001.0001

Paperback printed by Marquis Book Printing, Canada
Hardback printed by Bridgeport National Bindery, Inc., United States of America

Contents

PART I

Acknowledgements

All books are collaborative efforts. Ours has two authors, and many to whom both authors are indebted. We would like to thank the audiences and commentators at two manuscript workshops, one online organized from Bern by Sabine Hohl and Anna Goppel, and one in Louvain-la-Neuve, organized by Axel Gosseries and Manuel Valente. Commentaries were provided by Teresa Baron, Alain Loute, Tim Meijers, and Cleo Salion. We are very grateful for these opportunities and the helpful feedback.

Anca Gheaus is also grateful to Teresa Baron, Zlata Bozac, Paula Casal, Matthew Clayton, Andree-Anne Cormier, Daniela Cutas, Axel Gosseries, Sabine Hohl, Connor Kianpour, R. J. Leland, Erik Magnusson, Tim Meijers, David O'Brien, Serena Olsaretti, Gregory Ponthiere, Riccardo Spotorno, and Isabella Trifan for discussions about the issues at stake in the book, or written comments on previous drafts, or both. She dedicates this book to Jens.

Christine Straehle would also like to thank Costanza Porro and Oliver Hallich for valuable comments. Her interest in surrogacy was prompted by a workshop co-organized with Vida Panitch at the University of Ottawa and Carleton University, and thanks are due to Vida for getting her going on the topic. Particular thanks are also due to Christine Overall, whose work on surrogacy has provided intellectual companionship.

Special thanks to David Archard, Colin MacLeod, and Adam Swift, who read the entire manuscript and met twice with us to discuss it. Finally, the authors would like to extend particular thanks to Kit Wellman for his interest in the book and his enthusiasm for the final manuscript, and to Lucy Randall, our editor at Oxford University Press, for her unfailing patience and support.

Introduction

Anca Gheaus and Christine Straehle

People have always used surrogacy—that is, the commissioning of a woman to gestate and give birth to a child for another would-be parent. Traditionally, this involved surrogates being (willingly or not) impregnated by the intending father through sexual intercourse. New reproductive technologies have made possible a new form of surrogacy, which has, over the past four decades, become an increasingly widespread practice. Nowadays, surrogacy usually has at least some commercial aspect and involves women consenting to carry babies for other people, sometimes conceiving with their own gametes, but more often than not using gametes obtained from the people who plan to raise the child, or by third parties.

Just as it is becoming more prominent, surrogacy also proves to be extremely controversial. As we explain, the practice raises several ethical questions, both in itself and in the highly international context in which it is used today. Our book is concerned with the legitimacy of the practice, at least in an ideal form. Its main question is whether surrogacy is or can be legitimate, as a procreative practice, as well as a way of becoming a custodian. In answering these questions, the discussion concentrates on two main issues, which bear on the justifiability of surrogacy:

(1) Whether providing gestational services is a permissible way of employing women's bodies—indeed, whether it is a legitimate form of work; and

Debating Surrogacy. Anca Gheaus and Christine Straehle, Oxford University Press.
© Oxford University Press 2024. DOI: 10.1093/oso/9780190072162.003.0001

(2) Whether the children born out of surrogacy are in any way wronged by surrogacy agreements.

Christine Straehle proposes an account of surrogacy work as legitimate work for women, as a way to realize certain goals in women's lives through the fruit of their labour, literally and figuratively. Anca Gheaus believes that gestating for another could in principle be defended as within a woman's legitimate choice over how to employ her body, but that the private nature of current surrogacy, or of a reformed practice like the one defended by Straehle, makes it impermissible.

We also disagree with respect to the second question: Christine Straehle doesn't think that children are necessarily wronged by the practice of surrogacy, most notably, because she conceives of surrogacy as just one way to employ new reproductive technologies. Surrogacy is often chosen by the future parents after a long and arduous process of trying to conceive through other means. The intention to bring a child into the world is thus the same as with other ways of conceiving children. Anca Gheaus criticizes surrogacy by arguing that it always wrongs children—whether or not it also harms them— by disrespecting them. But since she doesn't deny that, under certain conditions, women may gestate without the intention to have custody over the newborn, she is open to some kind of post-surrogacy practice that would radically depart, in the allocation of legal parenthood, from any historical or currently proposed form of surrogacy. Here, we briefly introduce the reader to the basic facts and terminology of the book, to provide a sense of the diversity of current legislation concerning surrogacy and its current practices. We also review why surrogacy raises difficult ethical problems. Finally, we sketch the positions we defend in the book, making explicit their dialectic.

Surrogacy Defined

The practice of surrogacy involves a woman who gestates a child without the intention of raising her as her own, and with the intention that other people become the child's custodians; the latter's intention to parent the child predates the pregnancy and provides its motivation. This definition of surrogacy is meant to be strictly descriptive. In her chapter, Gheaus argues that surrogacy should be understood as an *attempted* transfer, privately agreed upon, of the moral right to parent; as we shall see, some contest that this model adequately captures what happens in surrogacy agreements.

In this book, Straehle calls the gestating woman "the surrogate" and Gheaus calls her "the surrogate mother." The people who aim to become the custodians of the child are called by Straehle "the commissioning parents," and both Straehle and Gheaus call them "the intending parents" or "the intending couple." Gheaus sometimes refers to "couples" for the sake of simplicity and, in some contexts, for precision, but with no intention to suggest that civil status, monogamy, or sexual orientation makes any moral difference to qualifying for custody.

One important distinction as far as types of surrogacy are concerned is between commercial surrogacy and altruistic surrogacy. Surrogacy takes a commercial form when the surrogate engages in gestation partly or entirely for the sake of financial gain—that is, when intending parents pay her above and beyond proper compensation for the costs of the necessary healthcare during pregnancy and of giving birth. In altruistic surrogacy, by contrast, surrogates gestate merely for reasons of beneficence, most typically because they want to help infertile people, often their own relatives, to become parents. The distinction between altruistic surrogacy and commercial surrogacy is central to the chapter by Straehle, who wants to defend commercial surrogacy, in part, by also tackling the main criticisms that have been levelled at it. Gheaus's criticism, by contrast, is aimed equally at altruistic surrogacy and commercial surrogacy.

Another important distinction concerns the surrogate's genetic contribution: in traditional forms of surrogacy, sometimes also called "partial surrogacy," the surrogate not only gestates the child, but is also one of its genetic parents. Indeed, all surrogacy was like this before in vitro reproduction became available; the other gamete sometimes came from the surrogate's spouse, and sometimes from the intending father. While traditional surrogacy still exists, it is increasingly displaced, with the help of technology, by gestational surrogacy—also known as "full surrogacy"—in which the surrogate has no genetic contribution. In such cases, both gametes can come from the people who plan to gain the custody of the child, but it is also possible to use an egg donated by, or purchased from, a third party. Indeed, some gestational surrogacy uses double donation, when neither of the intending parents use their own gametes but, instead, procure them from others. We assume that the selling or donating of one's gametes is permissible. Gheaus, however, believes that gamete ownership does not in itself entail any rights over, or in relation to, the child who may develop from those gametes, and this is a central piece of her account of the impermissibility of surrogacy. These distinctions are less salient in Straehle's chapter—which assumes gestational surrogacy as the norm—than in Gheaus's. For Straehle, the genetic relationship between the intending parents and the child becomes important in her answer to Gheaus. Gheaus argues that traditional, or partial, surrogacy and gestational, or full, surrogacy, lend themselves to different normative analyses because, in her view, the former but not necessarily the latter is always akin to private adoption.

A final term to be clarified, especially given its different use by Straehle and Gheaus, is "biological parents." Straehle uses it to refer to the genetic parents only. As Gheaus understands it here, biological parenthood can be either gestational or genetic. Thus, a child born through gestation can have three biological parents.[1] The possibility to separate, in practice, the genetic and gestational aspects of the relationship between a gestating woman and the (future) child, requires a normative analysis of the gestational connection in its own right. Some interesting lessons can be learned by looking at its significance. Straehle believes that a genetic link is a good indicator of who should have custodial rights, hence her choice to identify genetic gametes donors as "parents." Gheaus argues instead that both genetic and gestational kinds of biological connections between adults and children are widely believed to have normative relevance to the justification of custody, but not necessarily in the same way, and so the distinction is important to her argument; this explains her use of "biological parents" as either genetic or gestational. At this point, the reader may wonder about the point of using different terms to refer to the same thing (when referring to the woman who carries the baby) and of using the same term to refer to different things (as is the case with "biological parenthood"). When it comes to surrogacy, much of the language is normatively laden. For instance, participants in the surrogacy debate are likely to use "the surrogate mother" to refer to the gestating woman when they assume that her gestational connection to the baby has some implications for her potential claiming of custody; whereas those who deny any moral relevance of gestation to custody sometimes call her "surrogate."[2] Thus, Straehle never uses the term "surrogate mother," while Gheaus does. Similarly, critics of surrogacy who think it akin to child trafficking sometimes refer to intending parents as "baby buyers." Defenders who, like Straehle, think it permissible to commission a surrogate prefer the term "commissioning parents." Gheaus, who claims that custody over children can never be legitimately acquired by commission, sticks to "intending parents" to signal her belief that one cannot commission children, an expression that Straehle also uses at times, especially when talking about the ideational relationship intending parents have built with the child. The fact that normative disagreements are reflected to such an extent by the language used to talk about surrogacy indicates their depth: parties to the debate diverge even in what they believe to take place in surrogacy, ethically speaking. Part of this book's contribution is to make explicit different ways of conceiving surrogacy: as a form of labour in which some people commission the services of the surrogate, according to Straehle, and as an illicit attempt to transfer the moral right to parent, according to Gheaus. In this introduction we employ the least normatively laden terms—*surrogate, intending parents,* and *biological parents*—to refer to any kind of biological connection to the child.

Surrogacy and the Law

As an occasional practice, surrogacy has an old history. The story of the biblical couple Sarah and Abraham is a tale of surrogacy. Since the two could not conceive, but wanted children, Sarah asked her servant Hagar to conceive and carry Abraham's child, who was then raised as Sarah and Abraham's son.[3] But the first modern legal surrogacy agreement was made in 1976—a traditional, and uncompensated, instance of surrogacy.[4] The practice started to become notorious, and highly controversial, through the case of Baby M, born in 1984 as a result of Bill and Betsy Stern having hired Mary Beth Whitehead to be their surrogate. The Sterns paid Whitehead, who was also Baby M's genetic mother, USD 10,000; but upon the child's birth, Whitehead refused to release custody, and long-lasting legal battles ensued. Eventually, Bill Stern gained custody as Baby M's genetic father, and Whitehead received visitation rights.[5] Over the past decades, surrogacy has been rapidly growing: for instance, in the United States, between 1999 and 2013 gestational surrogacy increased 2.5-fold.[6] It is difficult, if at all possible, to obtain reliable data about the surrogacy phenomenon, not least because the legal situation is uneven worldwide and, in some places, is quickly changing. At time of writing, in 2022, some countries, including France, Germany, Iceland, and Sweden, have outright bans on surrogacy. However, the demand to change legislation is felt by governments in the face of dramatically evolving reproductive technologies. The German government, for instance, is planning to change the "Law for the Protection of Embryos" to possibly allow altruistic surrogacy.[7] If implemented, this would be a dramatic shift in a legal landscape that so far has been among the most restrictive reproduction laws in the world. Where it is legal, surrogacy is regulated in a variety of ways with respect to its commercial aspects, the allocation of custody, and the types of intending parents who are eligible. In the United States, for instance, there is no federal regulation, and different states have different legislation. Some states, including England, Canada, India, Ireland, Portugal, and South Africa, only admit altruistic surrogacy—and in some places, such as the State of Michigan in the United States, those who engage in any commercial form of surrogacy risk a prison sentence of up to five years and a USD 50,000 fine.[8] The federal government in Canada, again, at time of writing, has been considering a revision of the federal laws governing surrogacy to assess what expenses can be claimed in the course of surrogacy agreements. Similarly, the government of the United Kingdom is revisiting the Human Embryo and Fertility Act, and a new draft of the Surrogacy Bill was released in 2023. Where commercial surrogacy is legal, surrogates' fees vary widely. In some countries, the law recognizes those who enter contracts with a would-be surrogate as the legal parents of the newborn. In Ukraine, which has developed into a hub for many surrogacy agreements, the intending parents are immediately recognized as the parents of the child. In California and some other US states, intending parents can get a prebirth order that allows them to be recognized as the parents of the child at birth. Otherwise, they will have to obtain a post-birth order to claim parenthood. In other places, such as the United Kingdom, the surrogate is recognized as the legal mother at birth, and her husband or wife (if she is married) is the other legal parent.[9] Intending parents can only gain custody if they apply for, and are granted, a parental order. If parents in the United Kingdom want to bring a child born outside the UK to the UK, they have to request a UK travel document. Being able to get such a document requires that they are recognized as the parents, which explains the attractiveness to intending parents of countries that recognize them as parents at birth.

In some of the places where it is legal, surrogacy is only open to infertile, married, heterosexual couples—for example, in India, but only for Indian nationals; South Africa; and the US state of Louisiana. But other places have recently made surrogacy available to more people: in the UK, for instance, it has been available to single parents since 2019. And in some countries, gay couples can use it, for instance, in Ukraine or places that have no surrogacy legislation whatsoever, such as the State of Wyoming in the United States.

Given the outright bans on surrogacy that exist in some countries, and its unavailability in commercial form or for single people and gay couples in others, international surrogacy is a thriving phenomenon. Before 2018, when it started to enact its highly restrictive legislation, India was the world's largest surrogacy hub; at the moment of writing, it is, as noted, Ukraine. Fees in both countries were and are significantly lower than they are in the US states that have permissive legislation, and both countries therefore attract a significant number of international clients. Yet to date, there is no international regulation of surrogacy, and therefore the legal rights and duties of the parties involved are unclear. The internationalization of surrogacy practices, especially against the background of large global inequalities of money and power, raises significant normative problems. But surrogacy is ridden with such problems anyway.

Ethical Issues Surrounding Surrogacy

It is unsurprising that a practice whose main result is the creation of human beings, whose main motivation is bringing children into existence and acquiring custody of them—that is, moral and legal authority over them—and whose main tools are women's reproductive powers, should pose serious ethical issues.

Perhaps the most formidable charge against surrogacy is that it amounts to the selling and buying of babies[10] and child trafficking, since commerce in human beings is illegal on moral grounds. In this respect, surrogacy has been compared to children's slavery.[11] Thus, philosophers who seek to defend the practice in some form have primarily aimed at showing that surrogacy should count as one way of realizing the good of parenthood and does not involve selling children but, instead, merely paying for the service of surrogacy and selling rights over children—or, in altruistic cases, signing parental rights over for non-commercial reasons.[12] Gheaus, whose thesis is that surrogacy is illegitimate for child-centred reasons, addresses this issue and argues that (an attempt to) transfer parental rights at will, is, in fact, on a moral par with selling children.

A second, more complex set of moral questions fundamental to surrogacy concerns the would-be surrogates. Some criticize surrogacy on the grounds that gestating for others is not a morally permissible form of employing one's body, because it is unavoidably alienating. If so, it cannot be legitimate work. In this respect, surrogacy has been compared to prostitution.[13] Straehle addresses this criticism in much of her initial chapter, arguing instead that professional surrogacy should be allowed if a woman chooses to work as a surrogate in a free and non-coerced way. Surrogacy, in her view, is a profession that allows women to realize goals in their lives just as other professions do. Further, some feminists criticize surrogacy because it requires women who gestate to distance themselves emotionally from the baby.[14] Based on empirical research, Straehle resists this claim, too, suggesting that it is indebted to a particular kind of biological determinism. Gheaus, on the other hand, subscribes to this particular criticism, and takes it as one reason for ensuring that surrogates have at least visitation rights in any post-surrogacy practice. Besides these foundational ethical questions that surround *any* surrogacy practice, there are further debates about specific surrogacy arrangements that present, at least in principle, more tractable questions. We thoroughly addresses some of these questions as they pertain to our individual arguments; we engage less with others, but we mention them below, with references, in order to provide a comprehensive account of the normative landscape of surrogacy.

In its historical form, surrogates have often come from vulnerable economic and educational backgrounds. The vast power differential between the parties involved naturally raises the issues of domination and exploitation in surrogacy.[15] Not only are surrogates sometimes coerced by poverty, but once they sign a surrogacy contract, they put their body at the disposition of their clients around the clock and for a significant period of time, with no off-shifts, weekends, or holidays. For these reasons, surrogacy has been compared to women's slavery.[16] Gheaus, who is critical of surrogacy for the fundamental reasons sketched above, doesn't discuss surrogates' exploitation and domination—rather, she assumes that any legitimate form of gestation for others should avoid them. But Straehle, who defends a properly regulated form of surrogacy considers the question of what it would take for surrogacy to be non-exploitative. A central problem here is what kind of remuneration is owed to surrogates if they are to avoid exploitation. If surrogacy is work, it is of an unusual kind due to the fact that preparing the body for a pregnancy, achieving the pregnancy, carrying the baby to term, and giving birth is a very long, round-the-clock process; moreover, it involves significant health hazards and opportunity costs. Straehle briefly addresses this issue, as well, and argues for a system of remuneration based on a minimum hourly wage for twenty-four hours a day, and for the whole length of treatment and pregnancy, at least ten months. Finally, a non-exploitative and non-dominating kind of surrogacy would presumably also be one in which women are not psychologically pressured to accept gestating for others by social expectations about their femininity—or, in the case of altruistic surrogacy, by the relatives or friends for whom they gestate. In social worlds that associate femininity with care in general, and maternity in particular, this is a challenge.

Another normative question with a significant bearing on the shape of any ethical form of surrogacy regards the way in which people acquire the moral right to parent a particular child. In this context, it concerns the significance, if any, that biological connections have to the moral basis of custody. This, of course, is a large and much-debated issue beyond discussions about surrogacy. One account of acquiring the moral right to parent singles out intention as the relevant criterion.[17] But in existing practices and legislations, intention alone is never a ground for claiming custody; this is given, by default, to the biological parents. Since genetic and gestational connections do not always go together, the question is which, if any, has more moral weight. Legislations across the world differ in this respect: in the United Kingdom, a birth mother is always a legal custodian. Not so in the United States, which is generally more favourable to taking genetic connections as the most relevant.[18] Gheaus discusses this issue, arguing that the gestational connection is a better proxy than the genetic one for what matters morally: improving the chances that newborns will enjoy a loving attachment to their parents. But she thinks that none of these proxies are perfect, hence the moral right to raise a particular child may be held by people with no biological relationship to that child.

Two particularly pressing problems in current surrogacy practices that we do not discuss comprehensively, but which are too important not to at least flag concern the fate of children born out of surrogacy. The first is about the rights of children and, especially, their right to a parent. As one is occasionally reminded by scandals that break out in relation to international surrogacy in particular, the intending parents sometimes refuse to claim custody—for instance, when the newborn has disabilities. A full defence of surrogacy, or of post-surrogacy practices, would have to explain who has parental duties, as well as parental rights, over these children. Do intending parents owe them parental care or do they owe them at least, to ensure that some individual or state is in charge of their fates? In cases of international surrogacy, do intending parents have a duty to at least accept legal responsibilities towards the children, and then put them up for adoption—for instance, in their own country of citizenship? Do surrogates themselves have any special moral duties towards the children—and which? The UK legislation, which is generally seen as surrogate-friendly, has the implication that the birth mother, as the default legal parent, incurs unexpected duties if the intending parents default on the agreement. How about the states that have overseen the surrogacy process; do *they* have special duties towards the newborn? Straehle argues in her part that states should oversee and regulate surrogacy agreements, and indeed, accept the responsibility for children left behind when the agreements are breached.

The other problem has to do with the prevention of child abuse and neglect by intending parents. This is, of course, a mere subset of the general issue of preventing the mistreatment of children by their parents, but in the case of surrogacy, it is perhaps more tractable, as we will explain.

The philosophical difficulty it raises is that people are not required to obtain a license to become biological parents, and at least in some cases, the intending parents in surrogacy are also genetic parents. Should states that permit surrogacy make an exception to this practice, and introduce a licensing requirement for parents who use surrogacy—or who use assisted reproduction in general— as some have argued?[19] A powerful consideration in favour of doing so is that permissible implementation seems a lot easier than in the case of non-technologically assisted parenthood: people failing to gain a parental license would simply be refused technological assistance, rather than asked to interrupt a pregnancy or to put the newborn up for adoption. However, in light of Straehle's account that justifies professional surrogacy, in part for egalitarian reasons, this seems problematic: if surrogacy is one way to help people realize their wishes to raise children, and possibly to compensate some for the bad luck of not being able to do so on their own, licensing some but not others adds injury to insult.

The Book

To conclude, let us present the general structure of the book. In Part I, Straehle presents a defence of surrogacy as a kind of work that advances women's autonomy by providing an opportunity to achieve individual self-realization and self-respect. Straehle explains that the argument is based on two premises: first, that individuals should be able to employ their bodies according to their own, nonharmful wishes; and second, that doing so provides the basis for individual autonomy. She then discusses possible objections to surrogacy— namely, that it harms others, and, indeed, the individual women hoping to work as surrogates—engaging with the critics of surrogacy along the way. In the section 4 of Part I, Straehle discusses the kind of regulated surrogacy labour that would protect the interests of individual women working as surrogates, and also the interests of intending parents. Importantly, part of this discussion also engages with the vexing issue of when termination may be warranted; here, Straehle suggests that the interests of the surrogate need to be weighed against the interests of intending parents.

The second part of Part I is Gheaus's criticism of surrogacy as an impermissible practice. Her argument is that children's interests are as morally weighty as those of adults, and hence, authority over them must be justified by appeal to their well-being, and not by appeal to how important it is for adults to hold such authority. The moral right to parent is held by the willing adult(s) whose possession of the right is in the child's best interest. If so, the moral right to parent is a privilege that adults hold on child-centred grounds, and which is therefore not theirs to alienate at will. If custody, and the grounds for holding it, can neither be sold nor gifted, then nobody can permissibly commission surrogacy work. Gheaus also notes that being the genetic or gestational parent of a child might make one, all things considered, more likely to be the best available parent for that child, and that the gestational connection is a better (albeit imperfect) such indicator. She leaves open the possibility of a permissible practice of gestating for others in which intending parents—especially when they are also the genetic ones—have good prospects to obtain custody, but no guarantees. Surrogacy, as we have it, is a private business between a few individuals—and this, according to Gheaus is not how authority over (vulnerable!) human beings should be allocated—but a different, non-private and legitimate practice is at least imaginable.

Straehle answers Gheaus in her contribution to Part II. Straehle discusses Gheaus's account of the interests of children, which Gheaus divides into *respect interests* and *well-being interests*, and argues that part of the respect interest of children is to develop their capacity for autonomy. For this, Straehle sustains, children need to have stable relationships that provide them with the possibility to be carefree. In this view, the social, genetic, and temporal relationship the intending parents have already established with the child warrants their being granted custody rights. Gheaus's answer to Straehle is her contribution to Part II. Her main objection is that Straehle's defence of surrogacy disregards children's moral status (for the reasons explained in Gheaus's main chapter) and also fails to do justice to the women who serve as surrogates: it either devalues or discourages the potential bonds created during pregnancy between surrogate mother and child; it requires surrogates to enter extraordinarily constricting labour contracts; and it wrongfully restricts the access of the surrogate to the child she carried.

PART I

Defending Surrogacy
as Reproductive Labour

Christine Straehle

Introduction

Surrogacy has become a mainstay of reproductive technologies in
our times. Yet surrogacy is probably also one of the most debated
reproductive technologies. Supporters of surrogacy propose that it
is one of the few ways that otherwise biologically childless couples
have of conceiving biologically related children, that it makes it
possible for homosexual couples to have biologically related children, and that it allows couples affected by illness to have biologically related children. In what follows, I will use "biological" in
the most commonly used sense, as it is also defined in the *Oxford
English Dictionary* when applied to individuals "as related by blood
or genetically." Opponents of surrogacy see it as one of the last
instantiations of the exploitation and commodification of the female body, of the child, and, for the cases of international surrogacy, of fundamental global inequalities, with surrogates coming
from poor countries, whereas intending parents come from rich
ones. Moreover, news stories of abandoned children born through
surrogacy, of surrogates who want to hold on to the children they
have borne, or of commissioning parents who change their minds
have made it such that surrogacy has become a political and ethical topic. Surrogacy has been put to national political and populist
uses, such as when the Indian government prohibited commercial

Debating Surrogacy. Anca Gheaus and Christine Straehle, Oxford University Press.
© Oxford University Press 2024. DOI: 10.1093/oso/9780190072162.003.0002

surrogacy contracts for non-Indian nationals and only allowed altruistic, non-paid surrogacy for heterosexual Indian couples. Similarly, surrogacy is encouraged and highly advertised in Israel, where rabbis arrange for willing surrogates to meet hopeful parents, yet only on an altruistic level, and not across religious lines.

My contribution to Part I of this book, will be to argue that remunerated surrogacy should be allowed. I call this *surrogacy work*. The core of my positive argument is built on three parts: (1) working as a surrogate is a legitimate employment of a woman's body for labour; (2) surrogacy when properly codified in (international) private law can serve as a means for women surrogates to realize important goals in their lives; and (3) surrogacy creates a life and helps couples who are unable to have biological children to become and be parents of biological children. In my view, surrogacy, including paid surrogacy, is worth protecting as a possible way to have children, and as a way of employing a woman's body within a highly gendered and unjust world. Thus, my contribution to this volume is based on two premises: first, I start from the assumption that surrogacy is labour; the challenge is to show how this affects our understanding of surrogacy, and to defend it as the kind of professional choice that is protected in liberal political philosophy.

My second premise suggests that surrogacy is an act of reproduction for the *commissioning* or *intending* parents, both terms I will use synonymously. I explain the analogy between biological parents and surrogacy for commissioning parents in section 4, in response to many critics. Both are the intentional and social parents, and in the case of gestational surrogacy, they are also the biological, genetic parents. For all intents and purposes, those who commission a child must therefore also count as parents. In this vein, surrogacy is on par with other reproductive technologies in that it allows those who are not able to conceive biological children of their own to have access to the good of rearing biological children. A further aspect of the premise is that surrogacy is a means for individuals to create a good—namely, that of a desired life. Most commonly, we accept the right of heterosexual couples to have children if they so wish. The arguments for having children have been well explained and analyzed in the philosophy of childhood, and will be reviewed in Anca Gheaus's contribution in Part I. I suggest that the protection of the good of parenthood should be extended to those whose children are born through surrogacy arrangements. If we accept parenthood as an important goal that many may have in their lives, and if surrogacy is accepted as one way to realize this goal, then, I suggest, this should count in favour of defending surrogacy. As Part II of this volume will illustrate, however, this may not be sufficient as an argument in support of surrogacy, since Gheaus argues that the commissioning of children by private citizens wrongs the interests of children. Thus, even though surrogacy is an act of reproduction for the commissioning parents, one could argue that it should nevertheless be prohibited to avert wronging the children born through surrogacy arrangements. I will respond to this charge in Part II.

My first argument establishes the freedom of occupational choice argument that underlies my position for surrogacy as work: I begin by explaining why freedom of occupational choice is an important aspect of many accounts of individual autonomy and self-determination. Professional choice oftentimes helps individuals to realize cherished ideas about themselves; it helps us to present ourselves to the world in the way we may wish to. In this vein, I explain that accounts of individual surrogates who take pride in helping otherwise childless couples are plausible and convincing descriptions of surrogacy work as self-constituting. Surrogacy *as work* provides surrogates with the kind of acknowledgement in interaction with others that supports their individual autonomy. In the final step, I argue that surrogacy should count as reproductive labour in the context of private law—that is, the context in which two parties to a contract can agree on the services a surrogate shall render to the commissioning parents, and on the kind of remuneration that these services would warrant, and what would be appropriate to compensation for them. Put differently, I suggest that individual women should have the right to employ their bodies for reproductive labour as a contractual right. To realize and protect the interests this interpretation of surrogacy work has as its basis— namely, that of freedom of professional occupation—the state's obligation is, first and foremost, to not prohibit commercial surrogacy, but instead, to frame it in contractual law, thereby stipulating what forms surrogacy contracts can take.[1]

Commercial surrogacy often raises the spectre of commercialization. Many critics have cautioned against allowing commercial surrogacy based on the fear that the kinds of contract entered would lead to a commercialization of children or of the surrogate's body or both. The fear is that such a market would introduce incentives into reproduction that it would be best to exclude for fear of lessening the worth of human life. Alternatively, some critics have suggested that the worry is not necessarily the commercialization of human life, but instead the commercialization of the act of childbearing. If childbearing were to become a market-driven activity, which my account of surrogacy work as reproductive work may suggest, societies would introduce market norms to childbearing where, instead, parental or family norms should reign. Finally, the fear is that commercial surrogacy would possibly wrong individual children or, at least, the wellbeing interests of children. I won't respond to this last worry here; I will address Gheaus's argument that commissioning children potentially wrongs them in Part II.

The worry about the commercialization of childbearing is an important one to address for my account, though. I begin my response with an argument for the value of surrogacy work as a means to realize important goals in the surrogate's life. I suggest that employing one's body to work as a surrogate should count as a legitimate means of providing for oneself and one's family. As part of this discussion, I examine recent accounts of surrogacy leading to the further exploitation and subjection of women, most problematically in the Global South. The worry is that women are now asked to work as surrogates against their will, based on the fact that women can carry children, and thus can potentially work as surrogates, and that surrogacy work provides great financial gains compared to other modes of work. The worry is that some offers are too good to be refused and may therefore lead to more danger of exploitation. More problematically still, some critics fear that commercial surrogacy in the unjust and gendered world we live in will be used as another way to sexually exploit women. A final concern is that in this unjust world, women from the Global South will be exploited not only domestically but also internationally. From a feminist perspective, in particular, this is an important worry. I argue, instead, that the current lack of a framework for surrogacy work juxtaposed to the demand for surrogates raises these concerns more dramatically, which supports my suggestion to establish an international codification of surrogacy contracts.

However, the lack of a framework doesn't address some of the criticisms. An important one of these is that surrogacy harms some aspects of society. Philosopher Elizabeth Anderson has argued that in commercial surrogacy, market norms rather than parental or family norms are applied to reproduction and pregnancy. This, she suggests, is wrong since it deteriorates the social fabric. My contribution in section 3, is an exploration of the moral wrong Anderson describes. Is it indeed the case that reproduction and the creation of a family is a sphere of life exclusively dominated by family norms? My first response is to say that attributing the family to the private sphere *only* has been the subject of feminist criticism in political philosophy: the assumption that the family is a sphere of love and emotions rather than a sphere in which norms other than those of love and care should be applied has often been used against the interests of women. My second response is that relegating reproduction to the private sphere, devoid of market considerations, is implausible considering the sheer market value of much of current-day reproduction. I cite the example of the United States to show that reproduction is, indeed, now an industrial complex, much like other aspects of life. The reproductive-industrial complex in the United States has an estimated market value of US$3billion annually.[2] Moreover, I investigate whether applying market norms to reproduction and pregnancy is qualitatively different than applying such norms to other forms of labour. This will be the second part of section 3: after arguing that surrogacy is reproduction, and hence, that as much as other reproduction, surrogacy provides commissioning parents with the good of parenthood, I will investigate whether the *circumstances* of reproduction may give grounds to prohibit surrogacy.

1. Surrogacy and Free Occupational Choice

1.1. Why Is Freedom of Occupational Choice Important in Liberal Theory?

If we believe in the right of all individuals to employ and dispose of their bodies freely, why should we put into question the right of a woman to employ her womb for surrogacy? The arguments against surrogacy as a contractual right that surrogates and hopeful parents should enjoy most often take the form of balancing the harms and goods the right may bear. The good worth protecting, on the one hand, may be the right of individual surrogates to be self-determining, to exercise jurisdiction over their own bodies, and to do so by entering into contractual relations with commissioning parents. Critics, on the other hand, offer a host of reasons why surrogacy work should be either restricted to altruistic surrogacy or prohibited entirely, particularly in arrangements between intentional parents in the developed rich world and intended surrogates in the developing world. The justification for prohibition most often offered is that of exploitation—the worry is that women would not agree to surrogacy arrangements if they weren't desperate, if they had other options for making ends meet. The argument from exploitation has a long pedigree in philosophical writing on surrogacy.[3] Against this trend, I want to suggest that paid surrogacy can be defended from the perspective of freedom of occupational choice. To be sure, some critics could argue that commercial surrogacy is inherently exploitative, independently of conditions and the ways in which it is carried out. I will return to the exploitation charge against surrogacy in section 2, when discussing the voluntariness of surrogacy work.

Many countries allow for altruistic surrogacy, including many countries in the EU and Canada, even though they don't allow for commercial surrogacy. Israel, for instance, officially endorses altruistic surrogacy, with Israeli society celebrating surrogates as giving a "gift" to otherwise childless couples, and the whole surrogacy process is overseen by government authorities.[4] Indeed, the Israeli high court recently decided that the existing surrogacy law needed to be changed to expand the protection of surrogacy arrangements, to provide single men and same-sex couples with access to surrogacy, and the restriction of surrogacy agreements to heterosexual couples was lifted on January 4, 2022.[5] Intending parents must apply for approval of their surrogacy agreement to the "foetus carriage agreements approval board," administered by the Israeli Ministry of Health, which decides whether or not individual surrogacy agreements can go forward.[6]

In contrast, *paid* or *commercial* surrogacy is most often what is at issue when critics disparage surrogacy arrangements. Commercial surrogacy is only allowed in a few countries, not including most countries of the European Union and Canada. The latter case is interesting: Canada, like the United Kingdom, regulates altruistic surrogacy arrangements through private law; and contracts abound in which surrogates and intending parents stipulate what kinds of expenses surrogates can request reimbursement for. These range from the obvious, such as health appointments, to massages and other services during pregnancy.[7] So, while payment for the reproductive labour is not allowed, or payment for "the product" of the labour, compensation for hardship is.[8]

We can surmise, then, that surrogacy per se, the act of carrying and bearing somebody else's child, is not at issue—unless we take the perspective of the potential harm that many assume will come to "the product" of surrogacy arrangements.[9] In this vein, one way to argue against surrogacy is to say that it is not labour or, at least, not only labour, since the "product" of surrogacy arrangements are children. In this part, I will focus on the fact that surrogates employ their bodies in exchange for remuneration, leaving aside the moral challenges that the product of their labour raises. For the purposes of my discussion in this part, I assume that surrogacy work provides a service. The moral status of "the product" and the possible limits it imposes on surrogacy work will be subject of my response to Anca Gheaus in Part II. I will also focus on gestational surrogacy arrangements, in which the surrogate is not genetically related to the child born. Gestational surrogacy is now the prevalent model of commercial surrogacy arrangements.[10]

As a rejoinder to those who believe that we should ban all, but especially commercial, international[11] surrogacy work (compared to "altruistic" surrogacy arrangements, say) I want to defend commercial surrogacy arrangements as a form of work that women can choose. I will contextualize the freedom as grounded in two concerns dear to liberal hearts: the concern to protect conditions for *individual autonomy*, and the concern to provide the means of *individual self-realization and the basis of self-respect*. I will follow this with an assessment of the kinds of limits on professional choice that liberal democracies typically accept, such as minimum-wage restrictions and the prohibition against selling oneself into slavery. These are standard limits that liberal societies set against the freedom of occupational choice, and I will explain how liberal democracies have justified such limits. I then assess whether we can use the same justifications when thinking about limiting or prohibiting commercial surrogacy work. Based on this discussion, I will argue that surrogacy contracts should be carefully regulated, akin to the regulations societies regularly impose on the exercise of certain other professions—but that it is not clear how we could justify prohibiting surrogacy work. I will explore what form the regulation should take in section 4 of this part I of the book.

1.2. Two Justifications for the Right to Freedom of Occupational Choice

We normally don't ask people their motives for choosing one profession over another. We may sometimes wonder at people's choices, but most often, liberal democratic societies respect that choosing a profession freely is a right that citizens should enjoy. In other words, liberal democratic states accept the right of their citizens to occupational freedom, and this freedom is normally taken to warrant the protection of the state.

Here a distinction may be in order. Rights as I construe them can be assessed according to what interests they aim to protect, and what claims they may entitle their holders to make. In a second step, these claims may be divided into two different categories: on the one hand, some rights give rise to positive claims against others, and often the state, to help realize the right in question; on the other hand, some rights simply entitle their holders to negative claims against others, which is to say that the rights holder can ask not to be interfered with when exercising the right. It should also be noted that it is not the case that important interests always warrant positive claims; at least in some interpretations, all that is needed is the absence of interference for the interest to be protected. In other words, claims need to be assessed from a perspective of the implementation of the right. When assessing the claims a right may generate, we need to ask what is necessary for the realization and protection of the interest at stake. To illustrate, think of the right to the bases of individual autonomy that many liberals hold dear, and which will be important for my assessment of the right to work in surrogacy. Some commentators argue that the interest at stake is to be able to shape our lives as much as possible according to our own choices.[12] Now, some argue that the claim resulting from a right to the bases of individual autonomy is simply to be free from undue interference, what we normally refer to as the *postulate of negative freedom*.[13] Others, however, argue that negative freedom is not sufficient to effectively realize the interest of individual autonomy—instead, the state needs to provide us with a set of options amongst which we may choose, and which alone will enable us to take the kinds of decisions that characterize autonomous living.[14] Suffice it to note that the right to pursue an occupation, and the right to claim what is necessary to be able to choose it, can be construed as both a negative right and a positive right. In my defence of surrogacy work, I will appeal to the negative aspect of the right to freedom of occupation: individuals should be free from prohibition as much as reasonably possible when choosing an occupation.[15]

Indeed, the right to "freedom of occupational choice," or the "right to freedom of occupation," terms I use interchangeably, is entrenched in several liberal democratic constitutions. For example, article 19(3) of the Dutch constitution, on work, codifies that "the right of every Dutch national to a free choice of work shall be recognized, without prejudice to the restrictions laid down by or pursuant to Act of Parliament." Similarly, article 23 of the UN Declaration of Human Rights stipulates: "Everyone has the right to work, to free choice of employment, to just and favorable conditions of work and to protection against unemployment." This implies that if there are jobs on offer, if there is demand, and assuming that a person has the necessary qualifications and training, she should be free to engage in the kind of work that she chooses. Put otherwise, individuals should not be prohibited from choosing an occupation unless exercising it harms another. Of course, this raises the question of whether individuals should be free to "design," as it were, professions for themselves. I will discuss how we usually think of professions and occupations later on.

A (second) note on terminology: the principle "do no harm" is a fundamental precept of ethics. It applies in medical ethics, for example, to questions of how individual patients should be treated; in public health ethics, to questions of how public policies should be designed in order to prevent harm to individuals; and in reproductive ethics, when we discuss different reproductive technologies and their consequences for all the parties involved.

What precisely the harm in question *is*, however, is a matter for philosophical argument. Most people accept that the bodily integrity of individuals ought to be protected; otherwise, they will be harmed in direct, obvious, physical ways. Hence the restrictions on some choices that people may want to make but that would harm others in these very tangible ways, such as very strict restrictions in most liberal democracies on the ownership and use of firearms.

Individuals can also be harmed in other, less-tangible ways, though. For instance, most people accept that individuals have basic interests, such as access to means of subsistence, shelter, and safety. Such interests are the subject of much human rights legislation, which stipulates that all humans share some basic interests that should be protected and safeguarded. If basic interests are not protected, then individuals are harmed, as their pursuit and realization of their basic interests is thwarted. Finally, and importantly, many philosophers assume that to lead a decent life, humans need more than just the protection of their basic interests. Instead, they also have interests that pertain to *how* to lead a life. Thus, in order to lead a decent life, human beings should also have the possibility to shape the lives they lead, to think about the course that they want to give their lives. This is the domain of *individual autonomy and agency*. What is important to note at this point is that autonomy interests can also be harmed, just as basic interests such as bodily integrity can be.

When individuals cannot realize and protect either their basic interests or their autonomy interests, or both—for instance, if they can't protect themselves against bodily injury, or if they can't protect themselves against interference in their life plans—they are harmed. If we can identify an actor, metaphysical or actual, who is responsible for the harm, then that actor has committed a wrong: they have acted against "the basic principle of ethics that it is wrong to act in such a way that subjects others to serious and unnecessary but avoidable harm."[16]

We can thus say that freedom of occupational choice aims to allow individuals as much as possible to choose the profession they wish to engage in, while also preventing professions that could potentially harm others.[17] Note that there are some exceptions to this rule—conscription into the military, for instance, is a case in point. Philosophically, conscription falls under very specific rules that are stipulated in the idea that citizens have duties to support the liberal state since such a state establishes the institutional context that guarantees access to rights. The institutions of the rights-granting state are thus necessary for any citizen to have access to rights in the first place, including the right to occupational freedom. Any fundamental freedoms within the state can only be curtailed if such curtailing is necessary for the protection of the rights-granting state. In other words, a violation of the negative liberty against interference by the state in an individual's choice of a profession can only be justified if it is necessary to protect the state that grants negative liberties in the first place.[18] This is how we can justify military conscription: if the state comes under attack from a hostile aggressor, members of the state may have to forgo their freedom of professional choice in favour of a profession that protects the state.

But in general, liberal states should not interfere with individual choices when it comes to specific professions. This precept has a long history in liberal thought, and has been defended by John Rawls against the critique of G. A. Cohen that the realization of social justice may demand restricting the freedom of occupational choice.[19] Rawls instead argues: "Citizens have free choice of careers and occupations. There is no reason at all for the forced and central direction of labor."[20] Note that Rawls here describes both the

negative liberty to be free from interference in choosing one's profession and the positive liberty to be free to choose any profession.
This suggests that freedom should actually always be thought of
as triadic: "Such freedom is thus always *of* something (an agent or
agents), *from* something, *to* do (not do, become, not become) *z*."[21]
I will return to a discussion of what makes a choice free further
below, in section 2, where I explain that professional choices ought
to be voluntary and free from coercion if they are to support liberal
values. Suffice it to say at this point that all the liberal state *can* do is
incentivize citizens to choose one profession over another.

We may wonder, of course, why freedom of professional choice
should have such a high value in political and moral philosophy.
Why should it be considered a liberty right, rather than something
that is weighed against the needs of the community, say, as it was
in earlier times?[22] I want to distinguish two different arguments
that can be used to ground the right to freedom of occupational
choice:[23]

  (i) Arguments from individual autonomy and agency
  (ii) Arguments for a profession as a source of self-respect

(i) Arguments based on concerns over individual autonomy and
agency can take different forms. Here I am concerned with the link
between the conditions of individual autonomy and agency and the
idea that individuals should enjoy bodily self-ownership. Following
Joseph Raz, I construe *autonomy* in the first instance very minimally, as being able to be part author of one's life.[24] To have access
to the basis of autonomy, Raz suggests, individuals need access to
a range of viable options from which to choose freely, i.e, without
being coerced into choosing one option over another, and which
they can then adopt for themselves. We can say that if we are autonomous, we have a sense of self;—we know what we stand for and
what values we endorse. Individual *agency* denotes individual capacity to implement—as much as can be reasonably expected—the

autonomous decisions individuals have taken to give a course to their lives. Thus, I construe individual agency as the implementation and realization of autonomous decisions.

Philosophers of different ideological persuasions have argued that one important condition of individual autonomy and agency is individual *self-ownership*. Self-ownership arguments start from the premise that human beings must be entitled to dispose of their own *bodies* as they see fit if they are to be able to have individual autonomy:

> Were a person to be deprived of this control—were others to have the right to block or manipulate the movements of his physical body—then his agency would be truncated, and he would be incapable of using his powers of intention and action to make something he (and others) could regard as a life for himself.[25]

The link between self-ownership of the body and individual autonomy and agency seems intuitively plausible if we think of cases in which we doubt that a person has effective control over her body, and when we concomitantly assume that individuals can't have agency, or shouldn't be assumed to have it, for lack of control over their body. For example, most national medical systems don't allow patients with severe dementia to take end-of-life decisions even in those jurisdictions where such decisions are now legally permitted for reasons of terminal non-mental illness. The rationale is that the brain, an important element in the decision-making process, is affected by the disease, the patient is thus *not* in full possession of her body and her bodily capacities. We should therefore be wary of allowing her to take fundamental decisions for herself.

Similarly, those affected by psychological and mental disease have, for the longest time, been barred from taking end-of-life decisions since, again, the assumption being that the disease affects their command over their body, which suggests that whatever decision they would take would not qualify as an autonomous decision.[26] Joel Feinberg illustrates the problem with a discussion of the play *Whose Life Is It Anyway?* The play describes the case of a young sculptor who is paralyzed from the neck down from a spinal injury he received during a car accident. The sculptor demands to be allowed to die after having suffered for 6 months, yet he is told that "he is suffering from depression and is therefore 'incapable of making a rational decision about life and death.'"[27] In his response to the judges and the doctors, and employing the principle of habeas corpus, the patient's lawyer suggests that "[the sculptor] is reacting in a perfectly rational way to a very bad situation."[28] In other words, the demand to die is quite reasonable for the sculptor since his situation is unchanging, and so the argument of "temporary lack of capability" isn't applicable.

The point Feinberg wants to make, and which is worth underlining, is that preventing someone from disposing of her body, or his in the case of the sculptor, as they see fit after a reasonable deliberation as to the best course of action robs a person of one of the fundamental ingredients for the realization of individual autonomous choice, understood as the "right to decide how one is to live one's life, in particular how to make critical life-decisions."[29] At least the *possibility* of individual self-ownership, as the possibility to dispose and employ one's body for one's own purposes, is necessary for individual autonomy.

A note about self-ownership is warranted here: In much of political and moral philosophy, self-ownership arguments are considered to defend libertarian ideas. The locus classicus of the idea that individuals own their own bodies can be found in John Locke's *Second Treatise on Civil Government*, where Locke writes that "every man has a Property in his own Person. This nobody has a right to but himself."[30] In particular, libertarian philosopher Richard Nozick has suggested that only if we accept individual self-ownership rights can we support and uphold liberal ideas about individual autonomy. Self-ownership rights are then tied to having the means to be autonomous and to leading one's own life, as I discussed them in the example of the paraplegic sculptor, just above.[31]

G. A. Cohen has investigated Nozick's claims about self-ownership in a detailed analysis; in particular, Cohen investigates to what extent self-ownership is indeed seminal for individual autonomy.[32] Since I want to argue that surrogates should have the right to choose surrogacy as labour because surrogacy work can be an autonomously chosen way of employing their bodies, it is important to my argument whether or not there is indeed a link between self-ownership and the basis of individual autonomy. According to Cohen, there are two different interpretations of the self-ownership argument as proposed by Nozick: the first interpretation suggests that *full* self-ownership rights simply mean being able to lead one's own life. This, according to Cohen, is not plausible, and I concur: even those who do not enjoy self-ownership can lead lives, albeit miserable ones. Think here of the accounts of former slaves in the American South, for instance. Even those who can't dispose of their bodies as they wish can have hopes and dreams; they can have ideas about the course they would wish to be able to give their lives. They have access to some aspects of autonomy, such as being able to *imagine* lives they wish to live, even though they don't enjoy the full range of autonomy-enabling options, such as the possibility of implementing choices in their lives. Since, I suggested, agency to be the capacity to implement and realize as much as is reasonably possible one's own choices about life, slaves don't enjoy agency.

Similarly, as David Archard has convincingly argued, Feinberg's account is too maximizing, because it prevents a nuanced analysis of different kinds of trespasses as harms to autonomy. In particular, Archard suggests that we should understand self-ownership and individual autonomy as separate concepts, not as the latter building on the former: "[T]he ideal of bodily sovereignty [as Feinberg construes self-ownership] does not seem to play the right kind of role in justifying the exercise of personal choice."[33] I agree that in some instances, such as the one Archard discusses about consent in medical intervention, getting to the harm done to individuals in non-consensual contexts is more complex than simply insisting that either their autonomy has been violated or their self-ownership has been violated. However, I don't agree that self-ownership and autonomy are not intertwined. Take another case Archard discusses, that of rape. To be sure, *solely* understanding self-ownership as *property* over the body doesn't yield the appropriate assessment of the harm of rape: "[R]ape on this type of account is only wrong because what is one's own is 'borrowed' without your agreement. Yet *that* doesn't seem to capture the specific and enormous wrongfulness of rape."[34] But it seems that precisely the case of rape illustrates that self-ownership needs to be thought of as *enabling* autonomy. Without self-ownership as sovereignty, individual autonomy is hampered.

Thus, I follow Cohen in his argument that the more plausible interpretation than the full-fledged libertarian one suggests that self-ownership is *conducive* to the full range of autonomy, not synonymous with it. It is plausible to suggest that self-ownership *enables* the full extent of individual autonomy—"autonomy" being understood as "denot[ing] the range of a person's choice,"[35] and not a personality or character trait: "For autonomy, the range of choice you have in leading your life is a function of two things: the scope of your rights over yourself, with which it varies positively; and the rights of others over themselves and over things, with which it varies variously."[36] Or, to put it into the language I have used so far, it is plausible to say that self-ownership is one of the rights that individuals must have access to if they are also meant to be able to be implement the choices that they wish for in their lives.[37]

How does this relate to freedom of occupational choice? In its negative interpretation, as a principle that justifies freedom from interference, self-ownership rights demand the protection of the body from harmful interference by others.[38] Note that I don't subscribe to the notion of *full* self-ownership if it is understood as maximizing the control function of self-ownership arguments to provide "protections from unwanted uses of our bodies"; instead, I see the value of self-ownership arguments insofar as they hope to protect "individual liberties to use our bodies." I agree with those who argue that a maximizing interpretation would go against many reasonable duties of assistance that individuals have towards others, but that "[i]t's possible to weaken the principle . . . while holding on to the general spirit of the self-ownership view."[39]

Interpreting self-ownership rights thus positively, as rights that set out what individuals ought to be free to do with their bodies, self-ownership rights imply the permission of employing one's body for one's own purposes:

> To say that one's body is included in one's sovereign domain then, is to say more than that it cannot be treated in certain ways without one's consent. It is to say that one's consent is both necessary and *sufficient* for its rightful treatment in those ways. The concept of a discretionary competence implies both negative rights (e.g., the right *not* to have surgery imposed on oneself against one's will) and positive rights (e.g., the right to have surgery performed on oneself if one voluntarily chooses—and the surgeon is willing).[40]

This passage also suggests a distinction that is not often discussed in the literature on self-ownership—namely, that between it and individual self-determination. As I have suggested, following Cohen, self-*ownership* enables the full range of autonomy, including the possibility of implementing one's choices. Self-*determination*, though, is a possible consequence of self-ownership: individuals can be self-determining if they have self-ownership. The two are not synonymous but, rather, interdependent: self-ownership is a condition for self-determination. Self-determination is thus a concept closer to Raz's idea of self-authorship. If we are self-determining, we are authors of our own lives: The way I construe the relationship here, self-determination is the act of adopting, as much as reasonably possible, our autonomously chosen goals in life as part of our self. Self-determination is thus the *internal* aspect of acting on autonomous decisions; agency is the *outward* realization of autonomous choices.[41]

The important thing to note, in the context of my argument, is that from the perspective of self-ownership, women, like all human beings, should be free from interference in deciding how to employ their bodies as long as they do so without infringing on somebody else's rights. Put positively, women should be free to employ their bodies for any kind of non-harming labour they wish to carry out. No other condition besides their consent is necessary for the rightful use of one's body, all else being equal, that is, their consent being freely given, and there being individuals willing to commission them to engage in surrogacy.[42] If women freely consent to work as surrogates, they should be able to choose surrogacy work.

A further note is warranted, however; this one about individual consent. The assumption that consent makes decisions morally unproblematic has been widely criticized in moral and political philosophy, in particular, by feminist philosophers. Instead of taking consent as a guarantee and a marker of individual autonomy and agency, feminists have argued convincingly that other things need to be considered when assessing if consent has been given freely. These include structures of power inequalities, dependencies, and a lack of alternative and viable options when taking decisions. Considering the circumstances in which consent is given is particularly relevant for women's taking decisions about their lives against the background of fundamental patriarchal structures that still govern women's lives.[43] The challenge, then, is to critically assess what *consent* actually means, while *also* and importantly, not to deny individual women agency by disregarding consent entirely and discounting individual decisions women take. I will return to the issue of consent in section 2 of this part, when discussing the conditions for individual autonomy further, including what it means to take a decision voluntarily.

So far, then, I have argued that the liberal right to freedom of occupational choice is rooted in ideas about how individuals should be able to dispose and use their own bodies, identified as the *individual right to self-ownership*. Persons need to have the possibility to employ their bodies as they see fit in order to be able to "use [their] powers of intention and action," as I quoted above. Only then can they be self-determining and have agency.

(ii) A second reason why freedom of occupational choice should be extensively protected as a liberty right is that the profession or employment we choose may be part of our life plan that provides us with the grounds for social self-respect. I have already discussed Rawls's take on freedom of professional choice. Rawls also describes the basis of social self-respect as a social primary good that all egalitarian societies should aim to distribute fairly. To recall, *primary goods* are "things which it is supposed a rational man wants whatever else he wants. Regardless of what an individual's rational plans are in detail, it is assumed there are various things he would prefer more of rather than less. . . . With more of these goods men can generally be assured of greater success in carrying out their intentions and in advancing their ends, whatever these ends may be."[44]

Having access to the social basis of self-respect is one such good. According to Rawls, self-respect has two aspects: "[I]t includes a person's sense of his own value, his secure conviction that his conception of his good, his plan of life, is worth carrying out. Self-respect implies further a confidence in one's own ability, so far as it is within one's power, to fulfil one's intentions."[45]

The "sense of our own worth" relies, in turn, on "(1) having a rational plan of life and in particular one that satisfies the Aristotelian principle;[46] and (2) finding our person and deeds appreciated and confirmed by others who are likewise esteemed and their association enjoyed."[47] To put this differently, persons will have access to the social basis of self-respect if they can engage and pursue a specific life plan that they deem good or valuable and that they find validated by others.[48]

Now, I believe it fair to say that the extent to which one's "person and deeds" are appreciated by others will in part depend on what kind of profession we carry out. If some professions are validated less than others, this can have an effect on how we think our life plans are validated by others, and how much our work can form part of the social basis of self-respect. One way to socially validate professional choices is remuneration—as I discussed earlier, liberal states can increase wages to attract more individuals into professions of high social value. However, remuneration is not the only way to express social validation: for instance, some professions are not necessarily highly remunerated, but are nevertheless highly regarded, such as being a professional firefighter.[49]

Of course, *why* professions are validated and regarded in individual societies, and *how* they are esteemed, is subject to social and cultural norms about labour and work, but also subject to ideas about the public and the private spheres, about family-making and the role women should play in society.[50] Feminist philosopher Susan Moller Okin has famously shown that reproductive work is not remunerated if carried out by women in the home, whereas it is paid work if contracted out.[51] And often, value is added to work that is paid work,[52] unless of course, it is deemed to belong to the private family sphere, in which work is supposedly carried out for love.[53] In this vein, it is interesting to consider some of the public comments that surrogates working in the United States have received: Many report that people have been supportive of their surrogacy arrangements if they describe them as altruistic projects motivated by the urge to help a couple to have access to the good of parenting a biological child. Put differently, when surrogates describe themselves as motivated by wanting to provide the gift of life, being a surrogate is esteemed. Thus, when surrogates describe their reproductive work *not* as work, but as providing a gift to others, they are lauded for their efforts. In contrast, if surrogates describe surrogacy as *paid* work, as a vehicle to earn money to be spent on their biological children, say, they are scrutinized and rejected as ruthless money grabbers or "womb whores."[54] Consequently, the surrogacy industry is at pains to downplay the financial, work aspect of surrogacy "journeys," as they are called, instead emphasizing the "giving" aspect. Moreover, surrogacy agencies, at least in the United States, carefully select surrogates for their intentions, arguing that if individual applicants are mainly motivated by the money, they won't be selected: welfare recipients and women below a socioeconomic threshold won't be chosen for fear that their monetary motivations will reflect badly on the agency. Representatives of surrogacy agencies also suggest that monetary motivations won't be sufficient to sustain individual surrogates over the course of the surrogacy process. In this vein, an important role comes in for the partner in a surrogate's life. Many agencies insist not only on surrogates having borne biological children before working as surrogates, but they also insist on hopeful surrogates being in stable relationship for the emotional and practical support they need over the course of the surrogacy journey. The picture of heterosexual couples with biological children of their own providing biological children for people who would otherwise be excluded from the good of parenting feeds into the social construction of surrogacy as valuable and as providing a service that should be socially accepted.[55]

This is to say that the extent to which professions are valued in society and thus can serve as the social basis of self-respect depends, in part, on how professions are framed within society. If a profession is valued in society—think of doctors or judges—it satisfies Rawls's criterion for providing an individual with the social basis of self-respect: a valued profession will provide a "sense of [one's] own value, [one's] secure conviction that [one's] conception of [one's] good, [one's] plan of life, is worth carrying out." The puzzling thing about surrogacy is that it is valued, at least in the United States, but think also of the Israeli example discussed earlier, but not as work. Yet this simply seems to reflect cherished ideas about family-making and childbirth rather than the reality of modern reproduction. I will return to this point in my discussion of Anderson's critique of surrogacy in section 3.

A critic of surrogacy as labour could object that it is not clear that the principle of liberty of occupational choice would protect surrogacy work. Some work, including possibly surrogacy work, might not be counted among the professions that support life-plans, as my brief discussion of the US surrogacy market and the perception of surrogates as working women just now suggests. Other work thusly disqualified may include sex work, for its degrading and alienating aspects, or other physically, socially, or morally stigmatized work, such as that done by refuse collectors, care-workers, or correctional officers.[56] My imaginary critic could argue that such work, even if we count it as a profession, doesn't help in the realization of life plans. As such, putatively unvalued work could not be considered to be protected by liberal ideas about freedom of occupational choice.

This raises the question of whether life plans have to conform to certain standards to enable individual autonomy and provide the social basis of self-respect. Should we evaluate the kind of goals and goods people pursue in their life plans? Presumably, we would want to be able to judge some life plans as worth pursuing, while we would find others possibly problematic from this perspective. Here, Rawls argues that a reasonable definition of what should count as a *good* for plans of life is to say that

> [a] thing's being a good X for K is treated as equivalent to it having the properties *which it is rational for K to want in an X in view of his interests and aim.* . . . We criticize someone's plan, then, by showing either that it violates the principles of rational choice, or that it is not the plan that he would pursue were he to assess his prospects with care in the light of a full knowledge of his situation.[57]

Note that the rationality condition is qualified later quite "personally": "if the agent does the best that a rational man can do with the information available to him, then the plan he follows is a subjectively rational plan."[58]

Rawls is at pains to avoid a prescriptive interpretation of a good life plan, allowing a wide array of individual life plans that should fall under the protection of the basis of self-respect. If individuals are recognized in pursuing a rational life plan, Rawls stipulates, they will have secured the social basis for self-respect. And one way of realizing one's life plan is, of course, to choose a specific profession: a profession is one way of realizing one's interests and aims. Women may choose to work as surrogates for diverse reasons. Most importantly for my purposes here, they may choose to work as surrogates to be able to realize some important goals in their lives. We now have many different accounts of the kinds of motivations women have to engage in reproductive surrogacy labour.[59] Predominant, at least in the United States, for instance, is the motivation to earn extra money for their biological children. In view of Rawls's non-perfectionist view of what counts as a rational life plan, it seems plausible to say that surrogacy work that allows surrogates to provide for their biological children, or that allows them to realize other important goals in their life is part of a rational life-plan.[60]

Earlier, I suggested that surrogacy as work can provide access to the social means of self-respect. I argued that the kinds of professions we choose can help us realize our cherished goals, as well as provide us with the recognition of others for these goals. The discussion of surrogacy just now, though, seems to suggest that the social status of surrogacy work is highly contingent—or at least very much dependent on changing the social norms surrounding family, reproduction, and women's work. If it is the case that social valuation of work is necessary for work to provide for individual access to self-respect, why, then, promote a kind of work that does not immediately provide social valuation?[61] It seems to me that there are two routes open for my argument to hold, nevertheless. First, we could say that social valuation is highly contingent on state sanction. In this instance, witness the Israeli system of surrogacy— which is highly regulated and state sanctioned. Of course, it is based on altruistic surrogacy—but we can imagine that a similar system would nevertheless be socially supported if surrogates were paid for their work—simply due to the social discourse around what surrogacy is—namely, a way to provide all hopeful parents with the gift of having a biological child.

On a more philosophical level, I believe it fair to say that individuals come up to the limits of self-chosen goals when demanding social recognition. As I said, autonomy requires that we are able to propose ourselves to the world as we intend, with the reasons and values we have adopted, and for the world to recognize us the way we intend it to. Only then can we be self-determined.[62] If we lack this kind of recognition, we won't be able to be the person we respect. We can't, however, control how the world will respond to us, if it will take our conception of the self and accept or understand it. This, we can say, is the "end of willing"; instead, we need to "take up an attitude of trust towards the world itself."[63]

To be sure, the assumption behind my discussion so far has been that surrogacy is work. It may be important to pause here to explain why I believe that surrogacy *is* work and that to work as a surrogate should be covered by freedom of occupational choice even though working as a surrogate is limited in time. To start with the latter, and drawing an analogy between surrogates and soldiers, I believe that nobody would deny that soldiers think of being in the army as a profession, even though not all soldiers stay in the forces for the entirety of their lives. Instead, individuals can be considered soldiers even if they have only worked in the army for a short period of time. This is to say that length of time is not the relevant criterion to designate an occupation as a profession. So how can we define what surrogacy is? According to the *Oxford English Dictionary*, a *profession* is "any occupation by which a person regularly earns a living." *Work*, on the other hand, is defined as an "action or activity involving physical or mental effort and undertaken in order to achieve a result, especially as a means of making one's living or earning money."

Now, I acknowledge that the regularity of surrogacy work is not necessarily given, albeit many surrogates have been reported to work as surrogates several times, rather than only once. In fact, return surrogates often earn higher wages, since they have experience, which is considered to assure as much as possible a "successful surrogacy journey."[64] Indeed, there are reports of agencies returning to specific surrogates in cases of intending parents who need special care. I believe it fair to say that working over, say, the course of five years as a surrogate, for instance, should thus count as being in a profession, much as being a soldier for this time period is accepted as a profession, or being an actor, even though both actors and surrogates have periods in which they are not engaged in their actual work. Recall that the actual period of surrogacy work is longer than the nine months of pregnancy: gestational surrogates need to have hormone stimulation therapy to make the uterus ready for an embryo transplant. However, the work period starts well before even that, during the selection of surrogates, the meetings between surrogates and intending parents, and the negotiation of surrogacy contracts, to name but the most obvious first steps of surrogacy work. If these parts of surrogacy work are considered, then it seems fair to say that surrogacy is work and that it is a profession over time.[65]

Another way to think about the question may be to assess whether professions help individuals to define themselves. Actors and soldiers identify and define themselves as such even in periods when they don't perform or carry out their duties. Similarly, many surrogates identify themselves as surrogates—that is, as somebody who has carried a baby for other people.

So far, I have discussed why the freedom to choose one's profession is regarded as an important good by many philosophers. I have suggested that one reason is the link between self-ownership, the right to employ one's body for one's own purposes, and individual autonomy. A deeper analysis of this link is the subject of section 2.

2. Surrogacy, Autonomy, and Individual Agency

How should we think about the link between a profession, individual autonomy, and individual agency? To reiterate: what is important, in line with Feinberg's consent clause, is that the profession be freely chosen, where *freely* implies "uncoerced." More precisely, the choice of one profession over another should be a voluntary one. This is important because, especially in international surrogacy arrangements, the claim is often that surrogates have not voluntarily chosen to engage in surrogacy. Some have argued that surrogacy is chosen under duress, or because no other options are available for women to provide for their families.[66] Some critics of surrogacy foresee a potential futuristic world, akin to that described by Margaret Atwood in her novel *A Handmaid's Tale*, in which the women of a future country are designated "living incubators," enslaved to the welfare of the nation and the lives of the women of the ruling class.[67] Obviously, all these cases are examples of coercion. Earlier, I suggested that consent is often taken as a marker of an uncoerced decision. However, I also noted that this notion has come under scrutiny, not least because the social, patriarchal, and gendered background against which women take decisions can make consent meaningless as an indicator of non-coercion. Paula Casal illustrates the problem of consent in economics with the example of Jack, who has a wide range of professional options available to him: "Unfortunately, every time Jack declines an occupation, an innocent person is murdered."[68] It is obvious that in Jack's case, consent given is meaningless for the circumstances in which Jack gives consent. Similarly, if women agree to work as surrogates because social conditions make any other decision harmful to them or their families, consent is void as a criterion for assessing a decision. If refusing to work as a surrogate implies not being able to provide for one's family, consenting to surrogacy work is meaningless in assessing the autonomous quality of decision. Instead, consent must be given voluntarily.

How should we think about voluntariness, though? For Bernard Williams, voluntariness is a statement about *how* we take certain decisions.[69] Agents act voluntarily if they have deliberated on their options and have decided to adopt one option over another. A voluntary choice is the result of deliberation and the active, intentional, decision to choose one option over another. Serena Olsaretti helps to clarify the point by carrying Williams's definition further. She suggests that non-voluntary decisions are those taken for lack of acceptable alternatives—in the example of Jack, we can say that there are no viable alternatives in his context of choice, unless he is prepared to sacrifice the life of another person.[70] In this vein, we can wonder if surrogacy is non-voluntarily adopted. Different scenarios come to mind: It may be troubling to hear reports of moneylenders who suggest surrogacy work to women when they ask for an extension of the family loan. If women lack alternatives to earn the money needed to pay back loans, then the consent given to surrogacy agreements can't count as given voluntarily.

Alternatively, some critics, especially of international surrogacy agreements, worry because the offer of a surrogacy agreement is simply "too good to be true": some suggest that the money a woman working as a surrogate in India could earn from a surrogacy agreement is of such an amount that refusing to work as a surrogate is nearly impossible. Thus, what is coercive are the background conditions of women's lives, and the offers of surrogacy pay function as undue inducements. In such cases, the "coercion" is exerted by circumstances.[71]

What counts as an acceptable context of choice can be evaluated based on an objective standard, though, such as the promotion of individual wellbeing, the meeting of basic needs, or human flour-ishing. Both Williams and Olsaretti make clear that declaring a choice a voluntary one references an agent's *motivation* for making the choice. In contrast, to speak of a free choice is to say something about the *circumstances* within which an agent makes a choice. To push the point further, Olsaretti makes the distinction between free choices, "which are claims about *the options* an individual faces, and claims of voluntariness, which are claims about how the nature of those options affect an *individual's will*."[72] However, coercion *always* stands in the way of voluntariness. This is in line with Williams's account of the necessary deliberation that needs to precede voluntary choice: if there is coercion, the deliberation Williams stipulates can't take the form it ought to support volun-tary choice.

Thus, if we accept voluntariness as a statement about the motivations an agent has to choose one option over another, we refer to the *autonomy-enabling conditions* that need to be secured for agents to be autonomous. Only if voluntary choices can be made are these conditions given.

The challenge in assessing autonomy-enabling conditions derives from the tension: on the one hand, we have the argu-ment that people should be free to choose which profession they want to pursue, and which kind of work they want to engage in. On the other hand, however, we have the worry that women may be exploited by intermediaries or their partners, that they may be driven to work as surrogates against their wishes, that they may be caught in exploitative contracts and subjected to conditions of employment that are harmful; or that women deciding to do sur-rogacy work may be motivated to take the decision in line with their wishes, but that we will have to accept the non-voluntariness of their decision based on the coercive background conditions, such as a lack of alternative employment options, that govern their lives.[73] This is a serious concern, of course, since we would be hard-pressed to justify work that harms autonomy interests as an expression of individual autonomy and agency. Instead, it would be the opposite of what liberal defenders of occupational freedom intend since it would undermine the role that professions can play in individual lives. I will leave this worry aside since the exploitation charge, as well as the worry over undue inducements, has been extensively debated in the literature.[74] Moreover, I take Wilkinson's discussion as convincing and conclusive when he argues that it is not clear why surrogacy is singled out as being more exploitative than other forms of employment in a dramatically unequal world. Instead, I agree with Wilkinson that a strict (international) regime to regulate surrogacy is needed to protect as much as possible the decision-making context. However, no international surrogacy public policy will address and ameliorate the fundamentally unequal conditions of life in which women make choices.[75]

So far, then, and unless we want to say that commercial surrogacy work is *never* voluntarily chosen, or can't be, but is only ever engaged in because of coercive circumstances, I believe that we need to accept that surrogacy work would fall under the protection of the liberal principle that societies should protect freedom of occupational choice. The fact that surrogacy *can* be chosen as a part of a life plan, I would argue, may simply derive from the uses that surrogates make of the money they earn through their employment—to foster their own interests and provide for those of their family. Or it may be based on the fact that many surrogates have had biological children of their own and find some value in providing biological children to those who need help in becoming biological parents. Surrogacy work may also be chosen for the pleasure women have in being pregnant. Witness here some of Heather Jacobson's accounts of women who were heartbroken after the birth of their last biological child.[76] The challenge thus is to find a way to codify surrogacy to assure as much as possible that surrogacy is chosen under autonomy-enabling conditions, voluntarily, and free from coercion. This, I will suggest in section 4, is best achieved by demanding that contracts are overseen and enforced by the state. Importantly, though, freedom of professional choice is not absolute since there are justified limits, which I will discuss now.

2.1. Reasons for Limits: Harm to Self, Harm to Society, and Professionalization

Most liberal states limit people's choices often. We don't allow people to sell themselves into slavery. Put differently, a prohibition of selling ourselves into slavery is based on the fact that selling ourselves into slavery is incoherent—we can't use autonomy to create conditions of slavery.[77]

The prohibition also extends to a range of possible occupational choices. Ari Kaurismäki's movie *I Hired a Contract Killer* illustrates why this is a good thing. In it, Henry Boulanger wishes to die but fails to kill himself, which prompts him to hire a contract killer to do it, giving the movie its title. When Henry falls in love, though, and changes his views about the meaning of life, he is unable to contact the hired killer to avert his death. The movie recounts his run from the killer he himself hired and illustrates why some occupational choices are simply harmful for others, and for society, and are therefore rightly prohibited. More obviously and directly, they are not allowed since exercising them may harm individual people, unless, of course, those victims of harm give their consent to being harmed.[78] Of course, recent developments concerning assisted dying show that sometimes, helping somebody to die may be part of a profession and a valuable contribution to individuals leading autonomous lives.[79] Yet liberal states restrict individual choices in lifestyle and professions where the welfare interests of others are concerned and where professions affect them adversely. Recall here G. A. Cohen's definition of individual autonomy as being "a function of two things: the scope of your rights over yourself, with which it varies positively; and the rights of others over themselves and over things, with which it varies variously."[80]

In the category of those professions considered harmful for society, sex-work is probably the one most often discussed. Authors in different fields have tackled the question of whether this line of work harms individual women, all members of society, or both. Feminists but also those concerned with family values and people holding religious views about the sanctity of the body have pitched into the debate, which I will discuss further in section 3.

Finally, some occupations are not protected by the freedom to professional choice, and we can imagine that their prohibition can be justified, not only with the harm their exercise inflicts on others, but also with their limited value for individuals. As Carla Bagnoli has argued, mafiosi don't have a chance to engage in autonomous decision-making, and their occupation doesn't provide reasons for self-respect.[81] Similar arguments have been made about sex-work and sex workers, who are then characterized as being degraded by their profession.[82]

We also limit a person's freedom of occupational choice in other ways—we impose certain criteria for a person to be allowed to exercise certain professions, such as doctors, nurses, bus -drivers and train -conductors. We can justify the latter set of restrictions, however. We accept that doctors and nurses ought to have special and to pursue continuous training—we do so, though, not to bar individuals from these professions, or to prohibit the profession entirely, but in order to assure that the profession is carried out and exercised in the best way possible, where this is defined as the most socially valuable. Similarly, and more minimally, most would agree that it is defensible to impose specific requirements on bus drivers, taxi drivers, and train conductors simply to assure that those using their services won't come to harm. Finally, we regulate access to certain professions through salary conditions—as I mentioned early on, liberal democratic states hope to regulate the supply of labour by influencing salary levels, increasing the salaries in the professions that are in highest demand for society. Recall here that Rawls stipulates that all the liberal state can do is to incentivize people to choose one profession over another. Salary levels are one way to incentivize individuals to choose socially needed and valuable professions. Preventing women from working as surrogates— that is, preventing them from expecting remuneration for their surrogacy work, however, can't be justified by the concern for professional standards aimed at ensuring the best performance of a profession. In fact, if the underlying rationale *were* to assure professional standards, we can speculate that those advocating restriction and those advocating regulation of surrogacy arrangements *might* come to a consensus.

Liberal states also don't allow people to work below a minimum wage to ensure that people will earn a "living wage." This is where the parallel to prohibiting surrogacy work for fear of its exploitative and non-consensual nature may be strongest. The concern over the harm of exploitation that many invoke to justify restrictions and the prohibition of surrogacy is most akin to the rationale underlying minimum-wage restrictions. The condition of a minimum wage is justified as a tool to protect workers against exploitation or detrimental dependency[83] or, alternatively, as a condition to provide for effective protection of liberty rights.[84] Proponents of the latter argue that societies need to create conditions in which liberty rights, such as that protecting occupational choice, are meaningful and make sense. Put differently, a negative right against interference of the state in the choice of my profession only makes sense if I can also enjoy a minimum protection of my positive liberty to choose from a range of viable options. Minimum-wage legislation is meant to provide jobs that actually constitute a range of *viable* options. There need to be some viable professions on offer for me to be able to effectively make a choice.

Finally, minimum-wage legislation can be justified from a concern for (in)equality within society. If we accept that socioeconomic inequality is not only *intrinsically* bad since it deviates from the postulate of realizing moral equality, we may convince ourselves that it is also *instrumentally* bad for members of society, since it leads to worse societal outcomes.[85] More troubling, though, is that stark socioeconomic inequality that has not been chosen may rob persons of the grounds of self-respect. Recall that individual choices have to be presented to others and esteemed by others to ground the social basis of self-respect. The idea here is that social esteem is hampered by inequality. Yet if we follow Rawls in his concern for the social of self-respect as a primary good that all members of society should have access to, then conditions that rob individuals of the means for self-respect ought to be addressed. This, we may say, is what minimum-wage legislation hopes to realize.

2.2. Surrogacy and the Limits of Freedom of Professional Choice

I now want to assess if the restrictions on occupational choice that liberal democratic states accept can be applied to surrogacy. As we have seen, requirements for professional qualifications are motivated differently than those of minimum-wage legislation, and I believe that when applied to surrogacy agreements, requirements codifying how best to carry out a profession could lead to better standards for surrogacy agreements. This is to say that licensing surrogates, akin to licensing other healthcare providers, would be the best option, and one that takes seriously the argument from freedom of professional choice.

How can we think about professional qualifications for surrogates? I have already mentioned the common practice of US surrogacy agencies to only employ women with biological children and only those above a certain income threshold. Obviously, these are two different conditions for surrogacy work: while we can think of the first one as akin to a professional qualification—women who have born children know how their body responds to pregnancy, how they feel during pregnancy, what to expect during childbirth, and whether or not they suffer postpartum depression, for instance—requiring women intent on working as surrogates not to be on welfare is not a professional requirement. Instead, this condition for surrogacy work aims to forestall the worry about exploitation and financial dependency around surrogacy work. It is not clear that this practice can be justified, however—instead, when thinking about licensing surrogates, it will be more important to check for a range of health conditions, and to implement a minimum-wage equivalent for surrogates.

Next, I also believe that we can leave aside the prohibition of selling oneself into slavery as applicable to surrogacy. If we understand slavery to be the transfer of bodily self-ownership, as G. A. Cohen has done, then it is implausible to suggest that women employing their wombs for surrogacy for a set period of time are akin to slaves. While it may be true that surrogates hand over jurisdiction over at least some parts of their body, I don't believe that it is akin to permanent alienation. To be sure, we can agree that for twelve months, a surrogate or potential surrogate subjects herself to a regime of hormone stimulation, insemination, food and safety regimes, and possibly a caesarean birth at the behest of the commissioning parents or the agency negotiating between surrogate and intended parents. Importantly, though, her body "returns to her" afterwards. I don't deny that pregnancy leaves traces on a woman's body, but I find it implausible to compare such traces with the markers of slavery. Women are not indelibly stamped by surrogacy labour as alienated from themselves. Importantly, also, surrogates have and retain self-ownership. Indeed, as I have argued, their self-ownership—which slaves did not enjoy—is part of the argument why commercial surrogacy should be allowed.[86]

And in fact, liberal democratic states do allow individuals to choose various labour regimes that may take a heavy physical toll: think of the work of many seasonal labourers, or more strikingly still, of the work of soldiers in the military. We don't consider soldiers to be slaves; neither do we think of a military career as permanent alienation, even though soldiers use their bodies to earn their living and hand over jurisdiction over their bodies for the time of their military employment. One could argue, of course, that the analogy between surrogacy and the military only goes so far, since soldiers can opt out of active service by asking to be assigned to non-combatant tasks, or by opting out from the military entirely. This is not to say that I am making an analogy between surrogacy and working as a surrogate and active military service in a war. All I hope to show is that there are precedents for work that exerts a heavy physical toll without raising the spectre of slavery or unwarranted exploitation. In section 4, I will discuss professional rules for surrogacy, including that commercial surrogacy regulations need to take the exit option into consideration when thinking about how to establish a framework for viable and fair surrogacy work.

As we have seen though, many philosophers accept the value professions have for individual autonomy insofar as they help to provide the conditions for individual agency. The assumption underlying autonomy-based arguments for freedom of professional occupation is that they aim to promote what we may call a reasonable *context of choice*, and not a maximally attractive *set of options*. It is the reasonable context of choice that is protected by the right to freedom of occupational choice, and it is within the reasonable context of choice that voluntariness is relevant to characterize and distinguish autonomy-enabling freedom of professional occupation. Thus one way to justify the prohibition of surrogacy work might be to say that surrogacy is a non-required option in an otherwise reasonable—that is, sufficient—set of options amongst which hopeful surrogates may choose. In this vein, we may convince ourselves that surrogacy should not be protected as an option within a liberal argument from freedom of occupational choice.

Contrary to many, however, I argue that not being able to choose work as a surrogate can be considered an attack on the liberty right of professional choice. Prohibition shuts off the context of choice.

In the first instance, this is because, for at least some surrogates working in the Global South, the alternatives to surrogacy are equally if not more wretched. As Amrita Pande and Sharmila Rudrappa have shown in their respective volumes, women in India, for instance, are clear-eyed about the burdens and benefits of surrogacy.[87] Those who aim to prohibit commercial surrogacy out of concern for individual surrogates should, then, also be against the context in which surrogates make their choice for surrogacy[88] and need to explain why prohibition is the best option in a fundamentally unequal world.

The second reason why prohibiting surrogacy shuts off the context of choice for hopeful surrogates is that surrogacy work is a specific kind of work: it is not the case that surrogacy work is interchangeable with other work for those who derive significant meaning from providing a child to otherwise childless people. Some of those choosing to be surrogates want to do so not only in order to flourish and promote their own idea of who they are and what they stand for; but more importantly, hopeful surrogates may want to be . . . surrogates—that is, they may want to provide the gift of life, as is proposed, for example, in Israeli surrogacy arrangements. Or, they may want to be pregnant and experience the joy of having a life grow in their womb.[89] No other form of work can provide this experience, they could say, and it is an important aspect of who they are that they can experience it.[90]

We are left, then, with arguments for the regulation of surrogacy that are akin to arguments for minimum-wage legislation and arguments against surrogacy work out of concern about the harm that surrogacy work can bring to societies, including to the children born through surrogacy. I will address these in turn. As I said, the main motivation behind minimum-wage legislation is to enable positive conditions of individual choice. For freedom of occupational choice to be meaningful, persons ought to have the possibility of choosing between meaningful options rather than having to accept professions at any price. Second, I justified minimum-wage legislation to prevent fundamental inequality and dependence in society. Again, I believe that this is a reasonable concern. And this is, of course, where critics of surrogacy work as exploitative would weigh in, arguing that the protection afforded by minimum-wage legislation can't be used in international surrogacy arrangements, since the inequalities between those commissioning children and those carrying and bearing them are so vast. Moreover, we lack an effective state to implement an international version of the minimum wage, of course.

In response, I believe that this sort of worry is precisely what motivates the authors arguing for better regulation of commercial surrogacy agreements, international or national. Witness, for instance, the lack of regulation in the United States of brokers, agencies, and fees. The same applies to the lack of regulation of international surrogacy contracts. I agree with those who believe that international surrogacy markets should become part of international private law and that they should be codified, rather than that prohibition of so-called baby-selling should fuel an unregulated, black market in surrogacy.[91] This would allow to hold states in which surrogacy pregnancies are arranged accountable for implementing labour standards. It is the obligation of states to assure that women are properly remunerated for the work they perform when they carry a child; and that they are protected during pregnancy and when they enter into surrogacy contracts.[92] How to regulate surrogacy work is the subject of the section 4. Before that, I now turn to the limit on freedom of occupational choice based on the potential harm that some work can bring to societies in my response to critics.

3. Surrogacy, Commercialization, Reproduction, and Parenting

One of the most often voiced concerns about commercial surrogacy and the dangers it poses for societies is that it implies baby-selling, and that "some things should not be for sale" for violating their intrinsic value, as Debra Satz has argued.[93] Second, many feminists worry about the effects of surrogacy within gendered societies. Finally, and more broadly, an important criticism suggests that surrogacy transfers reproduction from the sphere of family values to that of market values. I will address these concerns over the harm that commercial surrogacy may bring to societies in turn.

3.1. Surrogacy as Commercialization versus Surrogacy as Parenting

How should we think about the charge that commercial surrogacy amounts to baby-selling? To answer this worry, I suggest to take a step back and think about the context in which surrogacy now happens. Many would argue that the healthcare services in developed states should provide couples with the possibility of having children if this were possible—as I have explained, having biological children and parenting them is a good that many hope to enjoy.[94]

In this vein, many states accept a responsibility to provide artificial reproductive technology for couples who have trouble conceiving without assistance. The argument for such assistance is that to have access to a family, some persons may need medical intervention. If we accept that it is a basic interest of individuals to have biological children and create a family,[95] and if the state can help realize this interest, then it should be easy to accept, also, that the state has a responsibility to help those of its members who cannot realize this basic interest without help. This stance was first advocated in the Warnock report, published in 1984, which served as the basis for the British Human Fertilization and Embryology Act of 1990, regulating access to and the licencing of assisted reproductive technology (ART) in the United Kingdom.[96]

To be sure, in-vitro fertilization (IVF) and other medical interventions are only advocated within the boundaries of the reasonable—Ontario, for instance, has for the longest time accepted to fund only one cycle of IVF for couples who suffer from infertility of all kinds.[97] It is also clear that no treating medical professional, or no state, can make promises about the success of IVF treatments. To provide context: in the United Kingdom, the National Health Service publishes annual success rates of IVF treatments for women using their own eggs and the sperm of their partners. Women who are under the age of thirty-five when treatment occurs have a 32 percent chance of a live birth, with the rate rapidly declining to 4 percent success for women between ages forty-three and forty-four.[98] Yet the principled part of the argument suggests that the state may have a responsibility to help individuals realize one of their important goals in life, which is to have biological children.[99] The argument for such claims is similar to those supporting many other services provided by the state—it underlines the state's responsibility to enable individuals to lead autonomous lives centred and organized on defensible self-chosen goals and projects. In this view, to procreate is a project individuals have and cherish, and societies that value the individual projects of their citizens should help realize them.[100] Many gay rights activists have therefore argued that surrogacy should be considered a reproductive *gay* right since it is the only possibility for them to have biological children.[101] Recall also the ruling by the Israeli high court I mentioned in the introduction to this part of the book to expand access to surrogacy to provide single men and same-sex couples with access to surrogacy.

Of course, one could reply that the good of parenting can be satisfied without having biological children. Some could argue that the interest to have children does not suffice to motivate justifying access to professional surrogacy since such an interest could be satisfied by means of adoption. The interest I have assumed so far, however, is the interest to have *biological* children.[102] Following the critics, we could argue that hopeful parents should adopt one or more of the many children who hope to be adopted and who need to find a home. This is a serious concern and one that often gets lost in discussions of reproductive assistance: to what extent does modern reproductive medicine provide those it assists with a good that is not, in the end, justice relevant or, indeed, that goes against other justice considerations, such as that of providing all children with a home in which they are cared for.[103]

The specific interest of having biological children may be prompted by different motivations:[104] for some, adoption in the current legal and international context is not feasible or is too lengthy a process. Others may fear that an adopted child may have special needs that they as future parents won't be able to satisfy; or, they may fear that they lack the intuition and understanding necessary to care for an adopted child, believing instead that a shared genetic heritage may make it easier to face the challenges childrearing may bring. Suffice it to say that we can't simply assume adoption to be as good an option for all hopeful parents as the option of having biological children.[105]

On a more positive note, some may have good reasons to hope for biological children. Anna may love some of her partner's character traits so much that she may hope to have a child with similar features. Or she may hope to recreate together with her partner some of the features that are prevalent in their families. Other hopeful parents may simply desire to continue life in the lives of their children, a kind of perspective that gives the parents' lives meaning and sense.[106] Most dramatically, of course, some parents may wish for biological children because they hope to thereby find a donor of a renewable organ for another ill child.[107] In general, we don't question people's motivation to have biological children, even though we may very well think that we should, from an ethical perspective.

Moreover, I suggest that we should also allow professional surrogacy for justice reasons: it seems simply unfair that some can have biologically related children, and are thus able to realize an interest and a good that they care for, while others are barred from this option. In this vein, allowing intending parents to acquire the services of a surrogate compensates some for the bad luck of being barred from biological parenthood.[108]

However, as we explained in the introduction and as I have stated at the outside of this part, oftentimes, the same states that support ART prohibit commercial surrogacy. So why would states that endorse ART as a way to provide for biological children prohibit commercial surrogacy as another way to do so? One way to justify prohibition may be to say that commissioning surrogacy is not actually an exercise of a procreative right. Instead, some argue that surrogacy is baby-selling or, in the case of commissioning parents, baby-buying. Elizabeth Anderson, for instance, has argued that surrogacy implies the relinquishing of a surrogate's parental rights, which is tantamount to baby-selling.[109] According to Anderson, commercial surrogacy commodifies children

> if it replaces parental norms with regard to rights and custody of the children with market norms. . . . [T]he pregnancy contract does this because it moves away from regarding parental norms over children as trusts, to be allocated in the best interest of the child, toward regarding parental rights as like freely alienable property rights, to be allocated at the will of the parents.[110]

To be sure, Anderson acknowledges that gestational surrogacy may change the setting since the surrogate should then not be regarded as the legal mother who has "no parental rights to relinquish."[111] What Anderson suggests, then, is that assigning parental rights depends on genetic link.[112] But this can't be the whole story. Indeed, Anderson's account of what makes a parent seems to be an inordinately biological, genetic one, and one that does injustice to different forms of family-making. For one, it neglects the role that adoptive parents play in the lives of their children. It also discounts the wide variety of family models, starting with LGBTQ+ parents, moving to broader definitions of family ties and culturally diverse family models.[113]

Moreover, and certainly in the case of gestational surrogacies, the commissioning parents are those who bring about the existence of the child, not only ideationally, but also practically. This is to say that they are those who need to count as the "causal," "genetic," and "intentional" parents;[114] commissioning parents have intended for and caused the child to come into being, by providing their genetic material and by commissioning a surrogate to carry the child to term. Here I am not addressing the question of how we should think about the different sources for rights and responsibilities that parenthood may bear. Instead, what is important for my purposes is that planning and bringing a child into the world through surrogacy also needs to count as an act of procreation and of generating parenthood. Commissioning parents must count as parents on the pain of misconstruing parenthood as something that depends solely on the act of physically birthing a child. And that seems implausible, since it would relegate gestational fathers, gay parents, and adoptive parents to the background of children's lives, rather than acknowledging the parental role they play. To be sure, Anderson posits that norms about childrearing should have the best interest of children in mind—but the assumption that intending parents, or adoptive parents for that matter, don't have the best interest of children at heart simply because of how a child comes into their lives seems unwarranted.[115]

This is the case even if we may debate to what extent the surrogate should also count as a parent: the surrogate mother may have parental status as a gestational parent, as she does in UK surrogacy law.[116] This may in turn confer some rights on her that are often employed to justify clauses in surrogacy contracts that allow the surrogate to renege on her original contractual agreement to release the child. Recall here that I accepted that the codification of surrogacy contracts must anticipate what should happen in cases where the surrogate and the commissioning parents no longer see eye to eye during the surrogacy journey. I suggested, in my analogy to soldiers who want to opt out of service, that surrogacy legislation needs to spell out under what conditions surrogates should also have the possibility to opt out of surrogacy contracts if they need to. Health concerns for the surrogate may come to mind first, and health concerns for the foetus, of course. In these cases, "opting out" implies terminating the pregnancy. I am wary to accept, though, that because of gestational ties, the surrogate should have the right to opt out of the original agreement to release the child. As I will argue, this would neglect the vulnerability of the commissioning parents; yet when weighing burdens and harms in surrogacy agreements, the harm that commissioning parents would suffer in cases of surrogates not releasing the child should weigh very heavily. I will discuss how we should think about such arrangements normatively in section 4, when discussing the framework of codification.

In response to the baby-selling charge, then, commissioning parents are simply exercising their procreative rights to become parents by entering into surrogacy agreements. Prohibiting surrogacy as simply baby-selling fails, on this account, since engaging in surrogacy has to count, at least in part, as the exercise of parental procreation.

So far, the argument has been that surrogacy should be considered as a means of helping to realize the fundamental interests individuals may have in having and parenting biological children. Now, we may accept this but suggest that the interest in parenting may protect the right to enter into surrogacy arrangements—altruistic ones—but that the interest in parenting may not justify the right to *work* as a surrogate. One could argue for this by insisting that commercial surrogacy is baby-selling, whereas altruistic surrogacy is not. This seems to be Anderson's strategy since she condemns commercial surrogacy but doesn't bedevil altruistic surrogacy. To wit, Anderson writes that her "arguments are directed only at surrogacy as a commercial enterprise."[117]

3.2. Surrogacy and Gendered Society

Despite her acknowledgement that gestational surrogacy may not pose the same challenge to family values through the specter of market values, as non-gestational surrogacy, as I have just discussed, Anderson remains critical and agrees with Debra Satz's argument against gestational surrogacy as commercial surrogacy. According to Satz, there is a specific harm that arises in the context of surrogacy when thinking about the gendered context in which surrogacy is brought about. By signing a contract, the surrogate relinquishes some control over her own body to somebody else for an extended period of time—namely, the period of pregnancy.[118] As I pointed out, this happens in other cases and other employment relationships: individuals sign up for military service all over the world, for example, thereby agreeing to be sent somewhere where they might not choose to go and to do things they might not choose to do.

What makes the case of surrogacy particular, however, is the fact that women sign over authority over their body in a societal context that has traditionally not protected women's interests. Instead, it has "historically subordinated women's interest to those of men, primarily through . . . control over women's sexuality and reproduction."[119] Satz acknowledges that "in a society in which women's work was valued as much as men's and in which child care was shared equally, pregnancy contracts . . . have the potential to transform the nuclear family."[120]

The worry about commercial surrogacy within the gendered context of societies is an interesting perspective, and certainly one that demands careful analysis. Satz seems to suggest that there is no inherent problem with commercial surrogacy but, instead, that it

is problematic in the context of the actual gendered division of labour, to which in the international context is added the racial and
socioeconomic aspect.[121] The question Satz raises, then, is whether
women should be allowed to employ their reproductive organs in
order to further their own goals, for fear of entrenching stereotyp-
ical and destructive gender structures.

In response, we may wonder if surrogacy cannot also play a different role; we may ask to what extent surrogacy and reproductive work can change women's position in their society of origin.
Against Satz's blanket warning, we may point towards those women
who—sometimes, together with their husbands and after having
had children of their own—decide to enter surrogacy contracts in
order to realize goals of their own, for example, paying for the education of their biological children.[122] One fascinating aspect of
surrogacy is that it is at least feasible that traditional gender roles
are put into question by such a new employment of women's reproductive organs. Especially in labour markets that restrict women's
access to properly remunerated work, surrogacy can allow women
access to gains that they would not be able to access otherwise.
To wit, through surrogacy, "women's reproductive capacities are
valued and monetized outside of the so-called private sphere. As
surrogates, women use their bodies, wombs and sometimes breasts
as instruments of labour."[123]

To be sure, surrogacy both challenges the gendered organization of society while also rewriting it: "just as commercial surrogacy subverts . . . gendered dichotomies, it simultaneously reifies
them."[124] The reification takes the very biological form of women
doing what only people with a uterus can do, that is, gestate a child.
Yet while Satz and other critics seem to focus on this second aspect
of surrogacy work in gendered societies, I maintain that we need
to also take the first into account. And while I accept that women
will not reform gender roles entirely through surrogacy work—
women, as I have suggested, often engage in surrogacy work to provide for their family members thus satisfying traditional gender

roles—surrogacy allows women access to pay that is not available to them otherwise. In this vein, Anderson's defence of *altruistic* surrogacy is actually perplexing: if the goal is to challenge traditional gender roles, then surely altruism should count as the perpetuation of a very noxious gender stereotype—namely, women as disinterested, self-effacing, and caring. It is not clear why altruism should be the form women's agency takes. Indeed, one could argue that it is only accepting commercial surrogacy as work, as I have argued, that would address the current global trend of what some have called "stratified motherhood—the hierarchical organization of reproductive fecundity and birth experiences that supports and rewards the maternity of some women while despising or outlawing the mother-work of others."[125]

A second harm to stem from commercial surrogacy is said to relate to the nature of the kind of work surrogacy demands of women. Following Carole Pateman, Satz draws a parallel between prostitution and surrogacy. Pateman argued in the 1980s that prostitution represented a sale of the self:

> Women's selves are involved in prostitution in a different manner from the involvement of the self in other occupations . . . the integral connection between sexuality and sense of self means that, for self-protection, a prostitute must distance herself from her sexual use.[126]

Pateman's argument also raises the question of women's autonomy and agency, two concepts with which I began my argument for commercial surrogacy. As I have suggested already, I believe it fair to say that some women choose surrogacy as a way of sustaining their families and themselves. However, if Satz were correct in applying Pateman's analysis of prostitution to the case of commercial surrogacy, then those who argue for surrogacy based on the value of individual autonomy have a problem: if we were to accept that surrogacy is justifiable because it is autonomously chosen, and if we subscribe to the liberal value of autonomy, then it would be problematic if surrogacy turned out to be *undermining* the conditions of autonomy. If it proved to be true that surrogacy led individual women to negate their own interests, then this would be problematic since one of the requirements of autonomy in the way I have construed it here is the idea of individual self-authorship. Put differently, if commercial surrogacy led women to negate their own autonomy interests, then the original assumption of the autonomy argument is void: we can't defend surrogacy as being based on autonomous decision-making if the decision will undermine a personal sense of self, thus making any further autonomous decision impossible. This, we could argue, would be analogous to allowing an autonomous decision to sell ourselves into slavery. As I explained, liberals don't allow such a decision, not only because it is irreversible, as, for example, suicide is, but also because it is incoherent—we can't use autonomy to create conditions of slavery.[127]

Anderson seems to have a similar concern in mind when criticizing (commercial) surrogacy's damning effects on women and their autonomy: one of the reasons why it should not be allowed derives from the fact that surrogates are manipulated and bullied into accepting surrogacy, which "takes advantage of motivations—such as self-effacing 'altruism'—which women have formed under social conditions inconsistent with genuine autonomy."[128] However, there is a tension in Anderson's argument on the subject of women's autonomy. It derives from what seems like a double-standard in assessing altruistic motivations—since Anderson wants to allow for altruistic surrogacy, but not for commercial surrogacy that exploits "self-effacing 'altruism.'" Presumably, if women serve as surrogates for altruistic reasons, they would do so only because of the motivations acquired within the autonomy-inhibiting circumstances of gendered societies? As I said earlier, the idea that altruism is what we should cultivate in women is clearly at odds with ideas of subverting traditional gender roles.

Anderson describes "true altruism" as the "autonomous and self-confident exercise of skill, talent and judgment"; whereas she ascribes only "lack of self-confidence" and "self-effacement" to surrogates.[129] If the concern is for women's autonomy, the distinction Anderson draws is not clear. What is clear is Anderson's idea about *what* women should choose were they *truly* autonomous. This is to say that Anderson's argument smacks of a prescriptive perfectionist idea of individual autonomy, which I don't share. In my definition of individual autonomy, provided earlier to support the argument for surrogacy as a professional choice, I more minimally argued for autonomy as self-authorship—I am loath to prescribe what shape the books of women's lives ought to take. To assume that market norms render autonomous choice impossible seems hard to justify.

To be sure, if we accept that a sense of self is an important background condition of autonomy, then acts that *undermine a sense of self also undermine a condition of being autonomous*. If Pateman is correct in postulating the "integral connection between sexuality and sense of self," and if surrogacy, like prostitution, involves a part of a woman's sexuality, then we can imagine that a surrogate would have to distance herself from this kind of work to preserve her sense of self. She would have to *not* think about employing her uterus to carry the foetus of another couple, including another man. Finally, we might then also accept that the kind of distance Pateman seems to observe is difficult to achieve as a surrogate.

In response to this argument employed by Satz, I want to raise two questions: first, we should ask if it is true that "for self-protection" women need to distance themselves from their sex-work, as Pateman claims; and second, we need to ask if it is true that prostitution is analogous to surrogacy in undermining a sense of self.

I am agnostic as to the first statement—I wonder whether it is a relic of a conception that many women now refuse to accept. For instance, witness the strong advocacy that sex workers have engaged in on their own behalf. In many countries in which prostitution is legal, for instance, sex workers have advocated for public improvements of their working conditions to make their work environment safer and better for them. Many have also explained the services they render to their clients. Their public stance and role doesn't verify Pateman's analogies; instead, it speaks to a healthy dose of self-respect and -esteem. More important is the fact that surrogates use their bodies in a very different context than prostitutes—for one, surrogacy need not involve the physical presence of the gestational father. Implanting the fertilized egg is a medical procedure—and in this respect at least, the analogy is not sustainable.

Instead, I have analyzed surrogacy as a service surrogates render to couples.[130] We may speculate to what extent gestational surrogacy may contribute to a positive sense of self that arises in relationships in which we can realize ourselves. As I explained at the outset, gestational surrogacy is characterized by women serving as surrogates to couples unable to biologically conceive, thereby helping them to have children and found a family. The relationship may be rewarding, since the surrogate is able to provide something the intending parents can't have without her. To wit, Pande reports how surrogates in India describe themselves as bearers of gifts to the commissioning parents, thus suggesting a highly positive sense of self. Surrogacy in this interpretation may even be construed to help the definition of the self. Moreover, surrogacy may foster a positive sense of self for the surrogate, not only in relation with the childless couple, but also for the surrogate in her relationship with her biological children: to be able to provide for them with the proceeds from the surrogacy contract may be an important aspect of a woman's identity and may help her define herself in a meaningful way. Unless the relationship between surrogate and those hopeful for a child is abused, I want to argue that this is not an inherently morally problematic relationship.

Recall now that I discussed earlier how we should think about the result of a surrogacy. Put differently, what is it that surrogates provide? If it were a product, then the worry that surrogacy is ultimately akin to baby-selling might gain traction. I hesitated to discuss the product of surrogacy and suggested instead that surrogates provide a service—thus the remuneration they receive is for their service of carrying the foetus to term; it is not for the product of their labour. Especially in gestational surrogacies, the focus of my discussion, this makes sense: the biological parents provide their gestational material, and while there may be some genetic material of the surrogate also involved in gestation, the baby is not hers to sell, as Anderson writes.

Anderson also argues, though, that to construct commercial surrogacy as providing a service for which payment is made rather than saying that the payment is for the product is disingenuous: it is as though we imagine that we are paying the baker for her service of baking the bread rather for the bread proper. However, the analogy is not only bad; it is wanting: the difference between the baker and the surrogate is what they employ to provide their service—we can imagine that we pay the baker for her service *and* the ingredients that go into the bread; whereas commissioning parents in gestational surrogacy pay for the service, having provided the extensive part of the gestational material themselves.

Now, one could believe that, in this view, paying for the service would oblige the surrogate only to bring the baby into the world—but not to hand the baby over to the commissioning parents.[131] Instead, what intending parents need to pay for is the custody of the child, as Gheaus will argue. Following Anderson, we could criticize this transferal of rights over children as baby-selling. In response, I believe that this objection to considering surrogacy as providing a service is based on simple fiat—namely, the decision to consider the surrogate as having custodial rights qua gestation. This, we could say, is based on the "foetus container model," which assumes that the surrogate is the necessary vessel for the foetus to gestate in, and that by providing the gestation vessel, the surrogate acquires custodial rights.[132] The foetus container model neglects the role of the commissioning parents as *parents* in the sense I discussed earlier: especially in gestational surrogacy, there is no embryo without them, without their genetic material, which is used to create an embryo that is then transferred into the womb of the surrogate; hence, they need to be considered as the parents. If the baby is not the surrogate's to sell, as Anderson says for babies born through gestational surrogacy, then surely, it is also not for her to have custodial rights that she could then sell.[133]

3.3. Surrogacy as Harm to Society: Applying Market Norms to the Family Sphere

The most important aspect of Anderson's argument, and the one most challenging for my account of surrogacy work as protected by liberal ideas about freedom of professional occupation concern her claim that commercial surrogacy applies the norms of the market to a sphere of life that should be outside of the realm of market norms. Anderson suggests that this move has harmful effects on individual surrogates, and that it violates ethical ideas about family and reproduction. The first claim I have already discussed.[134] In the remainder of this section, I want to address the second claim.

The family sphere has long been held to be the realm of human life that should be dominated by love and fellow feeling, care and concern. These, Anderson argues, make it such that children can grow up safely and develop. Put simply, growing up outside the sphere of market norms is what is in the best interest of children. In response, it is not novel to say that the private sphere is not a sphere dominated by feelings of love and altruism. Witness the history of feminist political philosophy that has called to attention how women's interest may be damaged by ascribing emotions to family relations and situating them in the private sphere—that is, outside the realm of considerations of gender justice.[135]

Moreover, the idea that child-rearing is outside the market sphere seems puzzling. Witness what I referred to early on as the "industrial reproduction complex" that is now worth US$3billion annually. Part of this industry are medical professionals, such as gynaecologist, reproductive endocrinologists, ART specialists, doctors, and nurses. Newer technologies, such as egg freezing and, possibly, womb transplants, are simply the latest steps in an industry that makes money from people's desire to have biologically related children. And these industries are not restricted to the markets of the Global North—more and more countries are becoming hotspots for those seeking fertility and the possibility of creating a new life.[136]

Of course, Anderson would argue that the question is an ethical one, not a legal or sociological one. However, we need to consider that many families wouldn't exist without the industrial reproductive complex.[137] Thus, especially from the ethical perspective, we need to ask whether it is better to insist on traditional models of family-making than to provide the good of family life to an ever-expanding circle of individuals. When weighing the supposed harm of commercial surrogacy against the good that it allows to realize in many lives, it seems implausible to categorically allow the worry about potential harm to outweigh the gains.

So far, I have discussed the possible harm to society that Anderson identifies as part of commercial surrogacy, albeit non-gestational surrogacy, and which takes the form of moving one aspect of life— namely, having children—from the sphere of family values and norms to that of the market. I have argued against this worry, proposing that the intending parents in commercial gestational surrogacy are already parents in the intentional and active sense of bringing the baby into being. I will discuss Gheaus's argument that surrogacy harms the wellbeing interests of the child in my response to her in Part II. Before moving on to considering surrogacy as work, though, one comment is in order about the original articulation of the commodification worry. Originally proposed by Titmuss, this worry is not so much about the details of the transaction and about what is exchanged; instead, it is about another kind of harm to society. The worry is that if societies establish a market in surrogacy services, rather than relying on altruistic surrogacy, the possibility of solidarity, and the possibility for people to provide a gift is undermined.[138]

However, this seems unconvincing: in altruistic surrogacy arrangements, just as in commercial surrogacy agreements, many people are paid along the way to make a pregnancy possible: ART specialists, gynaecologists, and endocrinologists are amongst the many highly qualified professionals whose services are required to make the surrogacy possible. And, indeed, they are not expected to provide their services for free. What those advocating for altruistic surrogacy seem to be suggesting is that everybody *but* the surrogate should be remunerated. But why should this be so? Is it because surrogacy would then constitute an act of solidarity and gift giving, or is it because societies don't value women's reproductive labour in a variety of ways, including surrogacy work? Recall my account of the social acceptance of surrogacy when it is altruistically understood, compared to when women acknowledge that they have been paid for their surrogacy work. The reaction to women working as paid surrogates of referring to them as ' "womb whores' " reflects gender norms that are based on assumptions what women ought to do and how they should behave, not on what solidarity demands. In fact, as I underlined early on, one justification for allowing surrogacy work should be the fact that it allows those not able to conceive to have a biologically related child. To enable people to have access to surrogacy services seems more in line with ideas about social solidarity than does leaving people to find an altruistic soul who will help them out.

This is not to say that the surrogacy market need not be regulated, and certainly more than has hitherto been the case. Especially in order to fulfil the original promise of the market as a sphere for self-realization and equality, to enable to each and every person to be valued for their labour fairly, and to prevent harm and hardship to surrogates, children born through surrogacy, and the commissioning parents, surrogacy markets—that is, the employment of women as surrogates—needs to be regulated. I will now turn to a discussion of the different aspects such regulation needs to consider.

4. Surrogacy as Work

In her introduction to a critique of noxious markets, Debra Satz writes: "Markets are important forms of social and economic organization. They allow vast numbers of people who are otherwise completely unknown to each other to cooperate together in a system of voluntary exchange."[139] As I illustrated in the previous sections, many critics of commercial surrogacy, including Satz herself, question to what extent this somewhat rosy picture applies to commercial surrogacy. In this section, I want to discuss how we should think of surrogacy as licensed work and what professional requirements could be stipulated for surrogates to be allowed to work. I will argue that surrogacy as work can serve the ideal of individual autonomy—that is, it can provide for a profession that is part of a life plan, and which can function as one of the bases of social respect if it is properly regulated by liberal democratic states. Through regulation, moreover, the danger of exploitation and the potential harm that can come to surrogates or to intending parents in underdetermined or unclear agreements can, as much as reasonably possible, be forestalled. Regulation can provide a level of certainty and a planning perspective that surrogates as much as intending parents may lack if planning is left in the hands of surrogacy agencies, doctors, and lawyers.

Several commentators have proposed policy suggestions on how to regulate surrogacy. For instance, Wilkinson suggests specific policies to address the danger of exploitation,[140] while Humbryds has used international fair trade agreements as a blueprint to design what she calls "fair trade surrogacy" for international surrogacy contracts.[141] Walker and Zyl have suggested to develop what they call "a professional model of surrogacy."[142] I am interested in the specific moral arguments for licensing and justifying professional requirements, along the lines of limits to freedom of occupational choice I have discussed in the previous sections, and how these can be justified morally.

Before discussing what form surrogacy work licensing and professional requirements can take, a note on who should regulate surrogacy. It is obvious that remunerated surrogacy happens in the shadow of legislation in many countries since it is illegal. But even in countries where commercial surrogacy *is* permitted, such as the United States, surrogacy is a domain of private contract law, and not specifically regulated by the state beyond the strictures of that domain of law. In this case study, I believe it fair to say that Satz's analysis of the market as noxious is warranted.

Canada has a model of compensation for hardship, which means that surrogates can claim expenses during the pregnancy, as I explained; yet Canada doesn't allow commercial surrogacy. In particular, the federal agency in charge of health—Health Canada—stipulates in section 6 of the Assisted Human Reproduction Act that it is illegal to "pay a surrogate mother for her services; pay or offer to pay another person, or place an advertisement to arrange the services of a surrogate mother; advise or do any medical procedure to help a woman become a surrogate mother when the person knows or should know that the woman is under 21 years of age."[143]

Similarly, the UK government stipulates that surrogacy agreements are not enforceable under UK law, and that it is illegal to pay a surrogate.[144] This implies that if one of the parties in a surrogacy agreement is wronged, UK legal authorities can't assist them.

Thus, we can say that many states try to reckon with the reality that surrogacy is now a way for their citizens to have biological children, but remain loath to endorse surrogacy work *as work*. Yet by taking this stance, countries that prohibit surrogacy work leave the field of surrogacy regulation open. This seems puzzling for several reasons: First, considering that Canada, the United States, and the United Kingdom are aware that surrogacy is a reproductive choice for some, we could assume that they have an interest in regulating it—if only to protect the *children* born through surrogacy. Liberal democratic states accept a special responsibility for children, and we could assume that the governments of these states have an interest in assuring that the children are born with the protection that the law provides—that is, based on reasonable contracts between the intending parents and the surrogate. When looking at the legislation in Canada and the United Kingdom, we can observe a tension between, on the one hand, the recognition of the reality of surrogacy and, on the other, the seeming lack of acceptance of the consequences of this reality, namely, that surrogacy should be considered a way for children to come into the world, and for this reality to be reflected in the law. Second, we could assume that governments have an interest in protecting their *citizens* who engage in surrogacy. Governments should protect intending parents, as much as possible, against the heartbreak that occurs when a surrogate decides to end the agreement; and governments have an interest in protecting the surrogate against the ills of exploitation already discussed. Indeed, this is the stance India's government had initially taken in response to reports of Indian surrogates being left to fend for themselves and their surrogate babies after the intending parents changed their minds.[145]

Finally, liberal democratic governments most often administer the health services that surrogates and the intending parents will use when the time comes to deliver the baby.[146] In times of scarce resources, governments of countries with publicly funded healthcare systems should have an interest in regulating and administering surrogacy contracts, if only to help avoid potentially difficult and risky pregnancies—for instance, by assessing the qualifications of women hoping to work as surrogates—that may cause higher healthcare costs for the surrogate and the child born through surrogacy. This is to say that I believe surrogacy regulation *should* happen through the state; moreover, *commercial* surrogacy should also be regulated by the state, much as other labour conditions and relations are regulated by states.

So how could states regulate commercial surrogacy? I will take the Israeli model as a starting point in discussing possible regulations for commercial surrogacy, even though surrogacy in Israel is only allowed altruistically and is not based on a commercial model. Israel has taken on surrogacy as one of the reproductive technologies that should be overseen by the state.[147] As noted earlier, the intending parents and hopeful surrogates must apply to the Israeli Ministry of Health and its ' "foetus carriage agreements approval board' " for permission to carry out the surrogacy.[148]

One of the tasks of the board is to "examine[] the physical and mental fitness of all those involved in the procedure," where the procedure is defined as gestational surrogacy, and gestational surrogacy only. If the intended mother can't provide an egg to be inseminated, then a donor egg has to be used since the agreement can't be based on an egg donation by the surrogate. The board comprises "two physicians holding a specialist degree in obstetrics and gynaecology, a physician holding an internal medicine specialist degree, a clinical psychologist, a social worker, a jurist public representative, a cleric, as per the religion of the parties to the agreement."[149]

To be sure, one can be critical of the selection of necessary professions to be on the board—one could also imagine a midwife to be a member of the board, for example, and wonder about the role of clerics in surrogacy agreements—but the legislation makes it clear that the State of Israel accepts its obligations to hopeful parents, the surrogate, and the child born through surrogacy. It also illustrates that surrogacy is accepted as a mode of assisted reproduction by the state.

4.1. Professional Requirements and Justifiable Limits

I believe one of the first lessons to be drawn from the Israeli model is about the importance of the physical and mental health of the parties involved in the surrogacy agreement: besides the obvious interest of the intending parents in finding a healthy surrogate to carry the baby, it is also plausible to stipulate that surrogates need to be able to expect that the intending parents will be healthy. This can prevent possible problems for the participants in the execution of the contract: especially the mental health of all involved will be an important aspect in order to make sure as is reasonably possible that intending parents and surrogates can have a respectful relationship. An analogy to this professional requirement could be the expectations and demands that astronauts have to satisfy: knowing that they will have to spend extended periods of time in close proximity with others in a small space, astronauts are not only evaluated based on their physical fitness and endurance, but also for the mental well-being and resilience. What it means to be healthy should be defined in a reasonable manner, in the sense that all parties should be free from genetically transferable or mental disease; it does not imply that intending parents can have exaggerated expectations of the surrogate.

In the same vein, surrogacy legislation needs to protect intending parents and the surrogate from other kinds of expectations. Weisberg, for instance, describes the case of intending parents who had numerous and extensive demands for every obstetrical visit of the surrogate during the pregnancy, which led the Israeli government to specify that surrogates and intending parents must agree on the level of privacy that surrogate should be able to enjoy during the pregnancy.[150] Similarly, intending parents can't hope to regulate the sex life of surrogates and their partners.[151] In exchange, surrogates also have to respect the privacy of the intending parents—how much access surrogates have to babies born is often considered a stumbling block after the end of the surrogacy agreement, that is, when the children are born. Of course it may be enjoyable for the surrogate to be able to play a role in the child's life, but it is not clear that she should be able to expect this. It certainly would be helpful to specify before the surrogacy journey begins what the intending parents anticipate and expect in this regard.

As I already mentioned, most US surrogacy agencies expect that women working as surrogates to have partners, since partners play a vital role in providing emotional and physical support to the surrogate. The Israeli government does not prescribe that women serving as surrogates should be in relationships; neither does it expect women to already have had children. Yet if the aim is to facilitate physical and mental well-being, knowing how a woman's body reacts to a pregnancy seems a plausible expectation and requirement: women who have been pregnant will be in a better position to know how their body reacts to the pregnancy and how they will feel after the baby is born.

In the context of establishing criteria for and the legitimate limits on surrogacy work, expecting surrogates to have been pregnant before their surrogacy work seems reasonable then. We may be wary about calling this a professional qualification, but in effect, this is what it is. As I mentioned in section 1, some surrogacy agencies have recourse to former surrogates when they have a particularly problematic intending couple—and experienced surrogates often earn more than first-time surrogates do. Moreover, women who already have been pregnant with their biological children are expected to be in the best position to know if working as a surrogate is working for them—if a pregnancy was hard with her biological children, then presumably a woman may hesitate before gestating a child for someone else. Moreover, biological children are often also credited with making release of the surrogacy baby easier—a surrogate will not leave the realm of children and childhood behind when fulfilling her part of the contract and bringing the baby into world without expecting to bring it into hers. Many commentators on surrogacy agreements worry about the surrogate's emotional well-being in surrogacy agreements, and especially in commercial surrogacy agreements—indeed, the Israeli legislation is cognizant of this worry by including a psychologist as a member of the board. And while mental health is obviously something to worry about, having already had biological children already may positively contribute to surrogates' mental well-being.

An important question in this regard is to what extent surrogates should have the option to change their minds during the surrogacy journey. Walker and Zyl, for instance, argue that this should not be possible—the intending parents would suffer tremendously if a surrogate were to end the surrogacy. I believe that taking the intending parents' perspective into consideration is an important and often neglected aspect of a reasonable assessment of commercial surrogacy. Much like prohibiting the intending parents' undue interference into the surrogates' private lives, I suggest that state regulation should tackle this question in a balanced way. A few things will need to be considered:

First, let's assume that the foetus is healthy and that the surrogate has had no mental or physical complications due to the pregnancy. In this scenario, it seems hard to justify were the surrogate to opt out, which is to say that an abortion would be hard to justify. This scenario resembles a simple change of heart, which is hard to justify in the context of a carefully planned and organized surrogacy. However, recall that I mentioned that surrogacy work doesn't only begin with the pregnancy but before, with hormone stimulation therapy and months of preparation. Opting out at this stage— before implantation—is certainly plausible to justify: a first-time surrogate would not know how this part of the process will affect her mentally and physically. Put differently, her genetic pregnancies would not have prepared her for this part of the process, so we could say that having gained new information and finding her position changed should be a plausible reason for ending the surrogacy contract. Surrogacy legislation should also consider the position of the intending parents. While it may be a hard experience for the intending parents to have a contract with one surrogate ended, after having searched for her, having found her, and having invested their hopes in her, as well as the time and money in collecting sperm and egg, a surrogate's decision to end the contract before implantation does not destroy the possibility of parenthood. The burden for the intending parents when a contract is resolved is lesser than the burden for the surrogate would be were she to carry the pregnancy through.

The balancing of harms is different once the embryo is successfully implanted and the surrogate is pregnant. Then, we could say, the harm to the intending parents' interest of having a child is greater, because the child is already feasibly in the making. The idea of a future together has already taken root, and intending parents will likely experience the loss of the foetus traumatically, much as genetic parents experience a miscarriage. Again, we need to weigh this loss against the interest of the surrogate—her reasons for wanting to opt out. I suggest that it is fair to say that they would have to be plausible and weigh heavier in the moral balance than the hardship the parents suffer in case of abortion.

What kind of reasons for termination could we imagine to be plausible and justifiable in this scenario? Imagine the case of a woman working as a surrogate who during the pregnancy wins the lottery, making the gain from surrogacy work pale in comparison to her newfound wealth. Presumably, most observers would be hard-pressed to find the lack of financial need a justifiable reason for cancelling her surrogacy contract with, for example, a gay couple in their late forties who have worked towards having a child for a considerable amount of time. It would simply seem unjustifiable. Now imagine, instead, that shortly after successful implantation, the surrogate's biological child is found to suffer from a rare disease. If there is to be any hope for a cure, he will need to be admitted to a specialist teaching hospital on the other side of the world to undergo experimental treatment. The surrogate is worried that she will not be able to travel to the bedside of her child, especially as the pregnancy develops. She is worried that she will have to neglect her parental duties, and feelings, if she carries on with the surrogacy. It seems plausible to say that in this scenario, and even in the absence of health concerns for the surrogate or the foetus, how the surrogacy contract can be completed, if at all, needs to be open for discussion.

If a surrogate has health complications, surrogacy regulations should be modelled on the rules for abortions in traditional pregnancies. The questions to ask, then, are: What are the rules for later-stage abortions, when can they be justified, and when are they carried out? The often-referred to standard of the "health of mother" is significant here—I don't believe that it would be justifiable to expect the surrogate to sacrifice her health for the life of the foetus.

In the parallel case, I would argue that the intending parents are justified in asking for termination if the foetus turns out to have serious health complications. This seems warranted, especially under my model of surrogacy work as service work, because presumably, if we accept that the intending parents pay for the service of the surrogate, and not for the "product," then it should also be plausible to say that the intending parents should be allowed to demand the end of the agreement if the health of the foetus is concerned. Special provisions for payment in these cases should be laid out, to assure that the surrogate is not disadvantaged by the intending parents' decision. Compensation for lost earnings would probably be too great a demand, but a set amount depending on the stage of the pregnancy would be justifiable. The measure used, again, is that of weighing the interests of the parties involved: the intending parents are the parents who will have to take responsibility for the life of their child, and just as genetic parents need to discuss how to proceed when a foetus is diagnosed with health complications, so should intending parents be able to discuss how to proceed.

In countries in which abortions are legal, non-medically indicated abortions are generally permitted up to three months after conception. After this, concern for the well-being of the foetus enters into consideration. This may be important to consider in cases of surrogates' developing serious mental health problems, such as depression. Any regulation of surrogacy should consider potential dangers to the foetus, and hence, to the intending parents' interest in having a safe surrogacy journey, while also protecting the interests of the surrogate. If the depression can be traced to the surrogacy, then it seems fair to say that the surrogate's desire to terminate within the three-month period, though it would still be traumatic and painful for the intending parents, may be in all the parties' interest and therefore justifiable. Indeed, on a practical level, and protecting, for instance, the interests of the surrogate to privacy, the idea of pursuing the pregnancy might imply supervising the surrogate and protecting her from self-harm. Especially in the context of my argument justifying surrogacy work based on ideas about individual autonomy, this course of action would be unjustified. I am not proposing an argument here about the debilitating effects of depression. Many artists have relied on their specific psychological make up to do what they hope to do—namely, to contribute to the world through their art. However, in the context of my argument about surrogacy as work, I find it implausible to expect a surrogate to subsume her interest in being able to lead the life she hopes to lead to outside surveillance in order to meet the terms of an employment contract. This is to say that while I accept the intending parents' vulnerability to suffering if a surrogate opts out of a surrogacy agreement, especially when such an agreement has sufficiently specified how conflicts of interests should be dealt with, I believe that the vulnerability of surrogates also needs careful consideration in any surrogacy regulation.

The vulnerability of the surrogate within a professional context as I have described it so far—that is, where women have knowledge about and experience with pregnancy and have biological children—remains that surrogates may find themselves with the child in cases where intending parents default on their side of the contract. In this scenario, the role of the state should be akin to that in other cases of child neglect. According to Walker and Zyl, the state should therefore be actively involved in surrogacy contracts, and social services should play an important role in the drafting of surrogacy agreements—so that social services can step in when the transfer is not happening as planned, and take charge of the child.[152] In this vein, ascribing parenthood to the surrogate may actually hinder her interests more than those proposing this set up have in mind: rather than put surrogates in the position of having to relinquish their parental rights to give a child up to adoption, effective state regulation of such scenarios should anticipate that the children are the responsibility of the state in cases of failed contracts.

A note on the challenge of releasing the child. How should we think about this crucial aspect of a surrogacy contract? Conceptually, I have sided with those who, like Anderson, argue that in cases of gestational surrogacy, the child is not the surrogate's to release—since it not "hers" in the first place. This is philosophically plausible, of course, but release may still challenge a surrogate emotionally. How should states regulate possible conflict over this part of surrogacy agreements? I believe any kind of surrogacy selection and contract should follow similar set-ups in bioethics: for instance, governments should look at studies investigating organ-donor remorse. Recent studies have shown that there are specific factors that increase anxiety and depression after organ donation; most notably, there is "an association between [donor] marital status and anxiety and depression and regret."[153] The authors suggest that these findings need to be taken into consideration in pre-donation counselling. Similarly, I would argue that comparable studies should be carried out among surrogates in order to assess the evidence for remorse among surrogates. One of the problems of unregulated commercial surrogacy is that we don't have sufficient evidence to assess the extent of the remorse phenomenon, and thus to formulate possible precautions that could be taken to help avert it. Moreover, it seems, according to Jacobson, that many surrogacy agencies, in the United States, for instance, have already realized the role of marital support for the surrogate, as I mentioned briefly before.

Finally, a note on a possible tension between my argument for surrogacy work based on the value freedom of professional choice has for individual autonomy, on the one hand, and proposals to codify surrogacy work, on the other: the tension, a critic could argue, stems from the fact that I propose quite a long list of scenarios in which surrogates *could* be asked to carry on with surrogacy work, even when they would wish to end it.[154] In light of my position based on the principle of bodily self-ownership as an argument for allowing commercial surrogacy, the fact that I allow regulations of surrogacy contracts in which surrogates may be obliged to carry the pregnancy to term even in scenarios in which they may want to end it seems problematic. After all, bodily self-ownership should protect precisely that, the sovereign right over one's body.[155] I suggest two considerations to defend the stipulations of surrogacy contracts that I have just provided. First, the analysis of the tension is made more complicated by the fact that the demands of self-ownership were satisfied "originally" in setting up the surrogacy agreement. This is to say that, as I explained, commercial surrogacy contracts only serve the ideal of individual autonomy if they are entered into voluntarily and freely. Surrogates originally agree to use their bodies for surrogacy work. Most importantly, they also agree to the stipulations in a surrogacy contract that discuss the possible scenarios for warranted termination. To put this differently, there is a moment of *original consent*. The question the critic thus raises is how we should think about bodily self-ownership when consent is withdrawn. Recall here that I argued for bodily self-ownership, but not for *full* bodily self-ownership understood as maximizing the control function of self-ownership arguments for "protections from unwanted uses of our bodies." Instead, I argued for a conception of self-ownership that aims at protecting individual liberties to use our bodies. In contrast, I suggested that *full* self-ownership would make any duties of assistance implausible. I also followed Cohen's analysis of self-ownership in the context of individual autonomy. Self-ownership thus is conducive to individual autonomy, but not synonymous with it.

Moreover, Cohen also allows for the contextualization of self-ownership as it relates to individual autonomy. While I accept self-ownership as a description of the liberties persons should have over their own bodies, I also accept that individual autonomy is delineated by the "the rights of others over themselves and over things, with which [individual autonomy] varies variously."[156] This is to say that once original consent to surrogacy agreements is given, a change in the decisional structure of the surrogate needs to be carefully evaluated in light of the interests of the commissioning parents. As I have explained, there are several scenarios in which the surrogate's desire to end the pregnancy should be heeded and realized. However, there are others in which the surrogate may have to satisfy the contract. As I said, surrogacy is not slavery, and a surrogate will have a set period of time during which to employ her body according to her earlier wishes, rather than her later ones.[157] And importantly, her body will return to her entirely at the end of the pregnancy. If the surrogate ends the pregnancy, however, one way to acknowledge the harm that the termination of surrogacy contracts inflicts on hopeful intending parents would be for the surrogate to pay compensation. In this vein, it would be important for states to implement an insurance system to protect surrogates against having to pay themselves compensation for possible termination.

My critic could object here that this argument could allow for all kinds of trespassing or abuse. Couldn't the rapist argue that a women consented to going on a date, therefore mutual consent was provided, and that, moreover, her body returned to her after the rape? I find this analogy lacking. As I said, setting up surrogacy agreements and expecting certain criteria, such as asking potential surrogates to have biological children and having medical professionals interview and assess the parties to the surrogacy contracts, is aimed at assuring as much as possible that the decision-making context for surrogates remains stable. Ideally, original consent is steadfast and carries the parties through the surrogacy contract. Changing a date to rape, on the other hand, is not confronting a woman with new facts in an agreed upon project. It is instead exchanging one category, a romantic outing, with another, physical abuse. Lack of consent is not what is wrong with rape, as David Archard has shown.[158]

4.2. Surrogacy as Licensed Work

In an interesting take on surrogacy, Walker and Zyl have argued that we should develop a professional model when thinking about surrogacy. Professional surrogacy could be based on the care professions and their characteristics. Note, though, that Walker and Zyl do not propose the professional model as a way to regulate commercial surrogacy:

> We think there is an alternative to the commercial and altruistic models of surrogacy, one that recognizes the caring motives women have while at the same time compensating them for their work. The professions offer the guide we need. They provide services that are fundamentally ethical in nature, but professionals are not expected to care without compensation. Surrogates provide a service, a form of care that is inherently ethical, and should, therefore, be compensated.[159]

In principle, I find the suggestion to think differently about surrogacy interesting—however, I find the deterministic ascription of female characteristics, having "caring motives," problematic. It suggests that a woman should only engage in and be compensated for surrogacy when she has the right motivations. As I stipulated in my discussion of life plans, it seems overly perfectionist to want to assess why people choose specific professions. Instead, the assessment of rational life plans for individuals should be based on whether they satisfy individual expectations and hopes, not whether or not they are engaged in with the right motivations.

This leaves the question what needs to be considered when thinking about licensing surrogacy work. In the first instance, states wishing to license surrogacy work need to assess the medical context in which surrogacy happens: this is to say that not only may surrogates need to satisfy professional requirements, but all medical professionals engaged in surrogacy need to be licensed. The particular content of this licensing is manifold: in the context of my argument for surrogacy as work, based on individual life plans, governments need to investigate and assess how surrogates are approached and treated in such clinics; that they are protected from undue interference, are able to give meaningful consent in the surrogacy procedure, and are not taken advantage of by doctors who hope to gain personally from the surrogacy. Again, in welfare states where healthcare is publicly funded, and where there is no two-tier system, this worry would not arise. But in all countries in which medical professionals can set up private practice it is important to assure that surrogates choose surrogacy work for themselves rather than that it is chosen for them.

Similarly with lawyers who will assist in drawing up the surrogacy contracts: ideally, states should develop guidelines that describe how such contracts can be entered into, what form of expenses should be covered and how remuneration needs to be dispensed. In earlier work I have discussed the limits of state provision in this regard:[160] since states don't have jurisdiction over the bodies of individual women, governments can't assure and implement a positive right to surrogacy. Such a right would imply that those who hope to have access to surrogacy have access to women working as surrogates—and this no state can do. States can only regulate and allow surrogacy work, either as private law or as part of accessible reproductive assistance, as in the case of Israel. Thus, we could imagine a state-regulated system of remuneration. Recall that I said earlier that states can only hope to influence the labour market through the wage regimes, including minimum-wage laws and increasing the salaries in professions of high social value. If states were to accept surrogacy as work and as a valuable tool for people to realize the wish for biological children, we can imagine a state-sponsored regime of surrogacy work, with state-regulated compensation. In this vein, Walker and Zyl's proposal for a professional model of surrogacy is convincing. Based on a recent ruling of the German Labor Court on the remuneration of live-in caregivers, the most plausible proposal for remuneration would be to pay surrogates a minimum hourly wage for the time of the pregnancy and the months beforehand spent on hormone stimulation. Assuming ten months in total, this would imply a wage of roughly $60,000 for ten months. In light of such costs, the argument for state-regulated surrogacy becomes even more urgent. Recall that one of the reasons for professional surrogacy is that it is one way to allow those unlucky in biological conception to have a chance of biological children. In light of the anticipated cost that fairly remunerated surrogacy would bear, I would further argue that states that truly want to compensate those not able to conceive, should also assist couples below an income threshold in accessing surrogacy.[161]

Conclusion

I have argued for a model of surrogacy as work, based on the liberal conviction that individuals should have access to the background conditions of autonomy. I have argued for commercial surrogacy work as flowing from the liberal conviction of individual self-government as it allows individuals to design and implement as much as reasonably possible the shape and course of their own lives. In defence of my proposal, I have argued that women working as surrogates need to be able to make the decision to do so voluntarily, without coercion and in the context of surrogacy work as viable work. I then, in section 3, addressed some of the criticisms against commercial surrogacy, most notably that surrogacy changes the norms of family-making and that it harms society. In the last section I have sketched how we should think about professional requirements for surrogates, the limits of enforcing surrogacy contracts in cases of ill health, and, finally, what licensing surrogacy would need to consider. In the next part, Anca Gheaus will explain her arguments against surrogacy in general, and hence also against commercial surrogacy.

Against Private Surrogacy

A Child-Centred View

Anca Gheaus

Introduction

More and more people avail themselves of surrogacy in the hope of
becoming parents. In my view, seeking parenthood through a variety of means is legitimate; but commissioning children, which is
what surrogacy as we know it involves, is not. My contribution to
this book examines the place of surrogacy in a child-centred upbringing: I consider both existing forms of surrogacy and a deeply
reformed version that, unlike the existing practices, could fulfil
people's desire to raise children and respect women's choice to gestate "for others" in a legitimate manner. I argue that surrogacy—
both as we have it now and in the more regulated forms that have
been proposed—is indefensible, whether commercial or altruistic. In a nutshell, the argument is that surrogacy involves a private agreement whereby a woman who gestates a child attempts to
surrender her (putative) moral right to become the parent of that
child such that another person (or persons), of the woman's choice,
can acquire it. Since people lack the normative power to privately
transfer custody, attempts to do so are illegitimate, and the law
should reflect this fact.

My criticism of surrogacy is part and parcel of what I consider a
just and humane form of childrearing, consisting of two desiderata.
The justice desideratum is the recognition that children's interests

Debating Surrogacy. Anca Gheaus and Christine Straehle, Oxford University Press.
© Oxford University Press 2024. DOI: 10.1093/oso/9780190072162.003.0003

have the same moral importance as the interests of adults. For this reason, the right to become a child's parent is not a claim right but a privilege justified by appeal to the child's interest, and this entails that private re-allocation for the right is wrongful. The humaneness desideratum is the recognition of how our membership in the animal (more specifically, mammalian) world bears on our wellbeing. Our embodiment, the fact that we have, or, perhaps more appropriately, *are*, bodies, and our typically mammalian need for secure attachment, most likely have some bearing on what is good for newborns. A humane and just childrearing, then, reflects both what we have in common with other animals—embodied attachment—and what sets us apart from them—the capacity to acknowledge that might is not right, and that the interests of human beings of all ages place strict limits on the legitimate exercise of power over them.

The moral right to become a parent, or to rear—which I believe should ground the legal right to obtain custody—involves the acquisition of a bundle of rights, including powers to control many aspects of a child's life for the child's own sake. Holding this right is justified by appeal to the child's own interest in a good life, as well as everybody's rights-protected interests, including the interest that children grow up to be autonomous and morality-abiding. But the right is not meant to serve the future custodian's own interest in being a parent, in spite of the fact that many of us desire, and have reason to value, raising children. If so, the moral right to become the parent of a child is held by those who express an interest in raising that child and whose exercise of the right would be in the best interest of the child;[1] given the justification of the right, custodians lack the moral freedom to sell or gift it.[2] These are decisive arguments against the permissibility of both commercial and altruistic surrogacy. But they don't imply that procreation and traditional forms of adoption are the only legitimate ways to gain custody over a child. A reformed version of surrogacy—indeed, so much reformed that it may deserve to go by an entirely different name—is, as far as I can see, permissible.

The background question that guides my contribution to this book is: Which aspects, if any, of surrogacy as we have it today are consistent with taking children's moral status seriously? Some aren't, I shall say. But the fact that people may not privately transfer custody doesn't mean that each and every component of the surrogacy process is impermissible. More specifically, parents have the freedom (albeit qualified) to surrender custody; however, people, even if they are genetically related to the child, cannot *acquire* it merely because they want to and because those who surrender their right want them to acquire it. This would be incompatible with acknowledging that we may not use children as mere means to advance other people's ends. Further, my argument doesn't entail that women are not morally permitted to bear children whom they don't intend to rear; for everything I say here, considerations of autonomy, and possibly of financial interest, might make this choice permissible. On this point, I don't disagree with Christine Straehle. Indeed, my positive view—which I sketch towards the end—is that it could be desirable to have a state-overseen practice involving surrogate mothers and allocating custody over the resulting children (assuming a morally and otherwise competent state). Crucially, the allocation of the right ought to be dictated by the child's interest.

As far as I know, this critical view of surrogacy has not yet been considered, let alone defended. But the literature on surrogacy contains several of its elements. The core moral principle driving my account—that the interest of the child is paramount—is endorsed by other writers on surrogacy. Some advocates of (a regulated version of) surrogacy, as well as some of its critics, believe that the sole consideration relevant to custody is the interest of the child.[3] Surprisingly, however, in formulating their arguments both sides seem to have missed the full implication of this claim for the permissibility of the practice. Second, several scholars insist on the ethical importance of an emotional bond between gestational mother and her foetus.[4] I agree with them and advance the additional claim that existing emotional bonds, because they serve the child's wellbeing, are also relevant to the question of which adults should enjoy a protected (but not necessarily custodial) relationship with the newborn. Third, many argue that surrogacy should be regulated to protect the interests of children born of surrogacy and of the women who bear them.[5] Yet the kind of practice that I envisage as potentially permissible goes well beyond some kind of vetting of intending parents and ensuring better conditions for surrogate mothers.[6] The principle that ought to guide regulation is that the newborn's interest dictates custody, to the extent to which this is possible and can be achieved by permissible means. In some cases, my account says that the surrogate mother has a right to raise the child she bears, if she decides to do so during pregnancy or soon after birth. This is not to say that surrogates should always have the opportunity to become the child's custodian; rather, in some cases they have (merely) the moral right to continue the caring relationship with the child that they carried—a right which, I will explain, is different from a right to custody. Most importantly, such a scheme does not ensure the intending parents' custody of genetically related children. Is it appropriate to call this practice "surrogacy"? Not according to what I mean by "surrogacy" in this book—but this, of course, is a merely semantic point.

Here is a map of the chapter. I start, in section 1, with an intuitive case against surrogacy, by inviting the reader to consider several highly stylized cases that involve the acquisition of custody of a newborn by people other than the gestational mother. Section 2 makes explicit my main normative assumptions, most importantly those entailing that the right to become the parent of a child is not privately transferable. To judge whether surrogacy is legitimate, it is necessary to first make sense of what happens in this practice. Therefore, section 3 discusses the main ways in which surrogacy has been understood: as trafficking children, as engaging in pre-birth adoption, and as providing gestational services (plus, sometimes, gametes). I explain that the first model collapses into the second and that the third is implausible. I conclude that the best model of surrogacy in all but one type of case is the private adoption model, consisting in an attempt to transfer the moral right to custody over a particular child, which makes it impermissible. Cases of surrogacy with the intending parents' gametes seem to escape this analysis; they are treated in section 4, where I explore how biological relationships between children and parents are relevant to custody rights. Even if genetic connections are a good proxy for the quality of parenting, their existence should not be seen as either necessary or sufficient grounds for acquiring custody, especially when genetic and gestational connections come apart. Moreover, the gestational connection is an even better proxy for what serves the interest of the child—i.e., bonding—and this provides a *pro tanto* reason in favour of the presumption, present in some legislations, that gestational mothers should be granted legal custody. But it is wrong to take either of these relations—genetic or gestational—to be decisive. I conclude that this type of surrogacy, too, is illegitimate. I then turn, in section 5, to what I consider the most important reason to permit surrogacy as far as children's interests are concerned: the fact that children born of surrogacy cannot in most cases be harmed by the practice, given that they would not have existed without it. I meet this challenge by explaining why, whether or not it harms children, surrogacy is wronging them; those who think they can appeal to the non-identity problem to defend surrogacy must accept many repugnant conclusions about permissible childrearing. In the concluding section I sketch the contours of a legitimate practice involving women who gestate with the intention of allowing other people to become custodians of the newborns. I also make the case for the unbundling of two kinds of rights that are currently held only by custodians: rights to control children's lives, on the one hand, and, on the other hand, rights to associate with children in protected caring relationships and to preserve such relationships once established. Gestational mothers, I argue, typically have (at least) rights of the second kind.

The child-centred considerations on the basis of which I criticize surrogacy indict many other aspects of current upbringing practices. For instance, courts sometimes decide custody disputes without prioritizing the child's interest;[7] this is wrong. We fail to license parents even when doing so would not be detrimental to children's interests, as is the case when we use assisted reproductive technologies;[8] in such cases we ought to license, even though licensing would fall short of ensuring that the best available parents raise children. Further, parents' legal rights are often excessive.[9]

Given my belief that much of existing childrearing is disrespectful of children's interests, I should clarify, up-front, two aspects of the view I advance. First, although I believe that we need to rethink upbringing in general, there is something especially troubling about surrogacy: because its core is an illicit attempt to transfer a moral right, surrogacy adds insult to injury. Second, establishing the wrongness of surrogacy does not in itself indicate *who* is blameworthy for wronging the children of surrogacy and, hence, who is blameworthy for becoming party to surrogacy arrangements. Possible answers include the surrogates, by attempting to transfer what they lack a moral power to transfer; the intending parents, by attempting to acquire custody in a wrongful way; and the state, for permitting wrongful transfer of custody. Here I only provide reasons for the third answer. Accepting my view about surrogacy does not entail the belief that gestational mothers or intending parents are always appropriate targets of blame;[10] indeed, in many cases they aren't. Surrogates are often pressured, economically or emotionally, into gestating for others. Since prospective parents cannot engage in child-centred practices of upbringing—this, as will become clear, would involve the proper reformation of parenting practices—they can only access parenthood *via* objectionable practices; and because people have a powerful interest in raising children, they can be excused for availing themselves of the only existing means to do so. My overall aim, then, is not to establish the blameworthiness of individual participants in surrogacy practices, but to explain why these practices must be reformed.

1. The Intuitive Case against Surrogacy

Before considering how to best understand what surrogacy is—what is being sold, or gifted, in a surrogacy agreement—and whether it is a permissible practice, I invite the reader to consider a few stylized cases involving the acquisition of a newborn's custody by people other than the child's gestational mother. The cases are meant to trigger intuitions about permissible venues into custody, intuitions which, once identified, will hopefully help bring out the appeal of the overall argument I propose. Read them assuming that no coercion of an adult by another is involved at any stage in these stories: all the adults involved make fully voluntary choices.

> Case 1: A pregnant woman decides she will not raise her newborn, who is her genetic and gestational child, and puts her up for adoption. The state, *via* a certified agency, determines which of the potential adopters would make the better parent for the child, and allow her, or him, or them, to adopt.

This is a run-of-the-mill case of adoption, which may well be morally innocuous in every respect (depending on the gestational mother's circumstances), and in which the adoptive parents have acquired custody in an irreproachable way. Now let us look at the following, rather different case:

> Case 2: A pregnant woman decides she will not raise her newborn, who is her genetic and gestational child, and surrenders custody, indicating that she wants a particular couple to raise her. Without any vetting, the state allows the couple indicated by the gestational mother to get custody over the child.

First, note that while most, or maybe all, states allow Case 1, only some, such as the United States and Canada, allow Case 2. That case is properly described as a privately arranged adoption, which is a private transfer of the right to parent; according to many legislations, children are not transferable by individual parents.[11] Rather, when a child finds herself without a custodian, the state automatically acquires custody over her in its capacity of *parens patriae*—that is, as the agent with the default power to be the guardian of people who cannot take care of themselves. It is therefore up to the state to decide who, if anybody, can acquire custody over the child, and it must do so by appealing solely to the interest of the child. This is the dominant view and, I will argue, the correct one. Thus, even if the couple in Case 2 happen to make good, even optimal, parents for the child, one may worry that the state fails to discharge its duty towards the child by allowing the adults in question to engage in an act of privately arranged adoption. This is disrespectful towards the child, and therefore objectionable even if the outcome in terms of satisfying the child's wellbeing interests happens to be desirable. Now consider:

Case 3: A pregnant woman decides she will not raise her newborn, who is her genetic and gestational child, and surrenders custody, indicating she wants a particular couple to raise her, on the condition that they transfer a certain, agreed upon, sum of money into her account. The indicated person transfers the money and, without any vetting, the state allows the couple indicated by the gestational mother to get custody over the child.

To the best of my knowledge, no state allows individuals to proceed as in Case 3. Indeed, we typically identify the behaviour in it as "child trafficking" and ban it. I believe we are right to be critical of the situation in Case 3, and to prohibit it, but it is hard to see why, exactly, the commercial aspect makes it more objectionable than the one in Case 2, assuming that all other things are equal, including the quality of people's will—i.e., that in neither case are they regarding the child as a commodity. Most importantly, imagine that the adoptive couple in Case 3 is just as fit to parent as the one in Case 2. Is Case 3 really more objectionable, morally speaking, than Case 2? Let us now move on to the next case:

> Case 4: A woman decides she does not want to raise a child, yet she is willing to conceive one with her own gamete, and indicates that she wants a particular couple to raise the child, on the condition that they transfer a certain, agreed upon, sum of money into her account. The couple in question transfers the money and, without any vetting from the state, is allowed to gain custody over the child.

The situation in Case 4 is a form of surrogacy arrangement in which the gestational mother is a partial surrogate. Indeed, if one introduces a variation and imagines that the adoptive father is also the genetic father of the child, this is a typical example of traditional surrogacy, as it was practiced before the advent of in vitro fertilization. Is Case 4 any less objectionable than Case 3? It is not obvious why it should be: indeed, Case 4 is identical in all respects to Case 3, except that the decision not to rear the child and the decision to engage in an economic transaction with the adoptive couple take place before conception. But why would the precise time of the intention-formation make any difference?[12] As we shall see in the next section, some philosophers argue that it does—as I believe, mistakenly so. Perhaps you are tempted to think that Case 4 involves morally permissible behaviour because, and only when, the adoptive father is also a genetic father. But, even if the genetic connection does make a difference in this case (a matter I discuss in section 4), there remains a major objection to Cases 2, 3, and 4: the state's failure to act in its role of *parens patriae*. That is, even if you think that the genetic relationship between the child and the

intending father grounds the latter's right to custody (in the variation on these cases in which there is such a genetic relationship),
one may object to the fact that the adoptive mother acquired custody as the result of a purely private understanding between the
parties.

In fact, as far as I know, states also disallow individuals' engaging
in Case 4 unless they enter a surrogacy agreement before the beginning of the pregnancy, and if the natural father, when different from
the intending one, surrenders his right to custody. Without these
two conditions met, Case 4, too, would qualify as "child trafficking"
and we would ban it just as we (should) ban Case 3, since there is no
morally relevant difference between the two. But surely, an agreement in itself cannot make the relevant moral difference, at least
not concerning the question of whether such an agreement has
the normative power to determine the custody of the child. Now
consider:

Case 5. A woman decides she doesn't want to raise a child. Yet
she is willing to get pregnant by having an embryo, genetically
unrelated to her, transferred to her womb, and to carry the
baby to term. She indicates that she wants a particular couple,
who provided the gametes, to raise the child, on the condition that this couple transfers a certain, agreed upon, sum of
money into her account. The couple in question transfers the
money and, without any vetting by the state, is allowed to gain
custody over that child.

This is a case of commercial surrogacy involving a full surrogate.
Is it a legitimate practice? Is it more legitimate than the practice in
Case 4? I submit that commercial surrogacy of the kind illustrated
in Case 5 is morally different from Cases 3 and 4 only if the genetic
connection between newborn and the gamete providers makes all
the moral difference to who has the right to parent. Let us consider
one last situation:

Case 6. A woman decides she doesn't want to raise a child. Yet she is willing to get pregnant by having transferred an embryo to whom she is not genetically related, and indicates that she wants a particular couple, who provided the gametes, to raise the child. She does this altruistically. The indicated couple is allowed to gain parental status in relation to that child without any vetting from the state.

Case 6, too, I submit, is morally dodgy. It differs from Case 5 only in that the surrogate's motivation is non-commercial. Unless genetic relationships make all the difference to the right to parent, Case 6, too, is morally similar to Cases 3 and 4. Some readers may be tempted to say that the surrogate mothers in Cases 3, 4, and 5 are *selling* their own child. In section 3, I discuss the question of whether we are right to think about these as cases of selling children proper, or of merely selling the right to parent, and whether it matters how we choose to portray them. Perhaps, then, the best reason to see Cases 3, 4, and 5 as illegitimate transactions is that people lack a moral power to sell their right to parent, since they have this right in virtue of how it serves the child's interests. An additional consideration, which I substantiate in section 4, is that often the child has an interest in not being separated from her gestational mother. The same objections, then, are triggered by attempts to gift the right, as in Case 2: the problem is the very attempt to privately transfer the right to another person, not its commercial aspect. If so, this also explains why Case 6 looks objectionable.

The general problem, then, is that neither commercial nor altruistic surrogacy are morally permissible unless one of these two claims is correct: Either (a) it is permissible to privately transfer custody, whether for commercial or altruistic reasons, or (b) the genetic connection between an intending parent and a child alone justifies the granting of custody to intending parents. The next two sections argue against (a), showing that Cases 3 and 4 are impermissible. In section 4, I argue against (b), and conclude that so are

Cases 5 and 6, that is, that we should also reject full surrogacy as impermissible. Before turning to a principled analysis of surrogacy, I lay out my normative assumptions.

2. Parents, Their Rights, and the Interests of Children

2.1. General Assumptions

People can bring children into the world permissibly;[13] assuming otherwise would be a nonstarter, since if procreation were always wrong, the same would obviously be true of surrogacy. I distinguish between procreators and parents; a child's parents are the people who rear her, whether or not they have also brought her into the world. I operate with a definition according to which surrogacy involves a woman who gestates a child without the intention of raising her as her own, and with the intention that other people become the child's custodians; the latter's intention to parent the child pre-dates the pregnancy and provides its motivation. This definition of surrogacy is intentionally strictly descriptive; later in the chapter, I argue that surrogacy should be understood as an attempted transfer, privately agreed upon, of the right to parent.

Much of my analysis concerns rights: children's as well as parents'. Unless otherwise specified, all references are to moral, rather than legal, rights. The right to parent is the same as the right to custody. "Custody" itself is a legal term: to have a right to custody, in this chapter, means to have the moral right to be a custodian.

2.2. The Right to Become a Parent

I assume some version of the interest theory of rights, according to which claim rights protect weighty interests of the right holder.[14]

In my view, the right to become a parent is a privilege, or liberty right, in the Hohfeldian analytical system of rights, that the parent has with respect to their child. To have a liberty right to become the parent of a particular child means not to be under a duty not to act as the parent of that child.

This goes against the most influential contemporary philosophical accounts of the right to parent, which see it not as a privilege, but as a claim right held by sufficiently good parents, and protecting their interest in being parents. On this view, people's interest in parenting is weighty enough to ground correlative duties in others, at the very least, not to negatively interfere with the right holder's exercise of the right.[15] These are so-called dual-interest views, coming in many shapes that share a common feature: the belief that the right to parent is grounded in a combination of children's and adults' interests. For reasons on which I elaborate at length in other work,[16] this view is incompatible with the most plausible understanding of children's moral status. The only feature that distinguishes children from adults, as far as their rights and duties are concerned, is their incompletely developed autonomy.[17] This feature makes it the case that adults may exercise authority over children, but only to the extent to which paternalist behaviour is needed to protect children's important interests. Children's moral status is otherwise no lesser than adults': in particular, their interests may not be sacrificed for the sake of protecting other people's interests any more than it is permissible to sacrifice the interest of an adult for the sake of protecting other people's interests. If so, the exercise of authority over them, including parental authority, must be justified by appeal to their interests, and not their parents' interests. The adults who raise children often see this activity, and their relationship with the child more generally, as a great source of value in their lives. To many, parenting brings joy, meaning, welcome challenges, and opportunities for self-development, and all these things can greatly contribute to the parents' own wellbeing. However, the adults' interest in enjoying such goods doesn't play a role in justifying their custodial rights, just as, say, the child's paediatrician's interest in practicing medicine doesn't play any role in justifying her role in administering medical treatments to the child. The right to become a parent does not protect the interests of would-be parents in holding custody; the right, therefore (and given my endorsement of the interest theory of rights), is not a claim but a liberty, or a privilege: the parent is morally free to control the child's life because, and to the extent to which, such control is in the child's interest.[18]

Since parenting is a fiduciary role, when several parties intend to bring up the same child, custody should go to the party who would make the better rearer for that child.[19] More generally, the moral right to become the parent of a child is held by the best available parent to that child, where "available" means that the would-be parent has expressed the willingness to parent the specific child. The fact that the right to become a child's parent does not track the interest in being that child's custodian is in line with how we usually think about fiduciary roles. Nobody believes that, say, an occupational therapist has a claim (that is, interest-protecting) right to guide her patients who suffer from dementia.

This understanding of the right to become a parent as a privilege will strike many as counterintuitive—although, as I explain elsewhere,[20] it need not be exceedingly so. One reason it appears counterintuitive has to do with the epistemic hurdles of making comparative judgements of parental excellence. I don't want to underplay this worry, and a fully fleshed-out account of how to allocate custody will have to say a lot more than I can say here about standards of parental competency. These standards should be set relative to the would-be parent's ability to protect children's interests, and I shall presently give a bit more detail about these interests and about the kind of personal qualities generally required for parental excellence. In many cases it will be difficult to make secure judgements about who is the better parent. All this shows, in my view, is that in many cases it will hard or impossible to determine who has the moral right to become the parent of a particular child. (There may also be cases, however, when there is no fact about this matter, if certain parental abilities are incommensurable *and* if, as a result, it is impossible to compare individuals with respect to their parental abilities.) But the epistemic challenge shouldn't be overestimated either. As a matter of fact, judges who take into consideration the interest of the child to settle custody disputes frequently make judgements about the claimants' relative parental abilities.

Tensions between child-centred views, like mine, and common-sense morality can easily be explained—in a debunking manner—by the long history of seeing and treating children as if they lacked rights. My child-centred understanding of the right to become a parent as a privilege is in line with the "best interest of the child" legal principle, which many take to be a guiding standard in cases when state agents or private institutions make direct decisions about children's lives. The principle is formulated in article 3 of the UN Convention on the Rights of the Child, from 1989, whose paragraph 3.1 says: "In all actions concerning children, whether undertaken by public or private social welfare institutions, courts of law, administrative authorities or legislative bodies, the best interests of the child shall be a primary consideration." According to the best interest of the child principle, in disputes concerning children, the interests of the adult parties are subordinated to those of the child, and should not be considered as potential counterweights to the child's interests. The principle is open to several interpretations, some of which are very implausible.[21] I assume that the principle is correct if it is interpreted to say that children's interest be given no less consideration than similarly weighty interests of adults. Amongst other things, this excludes the (unconsented-to) exercise of power over children in ways that serve the interest of the power holder in exercising authority; therefore, it also excludes a justification of the right to parent by appeal to the parents' own interests in being parents.

Individuals who hold privileges justified by appeal to *other* people's interests—for instance, to doctor—cannot sell or gift their privileges. My view of the right to parent obviously indicts as impermissible all those cases of surrogacy that are properly described as a privately organized transfer of the right: a privilege to exercise control over another person may not be privately transferred. Nor, more generally, can it be legitimate for an individual to transfer a control right that she holds only because the person over whom control is being exercised benefits from the fact that the first individual holds the control right. Just as a medical doctor lacks the normative power to sell, or gift, the right she has to treat her patients who are in a coma, so do parents lack a normative power to alienate their right to parent a particular child by transferring it to another party. This is not because the right to custody can never be alienated. It is permissible to put one's child up for adoption in certain cases; but then the allocation of custody should follow the child's interest and is not a matter of private agreement. As I explain in the conclusions, a form of surrogacy involving women who gestate with the intention to alienate their right to parent may be legitimate.

2.3. Parents' Rights and Children's Interests

The right to become a child's parent is analytically distinguishable from the rights *of* parents (or "parental rights"). In my view, the latter are, in Hohfeldian terms, a combination of claims, powers and liberties. To become a parent means to step into a fiduciary role which involves the acquisition of duties concerning the satisfaction of the child's interests.[22] To discharge their fiduciary duties, parents must be able to require compliance from the child—for instance, to be able to require the child not to engage in disproportionately dangerous action. They also need to be protected, in their interaction with the child, from disruptions that threaten the performance of parental duties. A mundane example of such disruption is others offering food to the child without parental permission; the food may be dangerous for the child, and hence the parent has a right to control its acceptance. More generally, parental rights enable and protect parents in the fulfilment of their parental role by making it possible for parents to create duties of compliance on the side of the child and of non-interference on the side of other people. Thus, parental rights are necessary for the successful exercise of the parental role, which consists in the creation of a, hopefully securely, attached relationship between parent and child, and in significant control of the child's life to the child's own benefit.

I don't provide a full account of children's interests,[23] but, for the present purposes, I note three elements of such an account. First, alongside interests in physical wellbeing, security, and education, children also have interests in emotional and relational wellbeing. Thus, there are several personal qualities that can qualify adults as good parents, which elsewhere I call "personal parenting resources."[24] They include patience, kindness, attentiveness, self-knowledge, sound judgment, a nurturing disposition, and emotional maturity. The more one displays such dispositions the more likely one is to be the best available parent for a child, as there is no such thing as providing a child with too much patience, kindness, good judgment, etc. By contrast, a person who is very rich because they have more than their fair share of wealth cannot claim custody on grounds that such wealth would benefit the child; not because the latter claim isn't true, but because the right to become a child's parent tracks not only the child's interest, but also the interest we all have in fairness.

Second, it is important to distinguish between (children's) wellbeing interests and their respect interests. The distinction between these two types of interests, and hence between two types of interest-protecting rights, is familiar from the work of Amartya Sen, Dabra Satz, and Harry Brighouse and Adam Swift. Brighouse and Swift distinguish between interests in "anything that contributes to her well-being or flourishing" and those in "having her dignity respected—in being treated in ways that reflect her moral status as an agent, as a being with the capacity for judgment and choice, even where that respect does *not* make her life go better."[25] I call the first "wellbeing interests" and the second "respect interests." Respect interests might be best understood as a class of wellbeing interests, in which case the claim should be that respect doesn't make children's lives better *otherwise*; I don't take a position on this matter here. In my view, respect interests protect not only the exercise of individuals' agency (and so, in the case of children, treatment in accordance with the level of developed autonomy of each particular child), but also the treatment of individuals in situations in which they cannot give consent: for instance, during childhood or while unconscious. They include an interest in not having one's own general interests set back in order to advance the interest of an adult in doing the controlling. For instance, imposing a setback of a child's wellbeing interests for the sake of allowing a suboptimal parent to satisfy an interest in rearing counts as disrespect. Thus, my view about the right to parent is fully supported by the constraint against allocating authority over children for the sake of satisfying an adult's interest in the exercise of authority.

Finally, attachments, and hence continuity in caring relationships, are very important to children's wellbeing. Children have a claim to the voluntary preservation of caring relationships with adults, as long as the continuation of such relationships doesn't set back their overall interests. To clarify this, I must introduce a last distinction, which I elaborate further below. It concerns the difference between parents' control rights and their associational rights. The first are powers that enable parents to control children's lives in a number of ways: for instance, the right to decide on children's diet, bed time, daily schedules, or discipline. To provide another illustration of a parental control right, one can create a duty in one's child to stop singing an offending tune and, in other adults, not to encourage the child to keep singing it. The second type of parental right protects parents' relationship with their child. But, in my view, *all* adults, association with whom would be in the child's best interest, have a right with respect to the child to initiate a relationship with her, and a claim right to adequate opportunities to seek such association.[26] This is controversial. A bit less controversial is the claim, to which I also subscribe, that adults who have successfully established such a relationship—including, obviously, the child's parents, but also other individuals such as members of the extended family and caregivers—are entitled to the protection of that relationship as long as it does not set back the child's interests. Because loving parents have a powerful interest in the continuation of their relationship with the child, and the dissolution of the relationship, when good, would harm not only the child but also the adult, they have a claim right that others do not prevent them from continuing the relationship. Roughly speaking, this distinction is similar to the one between having custody over a child and obtaining visitation rights.

While both the right to parent and the rights of parents are justified because they protect the child's best interest, existing practices of custody allocation and existing legal parental rights don't always track children's moral rights. Natural parents acquire custody over their children automatically, without any competence check, and lose it only in cases of proven, and usually egregious, parental abuse or neglect. In some jurisdictions, custody disputes are settled in ways that explicitly sacrifice the child's best interest.[27] And parents typically have, over their children, legal rights that are more extensive than what they need be in order to protect children's interests. Parents can irreversibly modify their children's bodies without medical indication for religious or aesthetic reasons that children may well grow up to disown. They can deny their children medically recommended treatments, enrol them in educational and religious practices independently from how such enrolment serves the child's interests, paternalize them in excess of what is justifiable given the development of the child's autonomy, and prevent them from establishing or continuing beneficial relationships. Therefore, there is a justificatory gap between the level of parents' power over children that is necessary to advance children's own interests and the level of parents' power over children that is actually guaranteed by states. Exactly how wide the gap is depends on my (controversial) view about the right to become a child's parent being a mere privilege. But the existence of a gap is widely acknowledged by contemporary family ethicists; many believe that parents have unjustifiably extensive legal rights over their children[28] and this belief plays an important role in my argument.

2.4. Two Caveats

This is the place to also clarify how I distance myself from other child-centred rejections of surrogacy. Mary Warnock, perhaps the best-known critic of commercial surrogacy, believes that surrogacy agreements degrade children by treating them as commodities.[29] In section 3, I explain why the trope of surrogacy as child selling is, most likely, a red herring: critics of commercial surrogacy can make their point just as powerfully if they see it as a (mere) transaction in the legal right to parent. In any case, nothing in my account hinges on the presupposition that children born out of commercial surrogacy are likely to feel degraded by the way they were brought into the world. It is not their procreation, but the way in which adults are permitted to acquire custody over them that disrespects these children.

I am also not exercised by the worry, raised, amongst others, by Elizabeth Anderson (1990), that children who know that they were born due to a commercial surrogacy agreement may be less likely than other children to believe that their parents love them.[30] This seems implausible, assuming that the parent-child relationship is otherwise good, and in particular if the child is securely attached to the parent. Other concerns about the wellbeing of the children of surrogacy, if warranted, generate reasons against both commercial surrogacy and altruistic surrogacy: children who know that their gestational mother carried them with the explicit intention of separating from them at birth may suffer from feelings of abandonment.[31] I am agnostic about the likelihood of this harm, and so my argument does not rely on it. This being said, section 4 contains a plea for childrearing arrangements that take seriously the more general emotional grievances of children who have been separated, at birth or soon after, from their birth mothers.[32]

Against this normative background, I now proceed to an account of surrogacy that goes beyond the merely intuitive one described above. I start by examining surrogacy models and their moral stakes.

3. What Is Surrogacy? Three Models

There is disagreement over how to understand what goes on in surrogacy, and this disagreement is normatively loaded. Critics of surrogacy often present it as the selling, or trafficking, of children. Some defenders of surrogacy who reject the child-trafficking model rely on the private adoption model, which consists in the transfer of custody. Yet others argue that surrogacy is a provision of services, and maybe of gametes. I discuss these models in turn, and argue that neither the private adoption model nor the provision of services model succeeds in its aim of showing that surrogacy is a permissible practice. But the private adoption model is, at least, conceptually convincing. However, as I explain, it is also closer to child trafficking than is assumed by those who defend surrogacy.

3.1. The Child-Trafficking Model

The moral difference between selling a child and selling custody over that child, I argue here, is of degree, not of kind. Critics of commercial surrogacy often claim that the practice is equivalent to child selling, or trafficking. Anderson says as much in her depiction of surrogacy as commodifying children.[33] And one of the most prominent complaints raised by the Warnock report is that "a surrogacy agreement is degrading to the child who is to be the outcome of it, since, for all practical purposes, the child will have been bought for money."[34] If this charge was correct, then, as Bonnie Steinbock notes, the objection against surrogacy would be of the same nature as that against slavery, because surrogacy would, in effect, create child-slaves: young human beings to be bought and sold.[35]

Defenders of surrogacy, unsurprisingly, deny that it is a form of child trafficking. Stephen Wilkinson, for example, notes that surrogate mothers cannot sell their child because they cannot own her, and what cannot be owned cannot be sold or bought. The object of the commercial transaction, he writes, is "a limited bundle of parental rights, not the baby itself."[36] Others make a similar point: Richard Arneson claims that the good being bought is the right and obligation to be the parent of a particular infant and that "[a] parent does not in any sense own her child even if she acquires parental rights and responsibilities by purchase."[37]

I find these replies convincing as far as they aim to show that surrogacy cannot involve child selling properly speaking—that is, as a transfer of (full) property rights.[38] Yet they are only superficially convincing; the worry that commercial surrogacy is similar to commerce in slaves isn't fully assuaged by noting that surrogacy involves a transaction in custody, that is, in parental rights, and not in human beings. The reason is that parents' legal rights *are*, largely, control rights over their children, just like property in persons partly consists in rights to control the lives of those persons. And, indeed, on some accounts, part of what makes slavery objectionable is the unjustified power aspect of the relationship between slave and slave owner. If so, the moral similarity between children and slaves cannot be dismissed merely by saying that rights over children don't amount to (full) property rights. (A fully reformed childrearing relative to the *status quo*, in which custody consisted only of a right to implement decisions over the child, but that the decisions were not made by parents—but by, say, childrearing experts—would be able to assuage the slavery challenge. In this case, parents wouldn't have any control rights over children. More generally, the more extensive parents' control rights over their children are—i.e., the higher the stakes of custody allocation—the more pertinent is the analogy with slavery.)

Let me elaborate. There is an obvious reason to resist the analogy between the predicament of slaves and that of children born though surrogacy. As Steinbock puts it, "there are important differences between slavery and a surrogate agreement. The child born of a surrogate is not treated cruelly or deprived of freedom or resold; none of the things that make slavery so awful are part of surrogacy."[39] Steinbock seems to assume that objections to slavery are exhausted by complaints about the *actual* treatment of the slave, which is typically harsh, exploitative and exposes the slaves to major unpredictable changes in their lives. But this criticism is not exhaustive: the mere arbitrary power that slave owners hold over slaves generates a serious grievance. One objection to slavery survives in the absence of any harsh, exploitative, or wrongfully unpredictable treatment of the slave. And this objection is powerful enough to provide the intuitive appeal of a distinctive strand in political philosophy: Neo-republicanism is specifically designed to capture the grievances of slaves who are well-treated by their kind, or perhaps morally enlightened, masters.[40] Above and beyond any *actual* harmful treatment, slavery raises the obvious objection that it unjustifiably places people at the mercy of others, who can then use their power with impunity. Liberals, too, can account for this particular wrong of slavery, even if, arguably, not as robustly as republicans.[41] Now, slave owners, in antiquity as in more recent times, have, indeed, very extensive legal rights over their slaves, including powers to kill, maim, or overwork them. Parents in most societies today lack

the legal rights to do these things to their children: in property par-
lance, they have nothing close to full ownership over their children.
Yet, parents do have extensive legal rights to control almost every
aspect of their children's lives—and the younger and more vulnerable the children, the more extensive the parental rights. Imagine a
practice whereby slaves may not be killed, maimed, or overworked
with impunity, but their lives are comprehensively controlled by
other people, from whose authority they cannot emancipate themselves. Whether or not this is proper "slavery," it raises prima facie
moral concerns of the same nature, though maybe not of the same
degree, as typical cases of slavery, and people subjected to it have a
serious grievance. As Frederick Douglass, once himself a slave, put
it, "it was slavery—not its mere incidents—that I hated."[42]

The situation of children in general, then, *is* strikingly similar
to that of slaves belonging to benevolent, indeed, often loving, and
occasionally adoring, owners.[43] Three conditions, when simultaneously met, can make all the moral difference between children and
(adult) slaves. The first condition is, I assume, always met: unlike
adult slaves, children lack the right to control their own lives to the
same extent as typical adults; this is why they are not wronged by
other people's control of *some* aspects of their lives, including by the
very fact of having custodians. The second condition requires that
custody be allocated *via* justified procedures, in which case individual parents occupy a position of legitimate power in relation to
their children, unlike slave owners, who never occupy a position of
legitimate power in relation to their slaves. The third condition is
that parents do not hold legal rights in excess of their moral rights,
in which case parents' rights do not constitute objectionable control rights over other human beings, and thus are entirely unlike
slaveholders' rights.

The last two conditions can be, but are not always, met. The most
coherent defenders of surrogacy, like Arneson and Cecile Fabre,
appear to ignore the second condition and defend their views by
assuming that the third is met. They, too, believe that the rights of

parents are justified, and hence limited, by the child's interests: "The rights that parents have to control their children's behaviour and to make major decisions affecting their lives while they are young are assigned to parents for the sake of their children's welfare and are supposed to be exercised for the good of their children. The point of parental rights is to enable parents to carry out their obligations to care for their children."[44] A similar view is defended by Fabre.[45] But this defence of surrogacy is successful only given an equivocation between moral and legal parental rights. I believe Arneson's and Fabre's claims are correct if taken to describe moral rights, yet they are implausible as a description of limits to current legal parental rights. As long as, in a particular society, parental legal rights are unjustified, the argument that surrogacy is not a form of trafficking because children, unlike slaves, cannot be owned is, *in that society*, unconvincing. In section 2.3 above I gave a few examples of how the legal rights of parents extend beyond what is justifiable by appeal to the interest of the child. The view that parents' moral rights do not extend beyond what is necessary to protect the interests of the child is perhaps not dominant, but neither is it particularly unusual.[46] On this view, then—and, more generally, on any account which indicts the extent of existing legal parental control rights as illegitimate— children are, to some extent, morally on a par with slaves. The difference is that the law allows more limited mistreatment of children than it permits in the case of slaves, in slave-owning societies. And perhaps the arc of children's history does bend towards justice: the extent of parental legal rights has been shrinking over time. While it's still bending, however, those who say that surrogacy is a bit like slave trafficking have a point. Their point—and this is not yet properly appreciated in the surrogacy debate—depends on parenting itself being a bit like slave-holding.

Similar things can be said about the second condition. Above, I explained why children's moral status requires custody-allocation procedures that track, as closely as possible, children's own interests. If so, then people who acquire custody by buying it or by receiving it as a gift occupy an illegitimate position of authority over a human being, similar to the slave owner—albeit to a lesser extent.

But it is interesting to note that, whatever the correct justification and extent of parental rights, it appears that selling custody is no less objectionable than selling children proper. Remember cases 2 and 3 in section 1, which looked a lot like "child selling." Imagine, for example, that the adoptive couples in those cases live in societies in which parents' legal rights map onto their moral rights; imagine also—*contra* my above-stated view—that the right to custody partly protects the interest of would-be parents, and hence, that the right may be privately transferred. It is difficult to see what difference it makes to call the transfer of custody over these children "child selling," rather than the mere selling of parental rights. And this is why arguments in favour of child selling don't appear to raise concerns that are *fundamentally* different from those raised by commercial partial surrogacy. For instance, David Boudreaux's proposal that we should allow parents to sell very young children (who, presumably, are still unattached to their initial custodians) draws its appeal—limited as it is—from the *proviso* that the buyers have no more rights over children than parents usually have.[47] Similarly, Fabre's defence of surrogacy seems to entail that the sale of (rights over) a child is, all things equal,[48] just as permissible as commercial surrogacy.

The sale of a child just *is* the sale of control rights over her.[49] Therefore, the polemic about whether commercial surrogacy is a form of child trafficking or a "mere" selling of custody seems merely semantic. What matters is not how we describe—as child selling or as rights-selling—cases when an intending parent pays a gestational mother, and, as a result, the intending parent is legally free to take home the child and raise her as their own. What matters, instead, are the interrelated issues of whether legal parental rights exceed parents' moral rights, and whether the holding of custody over children is adequately regulated. To the extent to which parents have excessive legal rights to control their children, their holding these rights is objectionable for the same reasons that make it objectionable for slave owners to hold control rights over slaves. And to the extent to which the conditions on acquiring or retaining custody fail to reflect the full extent of children's rights, holding custody amounts to having illegitimate legal control rights over other human beings, again, as in the case of slavery.

As I explained, my view is that legal rights to control children ought to be properly limited, in content, by the interest of the child. But this claim requires further interpretation. On a more demanding, neorepublican, account, it is not enough that the rights-protected interests of the child are not *in fact* set back by parental decisions. Rather, parents should not have rights to control children's lives in arbitrary ways, that is, in ways that *can* set back the children's interests. Fully unobjectionable childrearing would then require that the exercise of all legal parental rights be properly and effectively monitored to ensure they can only be exercised in the interest of the child.[50] On a less demanding, liberal interpretation, it may be permissible for parents to hold legal rights for the exercise of which they cannot be held fully accountable; on this view, it is enough that parents refrain from exercising power over the child in ways that are not justified by the interest of the child.[51] The proper limitation of parents' legal rights, even understood in the more modest key, will surely go beyond the typical requirements of not neglecting or abusing one's child, which, if satisfied, ensure the continuation of parental status in current societies. If so, then children who live in societies that fail to limit parents' legal rights are (whoever their custodian) in the normative situation that makes even benevolent slavery objectionable.

3.2. The Privately Arranged Adoption Model

If surrogacy is properly thought of as a private transfer of custody from the child's initial custodian (the surrogate) to the intending couple, then it is akin to privately arranged adoption—as in Case 2 (in section 1). Another feature that makes this kind of adoption unusual is that parties agree to transfer the rights before the child has even been conceived. Iwan Davies, for example, explicitly defines surrogacy as "adoption controlled by the parties, planned before conception and involving a genetic link(s) with one (or both) [intending] parent(s)."[52] In countries that allow gamete sale or donation, of course, the child need not have any genetic link with the intending parents.

The adoption model applies most obviously to cases of partial surrogacy, in which the surrogate, being both a gestational and a genetic mother, meets the legal conditions to qualify, by default, as the child's initial custodian in a variety of legislations. But while some countries, such as the United States, take genetic connectedness as the main or sole ground for the initial allocation of custody,[53] others allocate initial custody to the gestational mother, following the principle that the legal mother is the woman who gives birth. In such legislations, adoption appears to adequately model both partial surrogacy and full surrogacy. The reason behind this principle is that one can always be sure who the natural mother of a baby is (*mater semper certa est*). Yet, if one thinks about the legal mother as being the same as the genetic one, this claim is false given the current state of assisted reproductive technologies; alternatively, the claim begs the question of whether the gestational relationship with a child is more relevant to holding the moral and legal right to parent than the genetic relationship. Section 4 provides a pro tanto reason in favour of this principle.

To repeat, it makes little moral difference whether surrogacy is portrayed as the privately organized transfer of custody—which is the same as a private adoption—or as child selling. Indeed, one form of child selling itself has been defended as being on a par with commercial adoption.[54] If so, the legitimacy of surrogacy depends on whether the sale or donation of one's custody, as happens in private adoption and in surrogacy, is permissible. This, in turn, depends on the nature of the right to parent, and on the grounds on which it can be acquired. Claim rights in property—for instance, my right over my laptop or, closer to the issue at hand and hence also more controversially, one's right to one's pet—can be privately transferred. But if the allocation of custody must be decided by appeal to the best interest of the child, then neither markets in nor the gifting of custody is permissible. (That is, on the assumption that selling custody and gifting custody are not the allocative mechanisms that serve the child's interests best;[55] I find such assumption entirely convincing.) More generally, it is hard to see how a person can have the moral power to privately transfer a liberty right to control another's life, when the person in case has that right only because this is in the interest of the person over whom the right is being exercised.

Some scholars of surrogacy are aware of this problem and believe that appeal to the child's best interest is a reason to oppose both privately organized adoptions and, if it turns out to be the same kind of thing, surrogacy. In the words of Edgar Page; "Built into the law is the principle that children are not transferable by individual parents. This principle is also rooted in much of our moral thinking and it underlies many objections to surrogacy arrangements. Given the principle, it seems to follow directly that both total surrogacy and genetic surrogacy are unacceptable."[56] The same principle indicts private adoption as impermissible. It is unclear why philosophers such as Arneson, who agree that the rights of parents are entirely justified (and so, presumably, constrained) by appeal to children's interests, nevertheless think that a market in custody is morally permissible.

Here I have argued that if surrogacy is a kind of privately arranged adoption, it is wrongful since we have no reason to assume that markets in, or the gifting of, custody will match children with the best available rearers; as such, they are disrespectful of children. I next turn to the third model of surrogacy, as the provision of gestatory services and, in some cases, gametes.

3.3. The Provision of Services and Gametes Model

The private adoption model of surrogacy captures well (although it cannot justify) cases of partial surrogacy, when the surrogate, being both a genetic procreator and the gestational mother, has all the usual bases of custody allocation. But this model seems inadequate in cases of full surrogacy, especially when both of the intending parents are also the gamete providers. At least on the widespread view that genetic procreators have, by default, the right to custody, full surrogacy cannot be understood as a form of adoption, because, on this view, the full surrogate lacks the right. This result is welcome for those defenders of surrogacy who, like Page, worry that appeal to the child's interest makes surrogacy indefensible as a form of private adoption. Many argue for the permissibility of full surrogacy by conceptualizing it as the provision of a gestatory service.[57] If the right to custody is, by default, held by the child's genetic procreators, then in the case of full surrogacy the commissioning couple should automatically have custody when the baby is born. As Page puts it, "[T]he child belongs to the commissioning parents from the outset as they do not at any stage relinquish their rights and duties in respect of it."[58] I return to cases of full surrogacy, and explore the consistency between appeal to the child's interest and the view that genetic procreators have the default right to parent, in section 4.

Cases where at least one of the gametes has been donated or sold to the intending couple by donor(s) other than the surrogate, are more complicated. In those cases, too, the surrogate mother never had the right, and hence no private transfer of the right took place *from her* to the intending parents: she has merely sold, or gifted, her gestatory services. What is less clear is that the intending couple always had the right to custody over the resulting child in those cases: plausibly, it is permissible to obtain gametes from donors,[59] but the crucial question is whether the intending couple also acquire, together with the gamete, custody rights over the child developed from it. If they do—in virtue of a principle that says that the genetic procreators always have the right to first custody—this is only possible if individuals have the moral power to privately transfer custody. The problem with the privately or-ganized adoption model necessarily beleaguers full surrogacy with donor gametes. If the intending parents don't acquire parental rights merely by acquiring gamete(s), then the custody issue is yet to be settled, and hence, the act of surrogacy in question may or may not result in their having custody.

Even more ambitiously, Page attempts to extend the model of gestation as mere provision of services and donation to partial surrogacy.[60] If gamete donation or sale is permissible in general, it must also be permissible when the donor or seller is the surrogate herself. Page proposes that we should understand partial surrogacy as a situation in which the surrogate donates her own gamete *in utero*. On his view, then, surrogates sell, or donate, only services (if they are full surrogates) or both gametes and services (if they are partial surrogates). Since they either are genetically unrelated to the child or have transferred their gamete before conception, they never had a right to custody to transfer. Rather, the intending parents are the parents from the get-go: there has never been a time when the child had another parent. This is the intentional account of parenting. Obviously, this proposal, too, fails unless the genetic parent—in this case, the partial surrogate—is morally permitted to transfer custody over her newborn. Even if the surrogate can sell or donate the gamete, over the course of the pregnancy the moral status of the entity she transferred changes to that of an individual over whom nobody can have full property rights. For Page's ac-count to succeed, then, one needs an independent account of why the surrogate can transfer not only her gamete and services but also her right to custody.

Some believe it is impermissible to sell gestatory services in the context of commercial surrogacy,[61] sometimes even while accepting that gametes (or even embryos) can be permissibly donated.[62]

I don't subscribe to this view; that is, I take no issue with a woman's freedom to provide either gestatory services (including for pay), or gametes, or both. I resist the service and gamete-provision model of surrogacy on a strictly child-centred basis.

Conceptually, the difficulty with this model of surrogacy is the unclarity about the precise service that is being provided by the gestational surrogate. As Kajsa Ekis Ekman puts it: "[I]f pregnancy is a job—what, then, is the product?"[63] The most plausible interpretation of surrogacy as a gestatory service is that the surrogate provides just that: gestation. But this interpretation, as defenders and critics of surrogacy alike note, does not provide support to surrogacy. Discussing "Baby M," a widely publicized case of surrogacy from the mid-1980s, Steinbock notes: "If the surrogate were paid merely for being willing to be impregnated and carrying the child to term, then she would fulfil the contract upon giving birth. She could take the money and the child. Mr. Stern did not agree to pay Ms. Whitehead merely to have his child, but to provide him with a child."[64] Michelle Moody-Adams (1991, 175) makes this point when she asks, rhetorically, "[H]ow many couples would be willing to pay for a surrogate's 'services,' and then allow her to keep the baby?" And Fabre argues to the same conclusion by appeal to an analogy between partial surrogacy and baking: "although the surrogate mother, in partial surrogacy, provides her egg, commissioning parents are not buying that egg as well as her service, any more than in buying bread from my local bakery I thereby buy the flour which goes into the bread."[65]

If the surrogate merely provides the service of gestating the child, not the child herself—or, rather, the right to become her parent—then the question of who may raise the newborn needs to be decided by considerations independent of the agreement between the parties who engaged in the surrogacy process. It will obviously be in the best interest of the newborn to have a parent. In my view, that parent should be determined on grounds of the newborn's best interest. This is denied by some proponents of the service and gamete model of surrogacy, for instance, Page. His claim that the child belongs to the person whose body produced, or who legitimately acquired, the gametes from which the child develops, is not merely metaphorical. Rather, it is part of what Page presents as a quasi-ownership interest that people have in their genetically related child.[66] This ownership model of parenting is needed for his defence of surrogacy, and explains why, on this account, people can sell not only their gametes but also the right to rear any children that evolve from them. Page's attempt to rescue surrogacy as service provision fails because it shows too much: if his quasi-ownership of children thesis were correct, it would also vindicate, as permissible, private adoptions and, more generally, private transfers of custody—and thus the thesis runs afoul of the child's best interest principle.

Understanding surrogacy as the provision of services and, possibly, gametes, therefore provides no more justification for surrogacy than the privately arranged adoption model. It is, moreover, a less conceptually compelling model since it misrepresents what people seek from surrogacy as the mere provision of a service, and not of a "product." If so, on this model there should be no presumption that the intending parents are entitled to the custody of the child. But, surely, obtaining the custody of the child is *the*, perhaps only, point of surrogacy as actually practiced.

This leaves open the possibility that full surrogacy is permissible when both gametes are provided by the intending parents, because in these cases many will think that the intending parents' right to custody can be justified by appeal to the genetic relationship with the child. I discuss this case in the next section and criticize the view that genetic procreators have the right to custody *merely* in virtue of the fact that the child has developed from their gametes. Allocating custody to genetic procreators is compatible with the best interest of the child only in cases when they are the best available parents. But, as I argue, genetic connections with a child are, at most, a good *proxy* for the quality of parenting her. And while in some cases the genetic connection will be the best proxy, in other cases we may have better ones. For instance, gestation can be the best proxy for serving the child's interest, if a bond exists, at birth, between the gestational mother and her child and if the preservation of this bond is beneficial to the child. In such situations, both partial and full surrogates have a stronger, although not undefeatable, claim to custody than genetic procreators. In any case, if surrogacy is merely the provision of services plus, possibly, gametes, the intending parents have no automatic right to custody.

To conclude this section, the best way to understand surrogacy is as a private agreement between several parties, which consists in the attempt to voluntary transfer the surrogate's presumptive right to custody to the intending parents. Sometimes, this is accompanied by an attempt to transfer the gamete donors' presumptive rights to rear children born of their gametes. Yet, if the right to become a parent is a liberty right that an individual holds in relation to a particular child on the basis of being the best available parent for that child, such a transfer cannot be morally permissible. Neither markets in, nor the gifting of, the right to parent are legitimate.

4. Full Surrogacy with Intending Parents' Gametes

For a child-centred view like mine, the most interesting case of surrogacy, and the most difficult to assess, is full surrogacy with both gametes coming from the intending parents. As we have seen, this situation seems to (but, I will show, does not always) resist description as an attempted transfer of the right to custody from the surrogate to the intending parents. Common-sense morality, legal practice, and most philosophers assume that genetic procreators have a presumptive right to rear their progeny. A defender of surrogacy who accepts the child-centred account of the right to parent might say that, once the child is born (or maybe even before that), the intending couple's right is guaranteed by the genetic connection they have with the child; the surrogate never had the right. When such cases are of the commercial type, the intending parents pay the surrogate merely for her services, and therefore their payment of the surrogate does not, in itself, do anything to establish their right to parent; and in neither commercial nor altruistic full surrogacy—the objection goes—is there any need to transfer the right to custody from the surrogate to the intending parents.

Here I examine the most widespread justifications of the prevalent view that the genetic procreators are presumptive custodians. I do not oppose the view that a genetic connection is a decent proxy for serving the interest of the child in bonding, and this explains why a gamete provider ought to get custody when other parental qualifications are equal across all claimants. But in surrogacy they aren't, and the child's interest in bonding is more likely to indicate the full surrogate, *qua* gestational mother, as the holder of the right to parent. Both the genetic and the gestational connection, however, are mere proxies for one aspect of the child's wellbeing, and there may well exist (detectable) cases when a third party has, in fact, the right.

Therefore, a full treatment of the issue of surrogacy requires an analysis of the normative relevance of biological relationships between parent and child.[67] In particular, it is essential to clarify how appeal to the fact that one is a gamete provider can do some work towards establishing that person's right to parent the child developed from the gamete. Until recently, of course, gestational mothers were always also genetic procreators; but the separation of the genetic and gestational aspect of the relationship, enabled by assisted reproductive technologies, makes particularly salient the need for a normative analysis of the gestational connection in its own right. Some interesting lessons can be learned by looking at its significance.

I said that on a fiduciary account of parenting, it is the child's interest that establishes who has the right to control their lives, but so far I have said nothing about how to determine the first acquisition of custody—that is, what considerations are relevant to identifying the person who has the right to parent a newborn. The general practice, across places and times, is to grant custody on the basis of the genetic or gestational connection. (As well as, in many legislations, on the basis of being the mother's husband.) This is what makes surrogacy intelligible as a subsidiary practice of granting first custody to those designated by biological parents. It is far from obvious that the general practice of granting custody to genetic parents is *always* in the interest of the child, and hence legitimate; it is even less obvious, if the general practice is justified by appeal to the child's interest in being parented by her procreators, that the subsidiary practice of surrogacy can be justified.

My child-centred view is not inimical to a presumptive right to rear one's biological baby.[68] I look at child-centred appeals to the moral relevance of genetic connections between parents and children and then examine the prospects of gestational connections to justify the right to custody. The overall conclusion is that, in some cases, and other parenting qualifications equal, it is the surrogate mother who is more likely to have the right to custody than the genetic parent, even in full surrogacy with the gametes of intentional parents. If so, such instances of surrogacy, too, turn out to be attempts of transferring of the right to parent—the practice that I have criticized in the previous sections as illegitimate.

4.1. Child-Centred Appeals to Genetic Connections and the Right to Parent

The assumption that people have a default right to rear their genetic children is probably one of the most widespread moral beliefs. But many attempts to make sense of it are incompatible with a child-centred account of the right: by appeal to bodily self-ownership[69] or to a belief that children and parents are not fully separable.[70]

Some believe that people have an autonomy right to pursue parenthood with a body part that they own.[71] But if children's moral status is such that their interests are as weighty as adults' interests, then the pursuit of parenting cannot be protected by a claim to autonomy. Parent-child relationships involve control over the child, who cannot consent; hence, parenting is justified, when it is, as necessary for the protection of the child's interest, not required by the protection of the adult's interest in pursuing their conception of a good life.

More promising justifications of genetic procreators' presumptive right to parent have to do with the child's interest. Not all of these views, however, are successful in defending their intended goal, which is to justify the initial allocation of custody to genetic procreators.

David Velleman advanced the following child-centred argument, popular amongst philosophers: As he notes, many individuals raised in closed adoptions, or whose procreation involved anonymous gamete donation, spend a significant amount of time, energy, and money in search of their genetic procreators. Velleman thinks that the strong desire of which such efforts are indicative is explained by an important interest in self-knowledge that only close acquaintance with one's genetic procreator can satisfy. On this view, knowledge of our genetic procreators plays a crucial role in our identity formation: close acquaintance to our immediate kin provides us with a broader context within which to create meaning about our life than one could have in the absence of such knowledge. It is like having a special mirror that lets us understand and explore possible versions of ourselves. Velleman believes that an interest in close acquaintance with our genetic procreators is so weighty that it is morally wrong to bring into existence a child *via* gamete donation, and concludes that "other things being equal, children should be raised by their biological parents."[72] Some resist even the claim that acquaintance with one's genetic procreators is necessary for the satisfaction of the putative interests in identity-formation and self-knowledge.[73] But even if Velleman's thesis is right, it doesn't show that children's interest requires that genetic procreators raise them. Rather, it entails a child's right to (opportunities to) know, in a face-to-face context, the genetic procreator, and to have access to family stories. This can surely be achieved by recognizing and enforcing a duty of genetic procreators to make themselves available, in person and with sufficient disponibility, to their offspring, as well as by requiring gamete donation to be non-anonymous and adoptions to be open. While it is fully child-centred, and in this sense a good candidate for a proper account of the right to parent a particular child, Velleman's argument doesn't entail anything as strong as a right of the genetic procreator to control the life of the child in virtue of the child's interest in close acquaintance with the genetic procreator.

Another child-centred argument, defended by Melissa Moschella,[74] starts from the premise that genetic procreators and their children stand in a personal relationship generated by the genetic connectedness itself, a relationship the preservation of which is in the child's interest. The relationship is supposedly personal because our genetic make-up is, according to Moschella, essential to our identity; this gives the relationship a bodily aspect. But although the relationship is "bodily" (thanks to the genetic connection), it doesn't necessarily involve physical closeness. Moschella also believes that the genetic procreator's love is especially valuable to the child, and from this concludes that genetic procreators have a non-transferable duty to love the child, which usually implies a non-transferable duty to love and raise the child. Should another person take over the parental role, this would involve discontinuing the relationship between procreator and child. The genetic procreator can fulfil their duty, which is non-transferable, only if they have the right to raise the child. To the extent to which the view has appeal, it does not entail its conclusion. It is not clear why a relationship that is not embodied, even with someone who played a major causal role in determining one's identity, can be called a *personal* relationship. After all, the genetic procreators and the child may have never been in any kind of physical contact; and (hence) there is no assumption of an *emotional* attachment being formed. For the same reason, it is unclear why discontinuing the relationship should have a negative emotional impact on the child. Moschella indicates the potential worry that the child may feel rejected by her genetic procreators. I think such concerns should not be dismissed. But how likely feelings of rejection are will, in part, depend on background social expectations. Moreover, even granting Moschella's worry, at least in some cases, other people are so much better than the child's procreator at entering an intimate relationship with the child that, all things considered, the child will be emotionally better off with them even if the discontinuation of the "bodily," but not physical and in no way attached, relationship with the parent has somewhat offset the emotional interests of the child. Third, and more importantly, her conclusion that the genetic procreator has the right to parent does not follow, for the same reason as in the case of Velleman's argument. A genetic procreator can love the child they procreated and fulfil some of her emotional needs even without being the child's custodian. At most, the child's interest in having a relationship with her genetic procreators indicates that just childrearing arrangements will encourage genetic procreators to be part of the child's life in a loving capacity.

A promising account of how genetic connections are relevant for holding the right to custody, then, must fulfil two desiderata:

(a) It should be child-centred; that is, it should explain why somebody, in virtue of being a genetic procreator, is more likely than other individuals to serve the child's interests; and

(b) it should explain why the genetic connection matters in a way that is essential rather than peripheral to the fiduciary parental role—that is, explain how the genetic connection increases the likelihood of a feature of the parental relationship that is necessary to exercise control rights in the child's best interests.

Neither being the only person who can help the child gain important information about herself, as in Velleman's view, nor being
the only person who can give the child a unique kind of love, as
in Moschella's theory, will do, because neither feature is necessary
to enable the parent to serve the child's interest in a successful relationship with her authority figure. This is not to deny that both
features *can* contribute to the quality of parenting, and therefore
to singling out a genetic procreator as the best available parent in
specific cases. I now turn to the strongest argument in favour of the
claim that genetic procreators *in general* have a presumptive right
to parent on grounds of children's interests.

It is widely held that children have a powerful interest in being
raised by their genetical procreators because, in virtue of this connection, genetic procreators are more likely than genetically unrelated adults to bond with their children and to display the deep and
selfless love that motivates good parents.[75] If this empirical claim
is correct, it goes a long way to explain why genetic procreators
are presumptive custodians: to effectively direct a child's life for
her own good, one needs to have a good, loving relationship to the
child. One of children's main interests, of course, is in being loved,
and effective custodians are the adults who are most present in the
life of a child, especially when the child is young. They are therefore
best placed to provide children with the love they need. Further, a
loving relationship with the child facilitates (and perhaps it conceptually requires) knowledge of the child's needs. Finally, it is
plausible that children find it easier to trust and obey parental figures in the presence of mutual attachment. It then looks like one
requirement for a competent custodian is to be loving, where love
partly consists in attachment to the child. Note, however: this view
picks out more individuals than genetic procreators as presumptive
custodians, other things equal; the twin sibling of a genetic procreator may indeed have the same grounds for holding the right!

I don't take a stand on the likelihood that genetic procreators will
bond with their children quicker, or better, than other prospective

parents. Some philosophers think this thesis warrants high cre-
dence and point to studies finding that children are at significantly
higher risk of abuse by their adoptive parents than by their genetic
procreators.[76] But the relevance of these studies is unclear. First,
there are many confounding factors that could explain why adoptive parents abuse more than non-adoptive parents do,[77] factors
which are difficult if not impossible to isolate. Second, the studies
do not look separately at genetic and gestational procreators, which
makes it hard to conclude whether the genetic or the gestational
connection is responsible for the lower levels of abuse in genetically related families. Third, *other* studies conclude that the rates
of abuse in adoptive and foster families is very low, at least in the
United States and Canada,[78] and that biologically related parents
are more likely to abuse children than adoptive parents.[79]

In any case, the genetic connection is clearly neither necessary
nor sufficient for parental love as demonstrated by the existence
of bonded and loving adoptive parents and of unloving genetic
procreators.[80] So all that the thesis under examination here seeks
to establish is not *actual* bonding between genetic procreators and
their children but only its higher than average *likelihood*. But, as
David Archard observes,[81] the mere likelihood of bonding has
much less weight in establishing the right than does actual bonding.

If genetic procreators really are, other things equal, more likely
than genetically unrelated individuals to bond with, and love, their
child, this is a reason for them to gain custody when all of those
who claim it would otherwise make equally good parents of that
child. But this is not to say that genetic procreators automatically
acquire the right to parent merely by dint of their genetic relationship to the children; genetic procreative relatedness is only a proxy.
And, so, in cases of full surrogacy, intending parents who provided
the gametes don't automatically have the right to parent the newborn. First, there is no reason to assume that parents better than
the intending parents aren't sometimes available. It is possible that
some prospective custodians would make better parents for the

newborn than the intending parents on grounds other than like-lihood to bond. Mere likelihood to bond may not cut sufficient ice in favour of the intending parents, at least in some cases, thus making the latter less good, all things considered, than alternative custodians. Second, if the surrogate mother seeks custody, her case can be stronger than the intending parents' case *on the same count*, that is, with respect to fulfilling the child's interest in forming a loving relationship. Or so I argue next.

4.2. Appeals to the Gestational Connection

In past work, I have defended the claim that, typically, children come into the world being already part of an intimate caring rela-tionship with their gestational mother.[82] To some extent, the rela-tionship is based on the gestational mother's emotional responses to her pregnancy: anticipation, planning, hopes, imagination, and projection, but also anxiety and doubt. But the physical, embodied, nature of pregnancy, including its burdens, is also part and parcel of the formation of the relationship.[83] The relationship is also created through bodily interactions that, at least for the gestational mother, often have meaning and become part of the history of her relation-ship with the baby.

I talk about a "relationship" because there is reason to assume some degree of mutuality. While we cannot know what is going on in the minds of newborns, we do know that they react positively to the presence of their gestational mother, whose voice and heartbeat they can recognize during the last phase of gestation; and newborns respond preferentially to their gestational mother, physical con-tact with whom regulates the baby's hormone levels, temperature, metabolism, heartbeat, and antibody production.[84] Such findings provide some support for the plausible thesis that the bodily con-nection between newborns and their gestational mothers has at least a rudimentary psychological counterpart on the side of the newborn. They also sit well with the claim (possibly speculative but, I think, plausible) that physical proximity facilitates attachment in creatures like us—that is, in a mammalian species.

Both the child and the parent have an interest in maintaining an intimate and caring relationship; then, if gestation is the context in which such a relationship starts, there is a good *pro tanto* reason for the gestational mother's claim right to protection of the relationship. The relationship need not be custodial in order to be protected, but in cases in which other prospective parents are no better than the gestational mother on other counts, the fact that she is already attached (when she is—see below) makes her the best available custodian. My main argument has the following shape:

P1. The right to parent is held by the best available custodian.

P2. Gestation usually generates an intimate relationship between gestational mother and newborn; hence, it is a good proxy for the existence of parent-child attachment.

P3. It is in the best interest of the child to be reared by competent parents who are already attached to the child.

C1. From P1, P2, and P3, gestation generates a *pro tanto* reason to assign custody to gestational mothers, when they would make no worse parents than other adults willing to parent the baby, in respects other than actual attachment.

I also advance a secondary argument, whose full relevance will become clear in due course:

P4. Individuals have a right to continue their relationships unless (a) one of the parties does not consent to the continuation of the relationship or (b) the continuation of the relationship sets back the interests of parties that lack the power to consent.[85]

C2. From P2 and P4, gestational mothers whose relationship with the newborn does not set back the newborn's interests have a right to continue the relationship.

If successful, the main argument explains the child-centred case for sometimes giving priority to the gestational mother over the genetic procreator with respect to the right to rear—namely, when other aspects relevant to the prospective custodians' competence are equal. The second argument explains why surrogates who have already established a relationship with the newborn, and association with whom is beneficial for the newborn, have the right to remain in a protected caring relationship with the baby they brought into the world.

The second premise of the first argument has been contested. Some of my critics wonder whether the newborn can have an interest in the maintenance of the relationship with her gestational mother.[86] It is true that, at birth, this relationship is, in some important respects, unlike any other intimate relationship between adults, or between a child and an adult (or another child). The gestational mother sees the baby for the first time; the baby, being pre-verbal, can only show very little about her mental life, and so it is difficult to know with any certainty how she relates psychologically with the mother. On the other hand, gestational mothers do report powerful caring emotions towards, and, often, attachment to, the baby with whom they have been, for several months, as physically intimate as it is possible to be; and, as noted, babies seem, at birth, to prefer their gestational mothers to other adults. These considerations about the newborn's responses are also helpful in answering the challenge, raised by some, that what I describe as a bond is in fact a one-directional attitude of the mother to be explained "as responses to social or cultural cues, rather than as evidence of a two-way maternal-fetal bond."[87]

And yet, it seems very cruel—even inhumane—to separate newborns from their gestational mothers. This is especially so when the latter are unwilling, but perhaps it is cruel to the babies in all cases. The cruelty charge is best explained, I think, by the belief that a significant attachment is already in place. It is not difficult to see the appeal of this belief. The embodied aspect of the relationship may have a powerful psychological counterpart (which,

Caroline Whitbeck noted, is significant enough to help to debunk the myth of a mysterious maternal instinct[88]). Further, as Amy Mullin observes,[89] miscarriages late in a pregnancy tend to involve mourning, the depth of which is not plausibly explained by the loss of a mere hope or personal project; more likely, the mourning is explained, at least in part, by the existence of attachment, at the same time physical and emotional, to the baby. And, while the newborn's perspective is much harder to fathom, it seems plausible that many months in the closest proximity that is physically possible generates a bond with the gestational mother. Note, however, that even if the attachment is non-mutual, the argument succeeds, because the second premise states that newborns have in interest in being parented by someone who is attached to them—and hence has a stake in their wellbeing—whether or not the attachment is reciprocal. Admittedly, the presumption established if the attachment is non-mutual is very weak; but even a very weak presumption will do, since the aim is to establish that, at least in some cases of full surrogacy, parties seek to transfer the right to parent from the gestational mother to the indenting parents.

Moving on to the second argument, the claim is not that the relationship between newborns and their gestational mother is as developed as intimate relationships between older individuals. Yet, it is the most developed relationship that a newborn can possibly have, and, for this reason, it is worthy of protection. Facts about the complexity and richness of a relationship do not fully determine its relative importance for the individuals in the relationship. Compare, for instance, a rich friendship between two typical adults who are in close relationships with each other, but also with several other adults, to the attachment between a cognitively impaired adult and her caregiver, who is the only person with whom the cognitively impaired adult has a relationship. The second relationship might be much less complex in terms of relational exchanges, and yet be at least as important to the wellbeing of the cognitively impaired adult as the first is to the typical adult's wellbeing. And, for this reason, it may also be worthy of protection, in virtue of its value to at least one of the individuals involved in it.

Another objection to my account is that it fails to respect the parity principle, stating that "any fact by virtue of which a woman laid claim to be a parent could also be a fact in virtue of which a man with equal merit could claim to be a parent, and vice versa."[90] Some find this principle important,[91] and it is sometimes claimed that any adequate account of parenthood must respect it. I fail to see the principle's appeal. I accept that it is unfair if, through no fault or choice of their own some individuals—in this case, men—have less easy access to parenting. However, if parenting is a fiduciary role justified by appeal to the child's interests, then, like with any other fiduciary functions, some adults qualify and others don't; it may well be that women and men are not equally represented in the two groups. It is tempting to explain the intuitive appeal of the principle itself by the geneticist assumption that children have two parents, one of each sex; but this assumption is hard to justify outside a view of childrearing that is both proprietarian and relying on the traditional way of bringing children into the world. Be it as it may, I assume the greatest assumed worry with the account that I provide is that it excludes men in general from access to parenting; but the account certainly doesn't do this, at least in the version provided in this book, for several reasons. First, the existence of a bond is a merely *pro tanto* reason to claim custody; it can be defeated. Second, the account does not presuppose that children should have only one parent; most likely, it is better for children to have several. And, if so, it should be possible for prospective parents to acquire the right by means other than having a bond with the newborn (assuming the gestational bond is exclusive).

A final worry with my argument is its lack of universality, since not all gestational mothers will bond to their babies during pregnancy; some don't even know that they are pregnant, or are unwillingly pregnant and resent their pregnancy, and possibly the foetus/newborn. (It is an interesting question whether they can be attached to their baby even while harbouring resentment.) Perhaps gestational procreators who are not bonded at birth cannot claim the right to parent their newborn on grounds of an existing attachment; but this is fine, since my view does not say that gestational mothers always have the right to parent. Such a conclusion may, however, be too quick if the newborn's *own* level of attachment to the gestational mother is independent from hers. The newborn's attachment alone, if sufficiently significant, can provide a powerful child-centred reason for the gestational mother's right to rear.

In any case, gestation, too, is an imperfect proxy for the existence of a mutual intimate relationship. But assume that an actual bond between gestational mothers and newborns exists at least as often as it is merely highly likely to develop between genetic procreators and their children. Or, alternatively, assume that the actual bond exists less often, but that the likelihood of bonding between gestational mother and her baby after birth is no lesser than the likelihood of the genetic procreator's bonding with the baby. (That is, in cases when the gestational mother is not also a genetic procreator.) If so, an this "if" is highly qualified by empirical facts, appeal to bonding provides better overall support to the gestational mother's presumptive right to custody than to the genetic procreator's right—again, assuming the two parties are otherwise equally competent prospective parents. Sometimes, of course, the two parties will not be equally competent prospective parents; but the argument is only meant to show that the gestational connection provides *one* advantage over the genetic one when it comes to likely qualifications of parental competency vis-à-vis a particular newborn, relative to the genetic connection.[92] It is also worth noting that in cases when a surrogate changes her mind and desires to parent the child whom she carried, appeal to some level of attachment developed during gestation is a plausible explanation of the desire, as well as a reasonably good guarantee that bonding is actually present.

4.3. Creatures of Attachment: The General Impermissibility of Surrogacy Agreements

The best case in favour of the genetic procreators' right to parent is the higher than average likelihood that they will bond with the child. Attachment in general, I assume, is of great instrumental value to us, and especially so during childhood. But, since human beings are, for evolutionary reasons, "hard-wired" to seek attachment, bonding has also non-instrumental value: it is, in itself, highly satisfactory, at least when it doesn't take an unhealthy form. Once formed, the loss of an attachment is very painful. Moreover, attachment between parents and children is necessary if the parent is to adequately serve the child's interest. These considerations provide a powerful presumption in favour of organizing childrearing in ways that harness the (putative) higher than average chances of bonding that adults have with their genetic offspring. Yet, all these considerations provide even better support for organizing childrearing in ways that do not threaten the *actual* bonding that is likely to develop during gestation.

In the vast majority of cases, gestational mothers are also genetic procreators, so considerations of the former's actual bonds and considerations of the latter's likelihood to bond with the child do not support different practical requirements. But in other situations, and in particular in full surrogacy, the two considerations do result in different practical guidance. Where does this leave us with respect to full surrogacy with the intending parents' gametes—the easiest form of surrogacy to justify on a child-centred account? I conclude this section by noting that intending parents, *qua* genetic procreators, cannot automatically claim the right to parent the newborn by pointing to the best argument in their favour—namely, higher likelihood to bond with the baby; sometimes such a bond already exists between the newborn and the gestational mother. If it is in the best interest of the child that it be reared by the gestational mother even if *she* isn't attached to the child, but merely in virtue of a non-mutual bond that the newborn has formed, the cases may be indeed numerous. In all these cases, where the gestational mother has the right to custody, surrogacy could only be understood as an attempted transfer of the right; as I argued above, such transfer cannot be legitimate.

This, of course, is not to pass a judgement about how often gestational mothers will *in fact* have the right to rear their newborn. Such an overall conclusion depends on too many factors: not only those concerning actual or likely bonding, but also other aspects that determine parental competence and, obviously, on the existence and attributes of other willing prospective parents for the child. No doubt that in some, possibly many, cases the intending parents *will* be the best available custodians. The important point is that we have no reason to assume that they will always be, and that the surrogate herself will never be, the best available custodian. And, therefore, there is no reason to assume that intending parents in cases of full surrogacy always have the right to parent *qua* genetic procreators, and hence that the right needn't be, at least sometimes, transferred from gestational surrogates to them.

An account that gives attachment such a crucial role in acquiring the right to parent invites the question of whether it matters, for custody allocation, whether the attachment between the child and the adult who seeks custody has been wrongfully created. If it does matter, defenders of surrogacy could try another line of argument: perhaps surrogates are under a duty not to form such an attachment, which would in turn weaken their claim to a right to parent their newborn. I resist this line of reasoning, and, in doing so, I oppose the belief, assumed to be evident by some bioethicists, that the wrongful creation of an attached relationship with the child implies that the adult lacks a right to custody. Steinbock, for instance, writes (as it happens, in the context of discussing the Baby M surrogacy case): "We certainly would not consider allowing a stranger who kidnapped a baby and managed to elude the police for a year to retain custody on the grounds that he was providing a good home to a child who had known no other parent."[93] I think this is wrong. It is of course likely that the kidnapper could be disqualified as the best available custodian by various features that are strongly correlated with one's tendency to engage in crime. But, assuming this wasn't the case, and the kidnapper really was the best custodian, the mere fact that the (presumably, loving) relationship between the kidnapper and the child came about as a result of wrongdoing does not speak against the kidnapper's right to continue rearing the child. Nothing, in fact, could speak against that other than the child's own interest.[94]

The main objection to all forms of surrogacy that I provide here has to do with the general lack of normative power to privately transfer a privilege. Before concluding this section, I provide an additional rebuttal to the potential objection sketched above, one which contains a very different type of criticism to surrogacy. A practice which encourages gestational mothers not to bond with the babies they carry is, I submit, one that we have reason to reject as inhumane because it is generally disrespectful of, and possibly detrimental to, human beings' powerful interest in emotional attachment. The possibility that bonding happens anyway, as suggested by cases in which surrogates change their minds and try to rear their newborns in the face of adversity[95] or the possibility that the newborn has some attachment to the gestational mother independently from her psychological states, suggest that discouraging the formation of the bond can also be futile. But leaving futility aside, if attachment has great value for human animals, and if it cannot be taken for granted even in adult-child relationships—where it is most valuable—it is objectionable to systematically discourage it. This, I take, is one of the strongest objections that feminists raise against surrogacy, for instance, when they argue that, in Anderson's words, "[t]he demand to deliberately alienate oneself from one's love for one's own child is a demand which can reasonably and decently be made of no one."[96] This grievance against surrogacy, is not (or not only) that it demands of surrogates something that many find very difficult to do, i.e. to remain emotionally detached from the baby. It is also that it requires surrogates to deny, or at least disregard, in themselves, a tendency that is a valuable expression of one's humanity. To the extent to which it gives gestational mothers reason to resist being emotionally involved in their labour, the practice of surrogacy not only fails to promote or honour the value of attachment, but it is straightforwardly inimical to it.

5. Harm to Children? The Challenge from the Non-identity Problem

The most powerful rebuttal of a child-centred criticism of surrogacy would show that the following claims are jointly true: (a) the practice does not harm children; and (b) lack of harm to the children of surrogacy is sufficient to show they cannot be wronged, and to make the practice morally permissible as far as their treatment is concerned. I raise some doubts that (a) is true, then reject (b) and, with it, the challenge.

Claim (a) is open to interpretation, because it requires a specification of "harm." I cannot provide here a full treatment of this difficult matter, but I examine a few obvious possibilities before I conclude that the most plausible allegation of harm concerns the respect interests of children of surrogacy. "Harm" may be understood non-comparatively, as a state that is significantly bad for the harmed agent in absolute terms;[97] on such an account of harm, it is implausible that surrogacy as such is harmful to the children born through this practice. Even if the speculative claim that children tend to suffer when they know that their gestational mother has willingly given them up was correct (and if withholding the information is impermissible), such suffering would have to be significant, and maybe impairing,[98] in order to qualify as "harm" in a non-comparative sense.

"Harm" is more usually employed as a comparative term: an individual is harmed if their wellbeing is set back relative to a threshold. One may propose the following way to argue that children of surrogacy can be harmed: namely, to apply a counterfactual notion of harm to the decision to separate the child from the surrogate. The proposal is that surrogacy harms children relative to how they would do if raised by their gestational mother. If the correct account of harm was counterfactual, and people were to respond with emotional suffering at the separation from their gestational mother, such suffering could qualify as harm even if it did not amount to a particularly debilitating state. I have said that newborns are likely to have an interest in continuity of care with their gestational mother, especially if the latter is attached to them. There is also some evidence that separation from the gestational mother has a negative impact on children's adjustment,[99] which I take to be different from freedom from emotional pain. However, it is hard to establish that children of surrogacy incur harm in a counterfactual sense, *all things considered*. Continuity in care, adjustment, and freedom from suffering are important interests, but a lot more would have to be shown in order to establish that surrogacy is *always* harmful to children in the sense considered here. Maybe other important interests of children are better served if they are raised by the intending parents. Presumably, typical intending parents are highly motivated, and prepared, to raise the child while the surrogate, who wasn't planning to become a parent, is more likely not to be so. Most plausibly, children of surrogacy would sometimes be better off with their gestational mothers, sometimes with the intending parents, and sometimes with yet others who are willing to raise them.

Assume it could be shown that surrogacy harms children in *this* comparative counterfactual sense, i.e., when the considered alternative is for them to be raised by their gestational mother. Many will object to taking the transfer of custody, rather than nonprocreation, as the baseline of comparison. If transferring custody was wrong, people would have a duty to refrain from surrogacy practices. If they acted on the duty, surrogacy agreements would not exist. And so, the children in question would *not* be raised by gestational mothers; rather, they would not exist at all. In this case, neither their emotional suffering nor discontinuity in care, nor the negative impact on their adjustment can constitute harms in the relevant counterfactual sense—unless they make the children's lives not worth living, which, I assume, they usually don't. In a counterfactual world without surrogacy, those children would have never come into existence. But only if one's life goes so badly for one that it is worse than non-existence can that person be said to be harmed relative to not being born. This aspect of the non-identity problem seems to raise a formidable challenge to a child-centred criticism of surrogacy:[100] that it doesn't harm surrogated children relative to a world without surrogacy, in which they wouldn't exist. In other words, the challenge is that claim (a) is true on both the non-comparative and the comparative accounts of harm.

Against this challenge, I now explain why surrogacy is indeed wrong, and why it is likely to be wrong because it wrongs the children who are subject to it. Note that the challenge is real, rather than apparent, only if it is also true that lack of harm to children is sufficient to make the practice morally permissible as far as the treatment of children of surrogacy is concerned—which is claim (b). I don't believe (b) is true, and therefore I don't think that appeal to the non-identity problem can rescue the legitimacy of surrogacy. Here is an argument that, I hope, will appeal to most readers: If (b) were true, the non-identity problem would also make it formidably difficult to establish the illegitimacy, on child-centred reasons, of many other procreative practices which we believe are wrong. This is because a legal permission to engage in what it is generally recognized as child mistreatment can be necessary as incentives for certain instances of procreation. For example, there may be people who would only have children, or would have more children, if they were allowed to exploit them economically. An extreme case is discussed by Gregory Kavka:[101] a couple enters a contract with a wealthy man, whereby the former bind themselves to procreate and surrender the child to the latter for a large sum of money, with the understanding that the child will be a *de facto* slave for the couple. Slavery doesn't make this child's life as bad as not to be worth living, and therefore the adult parties' agreement doesn't harm (in the comparative sense of harm specified above) the child, who would not have existed in the absence of the contract. But it seems obvious that the contract is morally wrong. If so, then (b) is false. It may be tempting to object that, in the slavery case, what makes the contract wrong are the non-comparative harms that the child suffers as a slave; yet, as discussed above, plausible accounts of the wrong of slavery identify it as wrong even when the slaves are treated well by their benevolent masters who don't impose non-comparative harms.[102] Similarly, the economic exploitation of children would be wrong even if it didn't involve non-comparative harms, and even when needed as incentive for their procreation. Both cases are wrong because of how the children are being treated; the same is true of surrogacy.

As this analysis shows, the fact that children of surrogacy can have lives not only worth living but also free from non-comparative harm doesn't preclude all child-centred complaints against surrogacy—not unless one is willing to concede that enslavement, or the economic exploitation of a child whose procreation was exclusively motivated by the prospects of enslavement or exploitation, also involves morally permissible treatment of that child.[103]

I assume that most readers agree that the implications of (b) are widely implausible. Yet, a full account must not only reveal the costs of accepting (b), but also explain what makes all these cases of morally impermissible procreation wrong. One possibility is that they are wrong without being wrongful—for instance, it may be wrong to bring about suboptimal states of affairs even when nobody's interests are being set back in doing so.[104] If so, all the cases under discussion involve wrong actions when they make the world a worse place, all things considered. This may be true. But there is a complementary explanation of the wrongness of these cases, one that claims that children of surrogacy are themselves wronged even if they are not harmed.

People have grievances against unjustified setbacks to their respect interests. Enslaved people in general have grievances even when the masters are so benevolent as to not set back their wellbeing in the ways in which actual masters typically do (relative to either pre-enslavement or non-enslavement). Similarly, a person can have a grievance against economic exploitation even if the alternative to it is worse with respect to the fulfilment of her various interests—for instance, because she lives in dire poverty and she would benefit economically from exploitation. The fact that slavery and exploitation wrong those subjected to them doesn't seem to depend on whether, in the absence of these practices, those enslaved or exploited would have never come into existence: If, as I claimed, the private transfer of custody sets back a child's respect interests, it is wrongful even when it doesn't negatively affect any other interests of the child. In this case, children's grievance against surrogacy, or economic exploitation, or slavery, does not concern their procreation as such, but their treatment once they exist—namely, the settling of their custody by means of a private agreement. The very bringing into existence of children of surrogacy is not wrongful; the allocation of control rights over them after birth is.

It is worth noting two ramifications of this rebuttal of the nonidentity challenge. First, on one view about what makes life go well for people, being subject to injustice can be bad for them.[105] If this view is correct, then having one's respect interests set back is a form of harm and then it is possible that (a), too, turns out to be false. Accepting this would show that children of surrogacy are harmed in one respect; but it would probably be a long shot to show that the harm makes their lives not worth living, and so surrogacy imposes on them a net harm. Second, some accounts of the permissibility of procreation make it dependent on the intentions that motivate people to have children.[106] Such accounts could explain why procreation that wouldn't take place in the absence of surrogacy, and not merely the treatment of children of surrogacy once they exist, is wrongful. Since none of these ramifications is necessary to indict surrogacy as impermissible, I need not commit to any of them here.

To conclude this section, let me put its argument into a wider perspective. Procreation is, in itself, a morally suspect activity because of the harms it imposes on non-consenting persons.[107] A child-centred account may have particular difficulties justifying procreation, since simply invoking the ways in which it is good for procreators or third parties seems insufficient. More likely, procreation is, all things considered, justified by the benefit to procreatees of being alive. Or, alternatively, it is merely excused by the bads of a world with no children in it,[108] for instance the horror of the imminent extinction of humanity.[109] Assigning custody, i.e., control over persons, to procreators, by default, introduces another layer of moral risk, given that one's genetic and gestational relationship with a child is an imperfect proxy for the quality of that person's parenting. Perhaps we simply lack a better proxy, in which case relying on biological connections is overall justified when other things are equal. But existing surrogacy practices compound the moral reservations that one may reasonably have about procreation as such and about the automatic granting of the right to parent to procreators. Surrogacy, I argued throughout this chapter, is a practice whereby some people (intending parents) gain custody over other persons (the child); sometimes they gain custody because the initial holders of the moral right (gestational mothers) have these rights as a result of two morally risky practices (procreation and automatic allocation of the right to parent to procreators) and attempt to sell or gift those rights. At other times, when the intending parents are the best available, they gain custody in ways that are not overseen by any authority. This makes surrogacy extremely difficult to defend. The most powerful child-centred defence, in the face of these worries, is that, without surrogacy, the children over whom custody rights are being transferred would not exist at all. If the benefits of procreation are so great that they can justify, or at least excuse, the imposition of significant risks on non-consenting persons, one may think they can also render surrogacy permissible when the alternative is non-existence. And yet, I showed, this consideration doesn't dispel the child-centred objection to surrogacy,[110] unless one is also willing to accept as permissible a range of universally indicted practices such as the bringing into existence of children predestined to economic exploitation or slavery. For those unwilling to bite such bullets, an account of why surrogacy does after all wrong children is available: not because it (necessarily) sets back their wellbeing, but because it disrespects them.

Conclusion: A Respectful and Humane Form of Surrogacy

Many people who cannot procreate wish to become parents; I believe that society should provide them with adequate opportunities to fulfil this desire, if they would make adequate parents. Adoption is one venue into non-procreative parenthood but, for various (and potentially good) reasons, some people dis-prefer it. In particular, many people desire to parent genetically related children. I conclude this chapter by explaining how, and the extent to which, a child-centred account of childrearing can accommodate such preferences. Elements of this blueprint (in the broadest brush) of a radically reformed sort of surrogacy can be more or less easily grafted on the current surrogacy practices.

For everything I said here, it may be possible to defend a practice whereby women gestate "for others"—that is, without an intention to acquire custody over their newborns. The practice would be open to women willing to either gift, or sell, their gestational ability, as well as to intending parents, and could allow the latter to provide gametes in the hope, but with no guarantee, that they will gain custody over the child developed from some gametes. If genetic connections really are serving children's interest, these hopes would not be unfounded but, as I explain below, they would be merely reasonable hopes, not legitimate expectations, to obtain custody.

This practice would have three features that make it radically different from surrogacy as we have it now. First, any children born in this way would automatically become the charge of the state when the surrogate mother relinquishes custody[111]—as I argued in section 4, the surrogate mother *will* in some cases be the first holder of the right, namely, whenever she would make the best possible parent to the child.

Further, custody over a particular baby would go to the best available custodian, and therefore not *automatically* to the intending parents, no matter how intensely they hope to parent her, and in spite of having contributed one or both gametes to her procreation. In some cases, possibly a majority, either a strong desire to parent a particular newborn, or a genetic connection with the baby, or both, would make intending parents the best custodians of their genetic offspring. When surrogates changed their mind about wanting to raise the child themselves, they too would be considered as potential parents and, if my argument in section 4 is correct, in many situations they will indeed have a right to custody. Such situations could occur if the surrogate's already formed attachment recommends her as parent, and the genetic and gestational parent are otherwise similarly likely to be good parents. In any case, the interest of the child would have the last say in custody allocation— making the practice respectful towards the child—and no legitimate expectations could be formed on anybody's side (intending parents, the surrogate or any third parties) that they will become custodians. This feature would, indeed, make a dent in intentional parents' own interests, but a well- motivated one. As a result, the practice wouldn't involve contractual expectations, enforceable or not, that the gestational mother refrains from attempts to gain custody. Nor could there be any presumption that bonding during pregnancy is objectionable; the form of surrogacy that I envisage as legitimate would, in this respect, be humane. What, if anything, would surrogates who have changed their minds owe intentional parents for having used their gametes is a downstream question, requiring further investigation.

Finally, this practice would protect any bond that the gestational mother had established, during pregnancy, with the child she carried, and so it would ensure the continuation of the relationship between newborn and the gestational mother, whenever this is in the interest of the child. This, of course, is not the same as claiming that attached gestational mothers always have a right to custody; they don't if, in spite of such a bond, other individuals would make, all things considered, better custodians. But while surrogates lack the right to parent in such situations—that is, they lack control rights over their newborn—they do have the right to maintain a non-custodial relationship that is beneficial for the child. If we were to become reasonably sure that children in general have a powerful interest to remain in some sort of caring relationship with their gestational mother, then children may turn out to have a right to the protection of the relationship that is independent from the gestational mother's interests; this possibility raises another set of complications that are far beyond the scope of the present discussion. Maintaining the relationships could, in practice, justify a legal right to visitation. Since the right is partly grounded in the *child's* interest, and since the child cannot claim the right, let alone secure the means to exercise it, courts may require that intending parents and surrogates jointly ensure the practical conditions necessary to protect the relationship between the child and her gestational mother. Such constraints may be easily respected in cases of surrogacy relationships between, say, neighbours, and are likely to rule out most cases of international surrogacy.

In spite of its radical revisionism, this proposal, I hope, does chime in with our sense that surrogacy is not a morally neutral kind of work. Moreover, this reformed surrogacy would be quite similar in outcomes to some aspects of the existing practice as far as many surrogates and intending parents are concerned, albeit with a suitably expanded and more robust rights for surrogates to be involved in the child's life. Perhaps, then, my positive view, which I could only sketch here in the barest of details, captures the core of what people *should* want out of surrogacy.

When custody is allocated to individuals other than the genetic parents—in adoption as well as in a radically reformed surrogacy—one question is what remaining rights and duties do genetic parents have, if any. It is generally believed that genetic parents, when they procreate both intentionally and avoidably, incur significant duties of care towards the child—if not duties to directly provide for the child, then at least duties to ensure that the child is well provided for.[112] Lindsey Porter argues that one cannot fully divest oneself of such duties.[113] One can permissibly put a child up for adoption, for instance, in which case others will become primary duty-bearers in relationships for the child; but, should the adoptive parents fail to care for the child adequately, procreators would be under a duty to make up for such failure. Others have suggested that procreators have a right to ensure that the duties of care towards the child, which they incur in the first instance, as procreators, are discharged.[114] If either of these accounts is correct, then genetic parents, too, have a right to be part of the child's life to a sufficient extent to be able to gauge whether her upbringing goes wrong, and to step in and discharge their procreative duty in ways compatible with the child's overall interest. This applies to genetic parents who contributed gametes in the hope that they will, *qua* best available parent, gain custody; it may also apply to gamete donors who never had an intention to rear—but, of course, a separate discussion is required to establish this.

I remind the reader that surrogacy as we have it is driven by many adults' wish to parent genetically related children. My criticism of surrogacy is not dismissive of this desire. But if people really have a powerful interest in raising children developed from their own gametes, interest that is significant enough to warrant societal support, then we should also look favourably to the claim that alienation from their genetic parents can go against children's interest. The interest may be merely subjective, to be understood as a desire of the child—or future adult—that must be taken to be as important as individuals' desire for genetically related children. That is, at least in the absence of an account explaining why adults' desire in genetic children is significant, but children's desire to be acquainted with their genetic parents isn't. Or it may be an objective interest—for instance, in self-knowledge, along the lines suggested by Velleman. If either of these explanations is correct (and I remain agnostic about this matter), a full account of permissible procreation with the help of gestational surrogates must reflect children's interest in having their genetic parents in their lives in some capacity.

I end with the hope that my readers now see why existing surrogacy wrongs children by allowing adults to privately decide on their custody. In doing this, it fails to respect children's moral status, which requires all control over them to be guided by their, and not by their (potential) custodians', interests. Unlike most common criticism of surrogacy, mine does not find altruistic versions any better than commercial ones—unsurprisingly, since I am concerned with the child's interest. And, unlike other criticism, it is not in itself inimical to the use of assisted reproductive technologies, including help from surrogate mothers. Gestating with the intention that others raise the children may be morally permissible; "commissioning" children is not.

PART II

PART I

What's in It for the Baby? Weighing Children's and Parents' Interests in Commercial Surrogacy Agreements. A Reply to Gheaus

Christine Straehle

Introduction

Bringing children into the world is sometimes a fraught business. While in earlier times before there were reproductive technologies, those who couldn't conceive without assistance resorted to adoption—if they were allowed to—as the way to fulfil their wish for children in their lives, modern technologies today have made it so that many more people can realize the wish for biological children. Somehow, though, many commentators see a difference between having recourse to reproductive technologies to gain access to the good of childrearing, and having recourse to surrogacy. Most commonly, the worry motivating the criticism is over the treatment of surrogates, which I discussed in Part I. Sometimes, the worry is over the status of children born from surrogacy. The debate over surrogacy is, then, calling to adjudicate between the interests of the intending parents and the interests of the child, framed as being in at least potential tension. Anca Gheaus's contribution in Part I is part of this debate. In my defence of commercial surrogacy as reproductive labour, I argued that most liberal democratic states

Debating Surrogacy. Anca Gheaus and Christine Straehle, Oxford University Press.
© Oxford University Press 2024. DOI: 10.1093/oso/9780190072162.003.0004

allow individuals to freely choose their professional occupation; I made the link between professional occupation and a recognized sense of self, and thinking about freedom of professional occupation as a means for individuals to define themselves. If we accept surrogacy as reproductive labour, as I argued we should, then surrogacy work should be protected by the negative rights against interference into freedom of professional occupation. My caveat was, of course, that professions should be allowed only as long as they do not harm the interests of another or society at large—in this vein, I discussed possible harm to society, the degradation of women's position in society. Gheaus's contribution raises the important question of whether commercial surrogacy harms the interests of children born through surrogacy.

1. Where We Agree: The Interests of Children

According to Gheaus, parents have full control rights over their children, which makes it such that "[c]hildren's situation in general . . . *is* strikingly similar to that of slaves belonging to benevolent, indeed often loving and occasionally adoring, owners." (p. 111). This is problematic, and particularly so, possibly, in cases of surrogacy.[1] To motivate the particular worry over surrogacy, Gheaus argues that children have two different kinds of interests: first, they have *wellbeing* interests, and second, they have *respect* interests. These interests are harmed, or at least potentially harmed, in private surrogacy agreements since such agreements transfer custody rights to the intending parents without verifying whether they would also be the best available custodians.

Note that Gheaus doesn't argue in principle against surrogacy, but only against private surrogacy agreements; she suggests that a state-supported and regulated system of surrogacy could be defensible. In such a system, the wellbeing and, in particular, the respect interests of children—part of which Gheaus defines as to have and to be brought up by the best available custodian—could be protected and safeguarded, with the state screening applicants for surrogacy as to their capacity and willingness to provide and secure a child's interests. Recall here my discussion of the Israeli approach to surrogacy. In Israel, all hopeful surrogates and the intending parents have to be approved by the "foetus carriage agreements approval board," which is composed of medical professionals, including psychologists, and a rabbi. I have also discussed (in section 4 of my Part I contribution) Walker and Zyl's argument that social workers should be involved in surrogacy contracts to assure that state authorities can step in, in cases where parents renege on the surrogacy contract because of a change of heart, in order to protect the surrogate's interest not to have to take on the child born herself. Following Gheaus's proposal, states should become the warden of children born through surrogacy in all cases, to then place the child with the best available custodian: the surrogate or the intending parents, or somebody else yet again. Who gets to be the custodian—that is, who gets the child—would depend on how well the hopeful parents would score in this assessment, compared to the surrogate and others.

A custodian is meant to act in the child's best interests, which Gheaus divides into wellbeing interests and respect interests. The first set of interests is a widely acknowledged one, and we can assume that the basics of a child's interest are known as part and parcel of legislation in most welfare states: besides having their basic needs met, children should be loved and cared for. What, precisely, love and care imply may be up for discussion—but it is probably uncontroversial that children cannot be abused or neglected, that they should have access to the means to develop their capabilities, and that they should be able to develop and determine their own self over time. While the precise nature and context of children's interest can be debated, as I will do as part of my response here, Gheaus suggests that it is not debatable that as members of a mammalian species, humans have an interest in bonding and attachment. Indeed, Gheaus argues that one of the important features of a child's life as a member of a mammalian species *is* her attachment. As biological and vulnerable creatures, we rely on contact with others, and on the attention and care others bring to us. In this vein, children are constitutionally and biologically more vulnerable than adults, and, as I have argued elsewhere,[2] though this vulnerability need not raise moral concerns immediately, if we neglect to take this kind of vulnerability into account when designing legislation, then the background vulnerability of children may become problematic. Hence the need for legislation to protect children against abusive or neglectful custodians, and why the state steps in when abuse and neglect happen. Notice, though, that within the realm of child-protection legislation, states only step in when custodians show themselves to be bad ones: states only intervene in cases where custodians fail to protect children, or indeed, when they inflict direct or indirect harm on them.[3] This is to say that states only *retroactively* evaluate how parents perform in their custodial duties—they don't prescribe *prospectively* who should be the custodian of a child when there are seemingly obvious candidates at hand—that is, when a child is born to her gestational and genetic parents. Yet this is what Gheaus wants to suggest: her child-centred approach suggests that states should become wardens of children born through surrogacy, to then place them with the best available custodian.

How should we think of the best available custodian? We can piece together throughout the account that the best possible custodian protects their child's wellbeing interests, which include having emotional bonds and relationships, and her respect interests. We can glean also throughout the account that children should be loved and well-cared for. Selecting the person or persons responsible for the protection of these interests, Gheaus suggests, should be the task of the state. In particular, the impartial arbitration of the state would help protect the respect interests of children. These "protect not only the exercise of individuals' agency (and so, in the case of children, treatment in accordance with the level of developed autonomy of each particular child), but also the treatment of individuals in situations in which they cannot give consent: for instance, during childhood or while unconscious. They include an interest in not having one's own general interests set back in order to advance the interest of an adult in doing the controlling. For instance, imposing a setback of a child's wellbeing interests for the sake of allowing a suboptimal parent to satisfy an interest in rearing counts as disrespect." (p. 105).

Since parents have full control rights over children, parents have the power to dominate over children, thus setting back children's respect interests even in cases in which their wellbeing interests are protected. The best available custodian is thus the person or group of people who would protect not only the latter but also, importantly, the respect interests of children.

Most people would probably agree with Gheaus that children have a range of interests that need to be met. To state the obvious, there are physical interests—like all human beings, children should be kept warm and fed and out of harm's way. Children's physical and biological vulnerability in this sense is what motivates special protective measures, as those laid out in the UN Charter of the Rights of the Child;[4] since children can't protect their interests themselves, states bear special responsibilities towards children.

Of course, children's interests go beyond the satisfaction of mere physical need. Some philosophers, Gheaus among them, have argued that there are specific goods of childhood that warrant protection.[5] In this view, children have an interest in having a childhood because of the goods childhood provides. These goods can either be taken to be features of a childhood that we think is how a childhood *should* be. Or we can take the goods of childhood to be those goods that make for a childhood that will eventually lead to a good adulthood. In other words, we can have a view of childhood goods as intrinsically valuable, or we can take the goods of childhood to be instrumentally valuable, or both. Many philosophers of childhood have discussed what further interests children have—the interest of being loved, of having opportunity to play and experiment in life. I would go further and suggest that one important good of childhood is the disposition to be carefree.[6] *Carefreeness* in my view is an integral part of what it means to be a child; if children are prevented from being carefree, they are morally wronged.[7] From a moral perspective, then, and when thinking about what we owe to children, I propose that children are owed a childhood that allows them to be carefree. We can say that children have an interest in being carefree, since this is an important requirement to develop autonomy and agency over time.

This idea rejoins Gheaus's proposal for respect interests of children. As I have noted, Gheaus defines *respect interests* as those aiming to "protect not only the exercise of individuals' agency," but also the position a person should have in our consideration of different kinds of interests when agency is not given. I take this to mean that Gheaus wants to suggest that the respect interests of children should guide their custodians to protect and promote their autonomy and agency interests, as they develop over time.

How should we think about children's autonomy? In my defence of surrogacy, I spent some time discussing the basis for individual autonomy for adults. As I argued there, the way I construe autonomy is rather procedural—we should make sure that individuals have access to the background conditions of autonomy, which means that they should have viable options available amongst which to choose which shape they want to give their lives; that decisions can be made voluntarily and free from coercion; and that individuals can be recognized and accepted by others as part authors of a reasonable life plan. Importantly, individuals should enjoy negative liberty, i.e., freedom from undue interference in their decision-making process.

Children's autonomy is often considered a vexing subject, precisely because of this last characteristic of autonomy, since paternalism, if it is justified at all, is most commonly taken to be justifiable for the case of children. Whereas paternalist interventions in the lives of adults normally require meticulous justification and are often prohibited because of concern for individual autonomy, such paternalism is often justified when intervening in the lives of children. It is not always clear how to balance concern for children's vulnerability, physical and mental, with concern for their autonomy.[8] In this vein, some authors believe that we should accept that vulnerability is the opposite of autonomy.[9] The argument then goes something like this: because children are vulnerable, they are not autonomous. Therefore, parents, teachers and others interfering in children's lives to protect them against vulnerability don't violate the cardinal liberal value of autonomy: unless there is some kind of autonomy, there is no value to be violated. The dichotomy between vulnerability and autonomy then serves paternalistic attempts to protect children's interest and carries the dangers of serving to justify coercive and paternalistic acts. I believe this dichotomy doesn't hold and, moreover, is dangerous. Instead, we need to identify the specific kind of vulnerability that children experience; second, we need to assess if it is morally problematic. As I have stipulated at the outset of my response, liberal states accept their responsibilities to protect children because of their biological vulnerability. If custodians neglect to protect the children in their care, the state steps in. Paternalist interventions based on the argument from vulnerability, then, can be justified only when this kind of vulnerability is in evidence and when the intervention aims to address the vulnerability that hampers a child's interest.

But some further unpacking of children's vulnerability and their autonomy is needed. Besides the obvious physical vulnerability that children experience, Gheaus is certainly correct in putting her finger on the potentially problematic relationship between parents and their children, although I don't believe the relationship warrants the reference to slavery. Besides their physical vulnerability, it is certainly true that children experience a specific kind of vulnerability that is due to their dependency and relationships with others. So while relationships and dependency, and we might say, emotional and physical attachment, are part and parcel of a good childhood, they can also be grounds for a specific kind of vulnerability. Vulnerability in this sense can come in different forms; David Archard provides a good illustration when he discusses the specific need for protection children are usually held to deserve:

> Consider, as an illustration, the wrong of using another sexually against her will. In the case of a child's being so used most would judge that there is a special wrong. This might variously be expressed as a theft of the child's innocence, as an exploitation of her vulnerability . . . As an innocent the child should not be exposed to forms of treatment that cause her to lose that child-like understanding of the world that gives value to being a child. Moreover, such a theft of innocence is even more wrong because a child is less able than an adult, who is independent, strong, and confident, to resist such an abuse.[10]

The circumstance that makes the child vulnerable is not simply the fact that she deserves protection as a child (thus accounting for her physical vulnerability qua child) but the more specific context of being a child who depends on others for the protection of her interests. And it is precisely in this that children are vulnerable, they are vulnerable to come to harm without the possibility of protecting themselves against it: "disposed to trust the adults she knows, a child [will not] see such abuse by them as to be resisted."[11] The circumstance of being "easily" abused makes her vulnerable because this circumstance—instead of simply being a fact that comes with being a child—first, robs her of her interest in having the goods of childhood, including the possibility to be carefree; second, it hampers her ability to develop the capacity to develop autonomy and agency.

So parents, or custodians, have a set of responsibilities: first, and rather obviously, parents need to protect children's interests, including the interests of childhood. Second, parents have the responsibility to promote and further children's autonomy and agency interests. Recall here my discussion in Part I. There I argued that people's autonomy interests can be harmed, for example, when they don't have access to the background conditions of autonomy. Similarly, children's autonomy interest will be harmed if parents or custodians don't satisfy their duty to protect a child's developing autonomy and nurture her agency.[12] The ingredients of agency are, of course, debated—one important feature most philosophers can agree upon, however, is that it requires a sense of self.[13]

2. Where We Disagree: Relationships

This is where the value and role of relationships is important to consider. I would argue that one important ingredient in a child's gaining a sense of self is to have access to relationships that are secure. Children in secure relationships will be able to enjoy many of the goods of childhood: Take the good of unstructured imaginative play. In a childhood that many think is a good childhood,

> there is a sense of time as endless, as having one's whole life stretched out ahead . . . that one never has again in life. Likewise, there is the sense that all doors are open, and that anything is possible. . . . Finally, there is a kind of absolute trust in others, possible in childhood but never again.[14]

To actually *have* a sense of timelessness, possibility, and trust, however, may only be possible if a child can feel secure in a relationship, and can feel that their trust is not abused. Thus, secure relationships play at least two fundamental roles in the lives of children: in the first instance, it is through their relationships to responsible adults that they can arrive at a sense of self. If parents fulfil their duties qua parents (and, to a lesser degree, if other adults fulfil their lesser roles in the lives of the children), then children can feel nurtured and safe, they can learn self-confidence and self-respect, all of which is part of developing their own "me." The first role of relationships, then, is instrumental in the development of a sense of self in children. Second, the function of relationships in children's lives is to provide stability: besides having her basic bodily and safety needs protected, a child also needs to be able to have the emotional grounds to be carefree. In this need, I suggest that children *qua children* have a right to be carefree that distinguishes them from adults. Both adults and children have an *interest* to be carefree in aspects of their lives, but only the interest of children to be carefree can be the basis of a right to carefreeness. A sense of carefreeness enables children to *imagine* a future. Only when they are carefree can children engage in the exploratory and non-instrumental development of their own character that *will allow them* to have a future. The thought here is that children depend on carefreeness when thinking about themselves over time. Carefreeness, in other words, is an integral element in developing a sense of self, which in turn is a precondition for individual autonomy and agency. It integrally depends, though, on stable relationships, i.e., relationships that provide a narrative into the past and into the future. At least, young children importantly need to know that the adults they relate to will be there in their future.

So far, then, I have discussed, based on Gheaus's argument, how we should think about the interests children have, and the responsibilities parents or custodians have in the lives of children. I have argued with Gheaus that children have specific interests, interpreting children's autonomy interests and their interests in the goods of childhood as part of her analysis of a child's wellbeing and respect interests. But, whereas Gheaus pits the intending parents' interest in private surrogacy agreements against the interests of children born through surrogacy, I fail to see this conflict. One disagreement, I believe, is over the kind of relationship that counts—that is, the relationship that would embed children in the context in which their interests are protected and promoted.

The first distinction I would like to draw is that between physical attachments and relationships.

In the last part of her contribution to Part I, Gheaus discusses the particular role of the surrogate and argues that we should assume her to have established, over the nine months of gestation, a relationship with the foetus: "it is the most developed relationship that a newborn can possibly have, and, for this reason, it is worthy of protection." (p.132) This, says Gheaus, gives the surrogate the advantage on the score sheet in at least one respect over the intending parents. Since children have an interest in intimate relationships, and since, all things being equal, the intending parents don't yet have such a relationship with their child, the surrogate should be considered the one who, in the first instance, has a leg up on the intending parents in getting custody of the child.

I find this proposal problematic, for several reasons. First, as Gheaus discusses but dismisses, it disqualifies a lot of people, namely men, from being considered on par with women as "natural" born parents. Since custody in the child-centred view is a fiduciary relationship, it should be based on capacities and characteristics, and not based on equality demands. However, such a dismissal doesn't do justice to the problem here—since the simple fact of gestating and giving birth is ascribed a significance in terms of qualification that seems undue. More problematically, I find this explanation for custody rights for surrogates unduly biologically deterministic—it may be that surrogates have some kind of relationship with a foetus—but this relationship, one might argue, is an instinctive one on the part of the foetus—i.e., one that is driven by physical need. This doesn't qualify it as the only available relationship, and certainly not the only relevant one in light of children's interests discussed so far. To be sure, Gheaus preempts comments about the character of the relationship when she says: "Facts about the complexity and richness of a relationship do not fully determine its relative importance for the individuals in the relationship." (p.132) Maybe. But to speak of a relationship between foetus and gestating surrogate seems to overburden the facts. It may undoubtedly be the case that the surrogate has a relationship with the foetus—she cares about the physical wellbeing, about the arrival in the world, maybe also about the future—yet the foetus simply doesn't have a relationship if we understand a relationship to imply reciprocity, or at least cognizance. The biological dependency of the foetus on the gestating surrogate is just that, a dependency. It is certainly not the kind of relational bond that Gheaus stipulates forms an integral part of human wellbeing.

Compare this to the conceptual and social relationship the intending parents have to the child—they have planned and prepared for a life together and are deeply involved in the gestation of the child[15]—they envision the future of the child with them; they care for the child's wellbeing and respect interests. Indeed, if these two interests are at the basis of Gheaus's account, the turn to propose the surrogate as the first to have a relationship and thus custodial cred towards the end of her account is perplexing: surely, if we take protecting wellbeing and respect interests seriously, biological dependency should *not* be considered to be on par with the conceptual and social relationship that the intending parents have. To suggest that the only relevant relationship in this regard is the biological one seems simply wrong. Thus, I would argue that there is a tension in Gheaus's account: on the one hand, she proposes a child-centred view that challenges and questions many hitherto assumed facts about custody—the relevance of genetic link, for instance, and the link between intention of procreation and access to custody rights—based on the concern over wellbeing and respect interests. Yet, on the other hand, it isn't the concern for wellbeing and respect interests that motivates the argument for surrogates as custodians but an argument about gestational relationships.

Now, in response, Gheaus could argue that from a child-centred perspective, the link between the gestating woman and the foetus is the only relevant one, since it is the only one the foetus experiences; as I said, as mammals, we need attachments. However, this response supports my rebuttal more than refutes it: precisely because children are not only biological creatures, but importantly, also social ones in the making, to focus on the biological link between gestator and foetus is misguided; it should certainly not be used to ground claims for custody rights. Recall my discussion of the moral responsibilities that parents have as custodians—such as promoting autonomy interests. These are responsibilities over time, and in the context of the social world in which options for autonomous choice are provided.

Of course, some could hold that the prospective social relationship of a child is not the only relevant aspect in attributing custody—instead, we could also argue that the genetic link between intending parents and children born of gestational surrogacy, the type at the basis of my earlier discussion, should be considered the paramount reason why intending parents should be granted custody rights. In her argument in Part I, Gheaus discusses this move in the literature in section 4.1, where she writes:

"A promising account of how genetic connections are relevant for holding the right to custody, then, must fulfil two desiderata:

(a) It should be child-centred, that is, it should explain why somebody, in virtue of being a genetic procreator, is more likely than other individuals to serve the child's interests; and

(b) it should explain why the genetic connection matters in a way that is essential rather than peripheral to the fiduciary parental role—that is, explain how the genetic connection increases the likelihood of a feature of the parental relationship that is necessary to exercise control rights in the child's best interests."(p.126)

Gheaus discusses one promising view proposed by Archard, who suggests that genetically related parents will be able to provide "selfless love" to children, that genetic parentage motivates deep and selfless love (p. 127); but she then argues that the genetic connection is clearly neither necessary nor sufficient for parental love as demonstrated by the existence of bonded and loving adoptive parents and of unloving genetic procreators. So all that the thesis under examination here seeks to establish is not *actual* bonding between genetic procreators and their children but only its higher than average *likelihood*. But, as David Archard observes, the mere likelihood of bonding has much less weight in establishing the right than does actual bonding. . . . [G]enetic procreative relatedness is only a proxy. And, so, in cases of full surrogacy, intending parents who provided the gametes don't automatically have the right to parent the newborn. (p.128)

As I explained, Gheaus argues that the relevant relationship is the gestational one. Now, of course, we could say that the gestational relationship is also only indicative of a likelihood of a bond— witness the cases of women who don't have the kind of relationship with their newborn that many believe to be "natural," and instead suffer from postpartum trauma or other psychologically challenging circumstances that make it difficult to experience selfless love. More importantly, though, *all* possible custodians have only a "likelihood" of bonding with the child since we can only assume that they develop it over time. Whenever we engage in prospective analysis, we can only ever assume likelihood, since we don't know if parents will like and bond with the child born. Therefore, when assessing who should have custodial rights, the distinction between "actual" and "likely" bonds seems unhelpful. Instead, I suggest that the demands placed on intending parents should be based on the interests children actually have, not on romanticized ideas. And in this vein, it seems obvious that intending parents in surrogacy, much like intending parents in non-assisted pregnancies, have in principle the capacity and moral make-up to promote and further children's interests. Assuming otherwise is taking the nature of reproduction to indicate something morally problematic that just doesn't seem to be there.

3. Where We Disagree: The Role of the State

Finally, a note on Gheaus's proposal that the state should adjudicate who should have custody of a child born from surrogacy. In the first instance, as I discussed in Part I, many women working as surrogates have no desire to become the custodian of the child that is born. Indeed, as Jacobson reports, many surrogates, at least in the United States, explicitly don't want another child, but they enjoy being pregnant. To assume otherwise falls again into the biological trap that women, through pregnancy, are biologically determined to want to be custodians of the children they gestate. Moreover, if we were to change private surrogacy arrangements along the lines of Gheaus's proposal, that is, including the possibility that surrogates can be designated the child's custodian, then, at least, all those women who *don't want* to have another child would probably be deterred from working as surrogates, leaving hopeful intending parents with fewer surrogates to work with. Even if we assume that surrogates don't *have* to parent against their wishes, Gheaus leaves open the possibility that surrogates have to explain why they don't want to. And this, I submit, is not a justifiable expectation. Women working as surrogates should not be expected to become custodians of children they bear at the behest of intending parents; they should also not be asked to decide whether they want to.[16]

But assume this were not a hurdle—after all, as I argued, states can't be asked to guarantee the right to surrogacy, since this would imply their having jurisdiction over women's bodies to make them work as surrogates, so we might convince ourselves that fewer surrogates might simply be a supply problem—how should we imagine the implementation and, importantly, the consequences of Gheaus's proposal? In the first instance, we could be forgiven for being wary of making states the wardens of children—after all, not many states have an excellent track record in this domain. Witness recent cases of harrowing child abuse in many countries of the developed rich world that have happened literally under

the eyes of state authorities, or the recent allegations against the
UK government's decision to outsource social childcare to private companies.[17] Alternatively, recall the recent highly publicized
fallout from a long-held Canadian governmental policy to re-
move children from Indigenous families to place them with non-
indigenous ones, or to place them, more disastrously still, in
residential schools. Or the widespread and long-held practice of
putting single mothers in Catholic homes in Ireland, and taking
their children away from them to be placed for adoption. All of
these policies were implemented with the supposedly best interest
of the children at heart, against a racist colonial backdrop in the
Canadian case, or the forbidding catholic morality in the Irish one.
Instead of tasking states to find the best available custodian for
them, children would be better served if states invested in expan-
sive and affordable early childhood care, and into non-moralizing
parental support.

But more importantly, ultimately, Gheaus's proposal has
two possible consequences: prospectively, it suggests that possible custodians are screened for their custodial qualifications.
As I discussed before, here the assessment can only evaluate
likelihood—states could only aim to assess how likely a person is to
be a good custodian; then the question is, Why not opt for the traditional proxy of a genetic link to assume likelihood? Alternatively,
the proposal could suggest that we retroactively assess people's capacity to be good parents. The first challenge would be to define
criteria. Notice that one characteristic of the best available custodian seemed to be selfless love. We may wonder, of course, at this
idea: selfless love is a high threshold—why should we assume that
children thrive under conditions of selfless love, why should we not
assume that such love can turn out to be crushing and burdensome
for children? Especially considering children's budding autonomy
and agency interests, selfless love can be too much. I don't deny
that there are criteria of good parents that most people would agree
upon—just as most would agree that children have interests that

need to be protected. Parents who abuse their children are not good parents. But at the same time, I am wont to stipulate how parents ought to love their children.

Indeed, we might have a discussion about whether people need to be the best custodian or whether being good enough is, well, good enough. I believe it fair to say that many individuals would qualify as good enough parents, while the pool of the best available custodian is rather small. Against Gheaus's rather demanding view of parenting I believe that there is a threshold above which parents are good enough: parents need not excel at carrying out their obligations towards children in their care, they simply need to satisfy their obligations. To put it another way, if parents satisfy this sufficiency demand, if they protect and cherish the child and aim to promote their autonomy as much as is feasible for parents, then I believe that this satisfies the criteria to accept intending parents' expectation of custody.[18]

More importantly, though, should we assume that children whose custodians the state finds wanting will be relocated to people who seem more likely to be good custodians? Recall here my discussion of what kinds of relationships are important to protect and promote children's interests, including their autonomy and agency interests. One of the features of relationships I underlined is that relationships need to be secure to give children the background support and stability to actually enjoy the goods of childhood. Relocating children, even if it is a relocation from a good enough parent to the best available custodian will inflict harm to children's interests that even the best possible custodian might not be able to compensate.[19] If we think of relationships, not only as gestational, but also as social, the harm done through relocation seems to far outweigh the harm done by separating a child from the gestational surrogate. Moreover, we can imagine that some parents are excellent with small babies in their care—they love the cuddling and cooing that infants inspire—but they find dealing with a growing child difficult. Should we relocate children then, maybe, again? Put differently, when is the qualification period for custodians over? Against this, Gheaus could argue that the discussion she provides is only about initial allocation, and not about re-allocation. But if the rationale for the initial discussion is plausible—that is, that states have a responsibility to protect the wellbeing and respect interests of the child, then one could argue that consistency demands that these interests are regularly and periodically assessed against the custodial qualifications of the adults in the children's lives.

Conclusion

To recapitulate, I have suggested a map of my agreement and disagreement with Gheaus: we agree that children have different kinds of interests—we may call these wellbeing interests and respect interests, and I have argued to also consider children's autonomy and agency interests. We also agree that for children to develop the capacity to explore their own agency—which is at the basis of respect interests—children rely on relationships, in particular, on relationships with adults. Adults in children's lives have important roles to play to promote and foster not only their wellbeing but also their capacity to develop their autonomy and the necessary sense of self to be agents in the world. Our disagreement is about who is best placed to satisfy these needs. I believe that intending parents in surrogacy agreements, who spend considerable time and energy bringing their biological child into the world—certainly much more than many heterosexual couples do—have established some credentials as custodians, as the adults who will promote and protect the autonomy, wellbeing, and respect interests of the child. In cases of gestational surrogacy, their relationships to the child are not only social, temporal, and deeply invested, but also biological.

Gheaus's assumption seems to be that because of the power parents have over their children, they should have to qualify for the right to be their parents. Second, the assumption seems to be that the intending parents in surrogacy agreements prioritize their interests over those of the child. But I suspect that even if this last worry were assuaged—Gheaus would still be wary of private surrogacy agreements, since her third underlying assumption seems to be that something is deeply amiss in surrogacy transfers because custodial rights change hands before we have assessed if the intending parents might be the best available custodians. In response, I have argued that children's relationships are indeed important factors in protecting children's interests—but it is not clear that the state should adjudicate the relationships for children. Intending parents in surrogacy agreements have already worked on the basis of their relationship to the child, and should thus be counted as her custodian in light of their intentional and social relationship at birth.

Women and Children First. A Reply to Straehle

Anca Gheaus

Introduction

Surrogacy is morally complex: it affects several parties, both by potentially benefiting them and by potentially harming or wronging them. It's therefore not surprising that any two views about the value of surrogacy and its permissibility in some kind of form may agree on certain points and that they should also diverge from each other on other points. In the case of Christine Strahle's and my accounts, as given in this book, the potential overlap is fairly extensive. I shall outline the overlap in section 1 of this reply chapter; in a nutshell, I don't take issue with Straehle's claim that women may gestate children over whom they don't intend to have custody, and that they may do this in a profit-seeking manner. This is, indeed, part of my (very sketchy) proposal of a permissible practice.

The main ethical issues raised by surrogacy directly concern two kinds of participants: the women who serve as surrogates and the children born through surrogacy agreements. Many of these issues are independent of each other. In this book, my main concern is with how surrogacy wrongs children; Straehle's is with how it does not wrong women. Therefore, the area of our disagreement could, in principle, be fairly limited; that is, modifications of one or both of our views could be combined in an overall account of a permissible practice involving surrogate pregnancy. However, in the form defended

Debating Surrogacy. Anca Gheaus and Christine Straehle, Oxford University Press.

here, our views diverge considerably, and it is the main aim of this chapter to explain how and why. Sections 2 and 3 of this chapter focus on our disagreements by laying out my justice-based and value-based objections to the surrogacy practice defended by Straehle.

In section 2 I detail what I find objectionable about Strahele's proposal as far as women surrogates are concerned: First, that it either devalues or it discourages any bonds created during pregnancy between surrogate mother and child. (Doing this, as others have noted, is particularly concerning in societies shaped by histories of devaluing care and, more generally, devaluing women's contribution to social cooperation). Second, that it requires women who serve as surrogates to enter labour contracts that, in comparison to existing ones, are extraordinarily constricting; as such, it represents an illiberal proposal. And third, that it wrongfully restricts the access of the surrogate to the child she carried after the child's birth.

Section 3 zooms into my fundamental disagreement with Straehle about the way in which children's moral status prohibits adults from settling custody over children *via* private agreements. It shows why Straehle's proposal depends on the view that, in gestational surrogacy—where the surrogate carries a child created from gametes produced or purchased by the intending parents— the intending parents are always the moral parents of the child; if so, the surrogate is best described as selling a service, rather than as attempting to transfer the moral right to become the parent of the child she gestates. But if it is to justify surrogacy as we have it today, or as Straehle would like to have it, the service model must be paired with the belief that people have a presumptive right to parent the children created from their gametes; this belief is itself indefeasible without a proprietarian understanding of the child-parent relationship. But proprietarianism does not square with my fundamental assumption that children's interests are warranted the same protection as adults' interests. If so, then the surrogacy practice defended by Straehle is as disrespectful of children as is privately arranged adoption.

Straehle provides a hybrid defence of surrogacy as a form of legitimate work: she appeals both to women's ownership over their bodies and labour, understood as safeguards to their autonomy, and to the value of work for one's individual self-realization and self-respect. In section 4, just before concluding, I lay out some doubts about the stability of this hybrid argument. In some cases of real-world surrogacy, appeal to self-ownership will yield one verdict about the permissibility of that particular instance of surrogacy, and appeal to self-realization and self-respect will yield another. It is such hard cases that show why the defender of surrogacy as autonomous work must ultimately settle for one *or* another of these justifications.

Surrogacy, as we have it today, or in a slightly more regulated form as envisaged by Straehle, is not the only way to become a parent for people who cannot or would not have children the traditional way. Adoption is an obvious alternative, albeit not one that's likely to be seen as adequate by those who find biological parenting highly desirable. Straehle assumes, without explanation, that there is special value in raising one's biological child, and the people have an interest in biological (i.e., genetic) parenthood; if this is true, this interest can be satisfied by the type of arrangement I consider, and briefly outline once again, in the conclusions.

1. Where We Agree: Gestating for Another

As promised, let me start with my agreement with Straehle. She thinks that "employing one's body to work as a surrogate should count as a legitimate means to provide for oneself and one's family," and I see no reason to disagree. That is, as long as *surrogate* refers to a woman who carries a baby with the expectation that the baby will have a different custodian, under a regime of custody allocation that tracks the child's best interest, as explained in my main chapter. (This will pick out instances of surrogacy as legitimate work that are different from those that Straehle's account deems legitimate.)

To bring out this limited agreement, let me list several reasons why someone may resist Straehle's claim.

There can be different reasons for thinking that surrogacy as such (as opposed to particular, for example, coercive or exploitative instances of it) is not a legitimate form of work. One may object to surrogacy because one embraces a form of virtue ethics, perhaps of a traditional bent, according to which bearing and giving birth to a child inevitably makes one a mother, and a good mother is never willing to be separated from her baby. I do not endorse this view. More interestingly, one may question whether surrogacy can ever be mere "work," as opposed to being the beginning of moral parenthood; some believe that a surrogate is a biological mother, that children are always benefited by being raised by their biological mothers, and that children's interest must prevail in the determination of moral parenthood.[1] I share the child-centred part of this view, but not—as I made clear in my original chapter—the second premise. Even in cases in which children are benefited by being cared for by their biological parents, gestational or genetic, the benefits are not plausibly such that they require the biological parent to have custody over the child. A caring relationship alone will do. Finally, it is possible to think, like Lindsey Porter,[2] that procreators can never fully divest themselves of the duty to provide the child with a certain level of wellbeing. If the gestational mother counts as procreator, it follows, on Porter's account, that she is always the person (or one of the persons) of last resort to ensure that the child enjoys a good enough childhood. This would indicate that surrogacy can never be merely work rather than (also) entry into standby parenthood; or, at least, that it is indeed a unique kind of work, one the performance of which obliges the worker to take on unusually burdening and possibly lifelong obligations. I don't take a view on this last possibility. Even if surrogacy is not mere work (but also standby parenthood), what matters for the purpose of establishing its normative status is whether one may bear a child with the intention that another person gains custody.

Like Straehle, I think the answer to the last question is positive. But—and this is where our difference lies—I don't think one may engage in surrogacy work as part of a private agreement, the object of which is to ensure that the child's custody will be allocated to the intending parents, whether or not that will be the optimal custodial arrangement for the child.

Another, related, area of partial convergence between our views is that we both reject unregulated surrogacy practices. We both believe that gestating for another should be overseen by the state, and part of that oversight is meant to check that women who work as surrogates make voluntary occupational decisions. But unlike Straehle, I think the state ought to also license the intending parents and allow the surrogate and other parties to apply for custody. And I categorically reject Straehle's proposal that states are free to enforce surrogacy agreements by conditioning a surrogate's decision to withdraw from the agreement in the ways she proposes. I elaborate on these points below.

2. Where We Disagree: The Women

In Straehle's defence of surrogacy, women are the primary focus of concern and hence I start by detailing my disagreements with her as far as they concern the surrogacy practice my co-author envisages. As I say earlier in the book, my overall goal is to defend humane and just childbearing and rearing practices. The surrogacy practice proposed by Straehle seems to me to offend in one way against humaneness and in two ways against justice.

2.1. Humaneness

On the first count, Straehle proposes that surrogacy contracts be enforceable by states, making the gestational mother ineligible for custody, and nothing in the proposal suggests that surrogates may have rights to access to the child after birth, let alone a right to pursue a caring relationship with the child. But some surrogates bond with the child during pregnancy. This way of regulating surrogacy suggests that bonding during pregnancy is either ethically irrelevant to the questions of who should have custody and access rights to the child, or that surrogates have a duty—moral, but maybe also contractual—not to bond during pregnancy. It also entails that any surrogate is wise to refrain, as much as this is under her control, from developing feelings of attachment towards the baby she is carrying. Bonding—which we know can happen in surrogacy—is, under this regime, prudentially bad for the gestational mother, nothing but an invitation to suffer once the baby is transferred to the intending parents. But this, in my view, goes against impulses for which we, human beings, may be hardwired—namely, to feel attached to the child one is carrying to term. (In the next section I unpack the child-centred complaint against making bonding during pregnancy imprudent.) This impulse usually serves the good purpose of ensuring that the child is cared for, and is part and parcel of what it is, for human beings, to be creatures of attachment. If so, asking gestational mothers to refrain from bonding is at best difficult for some of them—no intention to generalize here!—and, at worst, cruel for surrogates who cannot help bonding. The requirement that women who enter surrogacy contracts shouldn't be able to exit them lightly only compounds this problem. This is, I assume, the thought behind Elizabeth Anderson's criticism, which is worth quoting again here: "The demand to deliberately alienate oneself from one's love for one's own child is a demand which can reasonably and decently be made of no one."[3]

Further, and finally, this is the place to make a point which is not, strictly speaking, about the humaneness of the gestational bond but about women's collective interest in preserving the recognition of the bond's value. I have some sympathy for the view that, when a socially accepted practice either denies the ethical relevance of this bond or encourages its avoidance, or both, this can be detrimental to women. Prevalent gender norms praise women in particular for being nurturing, and rightly represent pregnancy as a form of emotional, and not only physical, nurturing. The double standard is sexist; but, since emotional nurturing as such is an important good, valuing pregnant women for emotional nurturing is not objectionable. It is therefore not unreasonable to worry that a form of surrogacy that denies women opportunities to exercise emotional nurturing is not only harsh or even cruel towards some individuals but also undermining of a source of social valuing of women in general. In a world in which the social valuing of women is rather scarce, feminists have reason to object to the devaluation of attachments.

2.2. Justice

On the second count, concerning matters of justice, my objections are about the shape of the surrogacy contract and the gestational mother's rights after birth.

Straehle writes that there is little going back on the contract for the surrogate. She thinks that surrogates should typically not be legally free to opt out—that is, to interrupt an otherwise healthy pregnancy—because this would jeopardize the emotional wellbeing of the intending parents. Of course, the claim is not that the performance of surrogacy can *always* be required; Straehle thinks that the surrogate may choose to abort, but only for reasons that are sufficiently weighty to outbalance the disappointment of intending parents. Relatively few reasons will qualify, then—perhaps serious health hazards to the surrogate or the baby. But good reasons don't include, for instance, the surrogate's sudden financial abundance, like winning the lottery. She writes: "Presumably, most observers would be hard-pressed to find lack of financial need a justifiable reason for cancelling her surrogacy contract with, for example, a gay couple in their late forties who have worked towards having a child for a considerable amount of time. It would simply seem unjustifiable." If surrogacy is a mere service provision, I find this judgement puzzling. In the case of a regular pregnancy, where gestation is the first step into parenthood, we may think it is morally objectionable for a pregnant woman to abort merely because she won the lottery and better options for how to lead her life suddenly came up. Even if abortion is, at that stage, morally permissible, such a decision may cast doubts on the woman's motivation for becoming a parent. It is right to judge *that* situation by the standards of parenthood. (Presumably, even so, the woman should have a legal right to abort.) Yet, on Straehle's account, a surrogate isn't, or at least shouldn't be, generally judged by the standards of parenthood but by usual standards of service provision. She is a regular worker, albeit one performing a type of work with high emotional stakes. It is not right to morally evaluate her on the same terms as she would if she was also planning to become a parent.

Indeed, if a surrogacy contract is nothing more than a contract over the provision of a service, the claim that surrogates should not be legally free to exit the contract by deciding to abort is quite extraordinary. Common law, in general, rules out the enforcement of specific performance on labour contracts. Employees are free to quit, in which case they typically owe due notice and some reparation, but cannot be forced by law to provide what they said they would in their work contract. Rather, it is on the employer to find a new labourer. And if the process of recruiting a labourer, or the necessary materials, is particularly onerous to the employer, this should be reflected in the compensation owed by the quitting employee—but not in her legal freedom to exit the agreement.

All this is not to say that quitting surrogacy is never morally objectionable. Let's keep to the winning the lottery example. Usually, it is morally unproblematic for someone to quit her job in such a circumstance, but sometimes it *is* objectionable to do so as soon as the law allows it. Assume someone's job is to teach, and if she quits, some of her current students would face significant disruptions and difficulties finishing their degrees. They have come to rely on their teacher, and to plan an important part of their life under the assumption that she will supervise them. So perhaps quitting in such situations is wronging the students, or at least is breaching an undirected duty not to violate others' legitimate expectations. Even so, it is a long shot to argue that the law should prevent the teacher from quitting—that is, that this specific performance should be enforced. Why should it then be otherwise in the case of surrogacy?

There are some exceptions to the rule that labour contracts cannot be enforced by requiring specific performance: during wartime, soldiers are not legally free to quit their jobs. Yet this prohibition is justified, if it is, by appeal to the same consideration that is supposed to justify conscription—namely, the importance of defending basic freedoms. In surrogacy, at stake is not a basic freedom but the emotional vulnerability of people who were hoping to become the parents of a genetical offspring, and so the same justification for enforcing specific performance does not apply.

Another source of puzzlement is Straehle's claim that "if we accept that the intending parents pay for the service of the surrogate, and not for the 'product,' then it should also be plausible to say that the intending parents should be allowed to demand the end of the agreement if the foetus' health is concerned" and pay the surrogate less. Again, if surrogacy is a form of work in which the employee provides a service, then any such provision should be privately agreed upon (or not) by specific parties and appear in their particular contracts, rather than in a general regulation of surrogacy practices. Unless the parties specify otherwise in the contract, intending parents should pay in full. Consider an example: if I contract with you to paint my house and sometime during the process of painting, I change my mind because I discover, say, that something is wrong with the foundation and the house needs reconstruction, I typically have to pay you in full.

To sum up this point, I see no grounds to deny the surrogate the right to get out of the contract at any time and walk away. In section 3 I argue that, in addition, what she then does with her body—i.e., whether or not she aborts and, if she doesn't, whether or not she seeks to raise the child herself—are separate issues. One may, of course, think that a surrogate who walks away from the contract without terminating the pregnancy is leaving with something that is owned by the intending parents: the foetus. But, as I shall explain again presently, I reject this proprietarian view of how rights in relation to children may be grounded.

The second worry of justice concerns what I see as the wrong of a double exclusion of the surrogates: their exclusion from eligibility to parent the child and the exclusion from the life of the child of those surrogates who are willing and capable of having a beneficial, caring relationship with the child. I shall not elaborate more on the first exclusion, since that has been amply explored in my main chapter: if the moral right to parent a child is held by the best available parent, then there may be cases in which the right is held by the surrogate. Our disagreement is fundamental. Straehle writes that "when weighing burdens and harms in surrogacy agreements, the harm that commissioning parents would suffer in cases of surrogates not releasing the child should weigh very heavily." This, I take, is an indication that she rejects a child-centred account of the right to parent, since she factors the intending parents' interest into the balance of reasons that indicate who has the moral right to rear the child.

As for the second kind of exclusion, Straehle justifies it by noting that "surrogates also have to respect the privacy of the intending parents—how much access surrogates have to the babies born is often considered a stumbling block after the end of the surrogacy agreement, i.e., when children are born. Of course, it might be enjoyable for the surrogate to be able to play a role in the child's life, but it is not clear that she should be able to expect this." I can see that the privacy of the intending parents speaks in favour of excluding the surrogate from the life of the child. But in favour of allowing her access speak considerations that are much more important than how enjoyable it may be (for any of the parties involved) if the surrogate were to continue a caring relationship with the child after birth. As I explain in the main chapter and elsewhere,[4] I believe that, more generally, all those whose association with the child would be beneficial to the child have a right to seek such associations. This is a liberty right: they have no duty not to seek to become part of the child's life. But gestational mothers, of course, already are as much part of the newborn's life as anyone can be. So theirs should be seen as a right to continue, rather than to seek, the relationship. Given the powerful interest that we have in maintaining intimate relationships—and caring relationships are intimate—we have claim rights against coerced separation without very weighty reasons. When the child's interest is served by continuing to have the surrogate in their lives, such reasons do not include the intending parents' privacy. Similarly, no judge would (or, at least, should) deny visitation rights to a non-custodial parent merely for the sake of protecting the custodial parent's privacy.

3. Where We Disagree: The Children

In my view, the surrogacy practice proposed by Straehle wouldn't do justice to children, either. To clarify, my concern is not about the child's interests in general. There is no need to assume that most interests will be set back in all cases of privately arranged surrogacy—indeed, it is easy to imagine cases in which children whose custody was obtained *via* surrogacy agreements lead flourishing lives. Rather, when I complain that children are unjustly treated by the private allocation of custody, I mean that they are being disrespected: given children's moral status, control rights over them—as parental rights surely are—must be settled in ways that allocate the rights in a manner that suitably tracks the child's best interest (as far as this is possible). As I argued in my main chapter, and elsewhere,[5] respectful allocation of custody should track the interest of the child, and certain third parties' interests—for instance, in rearing future adults endowed with personal autonomy and a sense of justice—but not the specific interest of would-be parents in having custody. This, most likely, means that the allocation of the custody must be a public issue, in which the state is the warden of children of surrogacy. This is because, in spite of the states' epistemic and practical shortcomings, there seems to be no better agent, or procedure, to protect the child's best interest in custody allocations. It is not logically impossible that markets, or non-commercial private agreements, suitably track the relevant interests; it is merely very implausible. Children, then, may not be commissioned, and surrogacy as practiced today is disrespectful because it involves people trading in (or otherwise privately exchanging) the legal right to parent, under the guise of commissioning a service. I contend that my disagreement with Straehle is ultimately about the proprietarian understanding of the right to become the parent of a particular child, as I explain in the rest of this section.

Intending parents who produce the gametes—the case on which Straehle's analysis is focused[6]—can "commission" something from the surrogate only if surrogacy is the sale of a service, as Straehle assumes it is.[7] (If so, it is worth noting, against some of the formulations used by Straehle, that what parents commission is a service, not a child.) What usually motivates intending parents who engage in surrogacy agreements is not (merely) a desire to see yet another child gestated, but (also) the desire to acquire the custody of this child; but then, for surrogacy to be nothing but the provision of a service that leads to the intending parents' having custody, there must be an independent account of why intending parents are the moral parents of the child, i.e., those entitled to become her custodians. Absent such an account, the aim of surrogacy would be limited to the gestation and birth of a child, and would not include amongst its aims the obtaining of custody by intending parents.

Defenders of surrogacy as a mere service usually explain the intending parents' right to rear by appealing to the normative relevance of intention. On one account, because parenting is a project central to many people's lives, people have a right to pursue parenthood and those who initiate a particular parenthood project are also the moral parents of the child.[8] Someone who endorses this view may think, then, that intending parents have the right to claim custody in surrogacy cases, because raising the child is *their* project. But another custody claimant may reply that they, too, came to form a project of raising the same child. Perhaps the neighbour who first introduced the couple who were to become intending parents in a surrogacy agreement played matchmaker with the intention of rearing this couple's children. Or else, consider situations where the intending parents really are the first to form the project of raising the child, and others—maybe the midwife—form the intention to parent the same child at a later point: why should one assume that the first comers, rather than the late comers, have the right to custody? Isn't it more plausible to think that, of all those who seek to pursue the project of raising this particular child, custody should be given to those who would best serve the child's interest?[9] This is how we would judge in the case of other fiduciary relationships. The basic point here is that intention cannot ground parenthood, at least not on its own, since several people can intend to parent the same child. Therefore, while intention, or willingness, may be a necessary feature for somebody stepping into the parental role,[10] something else is needed to determine custody in cases in which more than one (group of) adequate parents desire to raise the same child.

What, then, can explain that the right to parent a particular child is held by the people who conceive the child, rather than by the neighbour who introduced them, or, in a surrogacy case, by the intending couple rather than by other people who may wish to raise the same child? The only morally relevant feature that distinguishes intending parents from other possible intending parties is that *they* produced the gametes from which the child was created. If so, the question is: How is the fact that they produced the gametes relevant to establishing their right to rear the child? One way in which it can be is because genetical connections predict better parenting. In my main chapter, I discuss some such child-centred ways in which genetical connections could be normatively relevant; as I say there, none of these decisively supports the conclusion that intending parents have the right to rear. Alternatively, gamete provision may be thought relevant on proprietarian grounds: on this account, whoever has property over the gametes has a claim to bring up the child that resulted from the gametes through legitimately acquired gestational services. Indeed, this is what Straehle indicates as her view, in the way she draws the comparison between surrogacy and the provision of baking services to clients who own the ingredients: "[T]he difference between the baker and the surrogate is what they employ to provide their service—we can imagine that we pay the baker for her service and the ingredients that go into the bread; whereas commissioning parents in gestational surrogacy pay for the service, having provided the extensive part of the gestational material themselves." But a proprietarian view of rights over children is incompatible with the belief that children have moral status. Even if intending parents own the gametes produced by their bodies (or obtained from other individuals), they do not thereby have a right to raise the child created from these gametes.

To be fair, Straele does not explicitly subscribe to proprietarianism. An additional, non-proprietarian, argument for her conclusion—that intending parents are the moral parents, and hence, surrogacy is a mere service—is perhaps available, and it is one that grounds the right to parent the child in a duty to care for one's progenee.[11] Such an argument, however, would be at odds with Straehle's view that "in cases of failed contracts" (meaning, I assume, cases when intending parents do not, after all, claim custody) "effective state regulation . . . should anticipate that the children are the responsibility of the state." If she believes that unwanted children of surrogacy become the moral responsibility of the state, then it cannot be the case that she also believes that intending parents have custody rights grounded in unalienable duties towards their progenee.

4. Is Straehle's Hybrid Defence of Surrogacy Stable?

So far, I have discussed substantive disagreements between Straehle's account of surrogacy and mine. In this pre-concluding section, I raise some questions about the stability of her dual grounding of the right to work as a surrogate: in women's self-ownership—understood as a safeguard to autonomy—and in their interest in freedom of occupational choice as a means to secure self-realization and self-respect.

The instability of this dual defence of surrogacy is brought out by situations when surrogates are at significant risk of exploitation. From reading Straehle's chapter, it was not clear to me whether she supports an exploitation-preventing licensing of surrogacy. Take, for instance, cases of international surrogacy where surrogates are recruited from amongst the poorest women in the Global South, women who lack alternative employment or, in any case, alternative decent work. In such situations, legislators may be duty-bound to allow desperate women to engage in surrogacy, thus respecting their self-ownership; as Straehle herself notes, this option gets further support from the fact that a ban would worsen their already wrongfully dire situation.[12] But when women want to serve as surrogates out of desperation, appeals to their self-realization and self-respect are not merely unavailable as reasons to permit surrogacy; rather, they count as reasons to ban it. Such surrogacy is non-voluntary, at least on the understanding of voluntariness which requires that agents have acceptable alternatives[13]—the view to which Straehle subscribes. It is not hard to imagine that non-voluntary engagement in the highly intimate work of surrogacy is corrosive to self-realization and possibly to self-respect.[14] Indeed, Straehle herself seems very reluctant to claim that surrogacy is permissible in these circumstances; for instance, in discussing the case of a woman who is offered surrogacy work in exchange for extending a loan to her family, she notes that such examples of surrogacy are morally troubling and, perhaps for good reasons, fodder to those who would like to see a ban on international commercial surrogacy.

Should we then think that Straehle's view yields an indictment against surrogacy when it is exploitative of women who live in dire poverty? This seems to be in line with her interest-protecting understanding of rights: in some situations, a ban on surrogacy may be the best protection mechanism, at least in the long run, against being pressured into it. And some of the protected interests are likely to be those in self-realization and self-respect. But a ban violates women's right to self-ownership and in doing so precludes the would-be surrogates from pursuing their life plans. That Straehle likely accepts this much can be inferred from her analysis in the note where she endorses Janet Radcliffe-Richards' judgement that a poor man who is banned from selling an organ to pay for his child's operation is denied self-ownership. Appeals to self-ownership can, arguably, even justify voluntary self-slavery.[15] Then why shouldn't they also justify one's decision to work as a surrogate for moneylenders? Moreover, if surrogacy is a type of work with no special normative status, as Straehle thinks it is, there is no more reason to prevent women from engaging in it in coercive or exploitative contexts than there is to prevent them from engaging in other types of coercive or exploitative work; working as a surrogate for the moneylender, on this view, should be seen as neither more nor less permissible than providing free domestic services, or car maintenance, or tuition in Latin for the lender's children.

This analysis brings to the fore the instability of defending surrogacy by appeal to both self-ownership, on the one hand, and to self-realization or self-respect, on the other, since the two grounds yield opposite conclusions concerning the legalization of surrogacy for women who lack any decent alternative employment. In just circumstances, this instability would not lead to practical difficulties—and we certainly have independent reasons to promote just circumstances. As Straehle herself puts it: "Those who aim to prohibit commercial surrogacy out of concern for individual surrogates should then also be against the context in which surrogates make their choice for surrogacy and need to explain why prohibition is the best option in a fundamentally unequal world." I can only agree with this point. But my agreement is compatible with thinking that a defence of surrogacy as morally and legally permissible in the existing unjust world cannot appeal to the thought that women's participation in surrogacy will always, or even most often, promote their self-realization or self-respect. In cases like the ones discussed here, self-respect speaks against surrogacy. Rather, the most robust real-world defences of surrogacy[16] appeal either to women's self-ownership, or to forward-looking considerations such as the belief that prohibition is likely to generate, all things considered, more harms than benefits for the would-be surrogates.

Conclusions

Straehle's main explicit concern, in her chapter, is to defend women's freedom to work as surrogates. In itself, this aim does not support any of the particular regulations of surrogacy that she proposes, with the exception of those meant to ensure that women can make autonomous decisions to engage in surrogacy work. This is why I suspect that my complaints concerning women and children are intimately related to Strahele's understanding of surrogacy as a practice primarily meant to serve the interest of intending parents in having biologically related children. (Why else give priority to these interests over a surrogate's decision to default on the contract?) She writes that "surrogacy, including paid surrogacy, is worth protecting as a possible way to have children." The excessive prominence given to this aim can explain the particular shape of her proposal, as well as the description of intending parents as "commissioning parents."

Straehle could have, instead, argued that intending parents ought to be at least licensed by state agencies, in the same way adoptive parents are, as Andrew Botterell and Carolyn McLeod propose.[17] Or, more ambitiously, she could have—as I propose—considered states to be the default custodians of any child born from surrogacy agreements, in which case states would have the power to determine whether intending parents provide the best available permanent custodial arrangement for the child. Intending parents, in this scenario, would not be "commissioning" anything—rather, they would contribute to the creation of a child whose custody they would quite likely acquire. Straehle could have also accommodated surrogacy agreements that allow surrogates to interrupt their pregnancies without having to provide reasons—as long as abortion is permissible—as well as to decide that they, too, are intending parents before or right after the birth of the child. Finally, she could have accommodated a form of surrogacy in which surrogates have the legal right to have ongoing caring relationships with the children they bear. All these details, however, would minimize the prospects for surrogacy to robustly cater for the interest that intending parents have in gaining custody—including the right to exclude other people from being caring figures in the life of the child, as per the *status quo* of custodial rights. Such a legal right to exclude is itself a mistake if, as I argue elsewhere,[18] there are independent reasons to want more people to have protected caring relationships with children.

To conclude, let me briefly remind the reader that I agree with Straehle about the fundamental good of a (suitably reformed, perhaps revolutionized) surrogacy practice. She writes that "we need to ask if it is better to insist on traditional models of family-making than to provide for the good of family life to an ever expanding circle of individuals." Like other egalitarians, I side with the second option. But it is possible to promote individuals' interest in parenthood—and potentially in biological parenthood—in a different way than the one proposed by Straehle. The arrangement I suggest provides no guarantee that intending parents will have custody of the child, even if the child is created from their gametes, but is overall justified because it provides fitting protection to the interests of children and of women serving as surrogates.

Notes

Introduction

1. We leave aside mitochondrial donation, which opens the possibility of children with four biological parents. See Catherine Mills, "Nuclear Families: Mitochondrial Replacement Techniques and the Regulation of Parenthood," *Science, Technology, and Human Values* 46 (2021): 507–527.

2. Yet another used term is "the gestational carrier." See Renate Klein, *Surrogacy: A Human Rights Violation* (Melbourne, AUS: Spinifex Press, 2017). Neither Gheaus nor Straehle uses this term.

3. In the book of Genesis.

4. Nayana Hitesh Patel and Yuvraj Digvijaysingh Jadeja, "Insight into Different Aspects of Surrogacy Practices," *Journal of Human Reproductive Sciences* 11, no. 3 (2018): 212–218, https://doi.org/10.4103/jhrs.JHRS_138_17.

5. Christie McDonald, "Changing the Facts of Life: The Case of Baby M," *SubStance* 1, no. 64 (1991): 31–48.

6. Kiran M. Perkins, Sheree L. Boulet, Denise J. Jamieson, Dmitry M. Kissin, and National Assisted Reproductive Technology Surveillance System (NASS) Group, "Trends and Outcomes of Gestational Surrogacy in the United States," *Fertility and Sterility* 106, no. 2 (2016), 435–442, http://www.ncbi.nlm.nih.gov/pubmed/27087401, accessed July 10, 2022.

7. M. Spiewak, "Unter schwierigen Umständen," *Die Zeit*, August 4, 2022, 35.

8. Lennlee Keep, "Surrogacy Facts and Myths: How Much Do You Know?" Independent Lens (blog), PBS, October 22, 2019. https://www.pbs.org/independentlens/blog/surrogacy-facts-and-myths-how-much-do-you-know/, accessed July 10, 2022.

9. Teresa Baron, *The Philosopher's Guide to Parenthood: Storks, Surrogates, and Stereotypes* (Cambridge: Cambridge University Press, forthcoming).

10. Elizabeth Anderson, "Is Women's Labor a Commodity?," *Philosophy and Public Affairs* 19 (1990), 71–92; Klein, *Surrogacy: A Human Rights Violation.*

11. Klein, *Surrogacy: A Human Rights Violation.*

12. Richard Arneson, "Commodification and Commercial Surrogacy," *Philosophy and Public Affairs* 21 (1992): 132–64; Cecile Fabre, "Surrogacy," in *The International Encyclopedia of Ethics*, ed. Hugh LaFollette (Oxford: Wiley-Blackwell, 2013).

13. Debra Satz, *Why Some Things Should Not Be for Sale: The Moral Limits of Markets* (Oxford: Oxford University Press, 2010).

14. Anderson, "Is Women's Labor a Commodity?," 71–92.

15. Vida Panitch, "Global Surrogacy: Exploitation to Empowerment," *Journal of Global Ethics* 9 (2013): 329–343; Stephen Wilkinson, "Exploitation in International Surrogacy Agreements," *Journal of Applied Philosophy* 33 (2) (July 2016), 125–145.

16. Klein, *Surrogacy: A Human Rights Violation.*

17. Baron, *Philosopher's Guide to Parenthood.*

18. Norvin Richards, *The Ethics of Parenthood* (Oxford: Oxford University Press 2010).

19. Andrew Botterell and Carolyn McLeod, "Licensing Parents in International Contract Pregnancies," *Journal of Applied Philosophy* 33, no. 2 (2016): 178–196.

Defending Surrogacy as Reproductive Labour

1. I do not go so far as to advocate a state-based system akin to that promoted by Gheaus, in which babies born through surrogacy become, in the first instance, wardens of the state, which then places them with the best available custodian. However, in such a system, if the state were to employ women as surrogates, the demands of my defence for surrogacy as reproductive labor would be satisfied. I will return to this point in my reply to Gheaus in Part II.

2. Heather Jacobsen, *Labour of Love: Surrogacy in America* (New Brunswick, NJ: Rutgers University Press, 2016), 157.

3. For a helpful overview of the different arguments, and a successful refutation, see Stephen Wilkinson, "Exploitation in International Surrogacy Arrangements," *Journal of Applied Philosophy* 33, no. 2 (July 2015): 125–45.

4. Kelly Weisberg, *The Birth of Surrogacy in Israel* (Tampa: University of Florida Press, 2005).

5. Tzvi Joffre, "High Court Pushes Fixed Deadline to Fix Surrogacy after Election," *Jerusalem Post*, March 12, 2021, https://www.jpost.com/israel-news/high-court-pushes-deadline-to-fix-surrogacy-law-after-elections-661692, accessed April 20, 2021. For the most recent approval of LGBTQ+

surrogacy parenthood, see https://www.reuters.com/world/middle-east/israel-lifts-restrictions-same-sex-surrogacy-2022-01-04/, accessed January 5, 2021.

6. See https://www.health.gov.il/English/Topics/fertility/Surrogacy/Pages/default.aspx, accessed January 2, 2022.

7. Mark MacLeod, "Reimbursement of Expenditures and Possible Sub-delegation of the Assisted Human Reproduction Regulations," in *Surrogacy in Canada*, ed. V. Gruben, A. Cattapan, and A. Cameron (Toronto: Irwin Law, 2018), 113–54.

8. Of course, alternatively, one could also understand the payments as providing the means for the pregnancy to be carried out, and maybe carried out in a comfortable and safe way, and ensuring that no extra financial burdens are placed on the surrogate. However, as MacLeod illustrates, some of the eligible expenses clearly aim to compensate the surrogate for the physical work that pregnancy involves. I thank Costanza Porro for pressing me on this point.

9. See Christine Overall, "Reproductive 'Surrogacy' and Parental Licensing," *Bioethics* 29, no. 5 (August 2015): 353–61.

10. Jacobson, *Labor of Love*.

11. The exploitation charge is most virulent in the international context. However, it would be misleading to assume that surrogacy arrangements might not also pose problems in developed countries, as the recent debate over legislating surrogacy contracts in Canada showed. See Dave Snow, "Measuring Parentage Policy in the Canadian Provinces: A Comparative Framework," *Canadian Public Administration* 59, no. 1 (March 2016): 5–25.

12. See Joseph Raz, *The Morality of Freedom* (Oxford: Oxford University Press, 1988).

13. Isaiah Berlin, "Two Concepts of Liberty," in *Four Essays on Liberty* (Oxford: Oxford University Press, 1986), 118–72.

14. Charles Taylor, "What's Wrong with Negative Liberty," in *Philosophy and the Human Sciences* (Cambridge: Cambridge University Press, 1985), 187–210.

15. See also Christine Straehle, "Is There a Right to Surrogacy?," *Journal of Applied Philosophy* 33, no. 2 (May 2016): 146–59, where I argue that there can't be a positive right to surrogacy since this would imply that the state had jurisdiction over women's bodies to make them work as surrogates. Similarly, there can't be a positive right to surrogacy work since a surrogate hoping to work as one needs access to intending parents to choose her—nothing a liberal state can provide.

16. Michael J. Shaffer, "The Publicity of Belief, Epistemic Wrongs and Moral Wrongs," *Social Epistemology* 20, no. 1 (2006): 41–54.

17. Should we also prevent professions that can lead to self-harm? Some authors think so: Peter de Marneffe, for instance, argues for the very strict regulation of prostitution because sex work putatively harms women. Peter de Marneffe, *Liberalism and Prostitution* (Oxford: Oxford University Press, 2009). Similarly, one could argue that women should be prevented from working as surrogates since surrogacy harms them. I acknowledge that possible self-harm could be an important consideration, especially in the context of my argument for freedom of professional occupation as important to individual autonomy. I agree with de Marneffe that the liberal state has a duty of care towards its citizens—but I am loath to be as paternalist as he suggests we ought to be, especially in light of a history of state policies that inflicted incredible pain on women because they policed how women should behave "for their own good." Think of the common practice, implemented by the Catholic Church, but sanctioned by the Irish state, of making single unmarried mothers give up their babies and then putting them to work in the Magdalene asylums. Or the forced sterilization of women who were considered mentally unfit to have children. While I acknowledge and explain in more detail later on that some requirements for surrogacy work are justified, and while it is important that individual women take the decision to work as a surrogate freely and voluntarily, the worry about protecting women from some occupations for fear that exercising them might lead to self-harm seems to me hard to justify. Thanks are due to Oliver Hallich for raising this point with me.

18. "Kant's political philosophy rests on a highly contentious claim that rational agents have a *right to freedom*, by which he means that their freedom can justifiably be restricted only for the sake of freedom itself." Louis-Philippe Hodgson, "Kant on the Right to Freedom: A Defense," *Ethics* 120 (July 2010): 791–819, at 791.

19. Lucas Stanczyk, "Productive Justice," *Philosophy and Public Affairs* 40, no. 2 (August 2012): 144–64; Gerald Allan Cohen, *Rescuing Justice and Equality* (Cambridge, MA: Harvard University Press, 2008), 2.

20. John Rawls, *A Theory of Justice* (Cambridge, MA: Harvard University Press, 1999), 241.

21. Gerald MacCallum, "Negative and Positive Freedom," *Philosophical Review* 76, no. 3 (July 1967): 312–34, at 314.

22. In earlier feudal systems, freedom of occupational choice was not a given. In guild systems, the children of guild members were expected to take up

the profession of their elders. One was born into a profession rather than that one chose it. In communitarian systems, such as socialist states, occupational choice was also hampered by the needs of the community.

23. A utilitarian argument might be a third, but I disregard that here.

24. Raz, Morality of Freedom.

25. Jeremy Waldron, "Property and Ownership," The Stanford Encyclopedia of Philosophy (Winter 2016 edition), ed. Edward N. Zalta, https://plato.stanf ord.edu/archives/win2016/entries/property/.

26. Belgium and the Netherlands now allow clinically depressed individuals to take end-of-life-decisions after a careful consultation process.

27. Joel Feinberg, Harm to Self (Oxford: Oxford University Press, 1986), 53.

28. Feinberg, Harm to Self, 53.

29. Feinberg, 54–55.

30. John Locke, Two Treatises of Government, ed. Peter Laslett (Cambridge: Cambridge University Press, 1988).

31. Robert Nozick, Utopia, Anarchy, and the State (New York: Basic Books, 1974), 34.

32. Gerald Allan Cohen, Self-Ownership, Freedom and Equality (Cambridge: Cambridge University Press, 1995), 236ff.

33. David Archard, "Autonomy and Self-Ownership," Journal of Applied Philosophy 25, no. 1 (January 2008): 19–33, at 32.

34. Archard, "Autonomy and Self-Ownership," 30.

35. Cohen, Self-Ownership, Freedom and Equality, 236.

36. Cohen, 237.

37. Cf. also Fabre, p. 3.

38. See here also Fabre's discussion of the extent egalitarian justice is challenged by self-ownership rights when the question is whether to compensate for inegalitarian bodily functions. We can't justify harvesting kidneys from healthy people to compensate those with kidney failure, even if egalitarian principles might demand such compensation.

39. Bas van der Vossen, "Libertarianism," The Stanford Encyclopedia of Philosophy (Spring 2019 edition), ed. Edward N. Zalta, https://plato.stanf ord.edu/archives/spr2019/entries/libertarianism/.

40. Feinberg, Harm to Self, 53; my emphasis.

41. For the link between self-determination and self-authorship, see Alexios Arvanitis and Konstantinos Kalliris, "A Self-Determination Theory Account of Self-Authorship: Implications for Law and Public Policy," Philosophical Psychology 30, no. 6 (April 2017): 763–83. I thank Colin Macleod for raising this point with me.

42. I assume for the purposes of this discussion that surrogacy work is *paid* work since that is at issue in many jurisdictions.

43. See the important discussion on consent in Amia Srinivasan, *The Right to Sex* (Bloomsbury: London, 2021).

44. John Rawls, *A Theory of Justice*, 2nd ed. (Cambridge, MA: Harvard University Press, 1999), 79.

45. Rawls, *Theory of Justice*, 386.

46. As a reminder, Rawls considers that "other things being equal, people normally find activities that call upon their developed capacities to be more interesting and preferable to simpler tasks, and their enjoyment increases the more the capacity is realized or the greater its complexity (TJ, 326/374). These general facts imply that rational people should incorporate into their plans activities that call upon the exercise and development of their talents and skills and their distinctly human capacities (TJ, 432,379)." Samuel Freeman, "Original Position," *The Stanford Encyclopedia of Philosophy* (Summer 2012 edition), ed. Edward N. Zalta, http://plato.stanf ord.edu/archives/spr2012/entries/original-position/.

47. Rawls, *Theory of Justice*, 386.

48. I have discussed the *social* conditions of having access to the social means of self-respect in Christine Straehle, "Solidarity, Social Deprivation and Refugee Agency: What Does It Mean to Stand in Solidarity with Refugees?," *Journal of Social Philosophy* 51, no. 4 (2020): 526–41.

49. See Joseph H. Carens, *Equality, Moral Incentives, and the Market: An Essay in Utopian Politico-Economic Theory* (Chicago: Chicago University Press, 1981).

50. Derek J. Ettinger, "Genes, Gestations and Social Norms," *Bioethics* 31, no. 3 (May 2012): 243–68.

51. Susan Moller Okin, *Justice, Gender and the Family* (New York: Basic Books, 1989).

52. Of course, the market was initially seen as an equalizer among people and as a way to integrate and join societies. See Judith Shklar, *American Citizenship* (Cambridge, MA: Harvard University Books, 1998).

53. Robert Titmuss argued that some things shouldn't be remunerated, because then they would undermine feelings of solidarity and rob individuals of the possibility of making a gift. He made this argument in the context of a sociological analysis of the example of blood donations versus a commercial system of generating donor blood. Cf. Robert M. Titmuss, *The Gift Relationship* (London: George Allen, 1970). I will return to this worry in my discussion of the commercialization worry in section 3.

54. Jacobsen, *Labor of Love*.

55. See Jacobson, *Labor of Love*, esp. chap. 4.

56. Nick Butler, Shiona Chillas, and Sara Louise Muhr, "Professions at the Margins," *Ephemera: Theory and Politics in Organization* 12, no. 3 (September 2012): 259–71. I will return to a discussion of sex work in section 3.

57. Rawls, *Theory of Justice*, 358–59; emphasis mine.

58. Rawls, 366.

59. See Jacobson, *Labor of Love*; Amrita Pande, "'At Least I Am Not Sleeping with Anyone': Resisting the Stigma of Commercial Surrogacy in India," *Feminist Studies* 36, no. 2 (June 2010): 292–314; and Pande, *Wombs in Labour: Transnational Surrogacy in India* (New York: Columbia University Press, 2014). See also Tanika Gupta, "Baby Farming," *Drama on 3*, BBC Radio 3. http://www.bbc.co.uk/programmes/b04003j9.

60. Janet Radcliffe-Richards makes an analogous argument for the wide range of goals in peoples' lives when she argues for a market in human organs: if selling a kidney is the only plausible way for a person to raise funds for a necessary operation for their child, or to save their mortgage, why should a healthy person not be allowed to sell a kidney? See Janet Radcliffe-Richards, *The Ethics of Transplants* (Oxford: Oxford University Press, 2012).

61. I thank Alain Lourde for raising this point with me.

62. Christine Korsgaard, *Self-Constitution* (Oxford: Oxford University Press, 2009), 204.

63. Korsgaard, *Self-Constitution*, 87.

64. Jacobson, *Labor of Love*; Pande, *Wombs in Labour*.

65. Of course, most critics might argue that the question is not whether surrogacy is work but, rather, whether it is morally non-objectionable work. I will return to this question in section 3.

66. Amrita Pande, "Transnational Commercial Surrogacy in India: Gifts for Global Sisters?," *Reproductive BioMedicine* 23, no. 5 (July 2011): 618–25.

67. Vida Panitch, "Surrogate Tourism and Reproductive Rights," *Hypatia* 28, no. 2 (Spring 2013): 274–89.

68. Paula Casal, "Occupational Choice and the Egalitarian Ethos," *Economics and Philosophy* 29 (April 2013): 3–20, at 9.

69. Bernard Williams, "Voluntary Acts and Responsible Agents," *Oxford Journal of Legal Studies* 10, no. 1 (Spring 1990): 1–10.

70. Serena Olsaretti, *Liberty, Desert and the Market: A Philosophical Study* (Cambridge: Cambridge University Press, 2004), chap. 6.

71. See, generally, Eric Lee, "Our Flawed Approach to Undue Inducement in Medical Research," *Bioethics* 33, no. 1 (January 2019): 13–18.

72. Olsaretti, *Liberty, Desert and the Market*, 140; emphasis mine.

73. The literature on this is plentiful. For excellent accounts from the Global South, see Sharmila Rudrappa, *Discounted Life: The Price of Global Surrogacy in India* (New York: New York University Press, 2015); Maria C. Inhorn, *Cosmopolitan Conceptions: IVF Sojourns in Global Dubai* (Durham NC: Duke University Press, 2015). For a particularly categorical take supported by predominantly women from the Global North, see the website Stop Surrogacy Now, http://www.stopsurrogacynow.com/#sthash.KMFtWEhV.dpbs. For a discussion on the different opposing feminist takes on surrogacy, see Sophie Lewis, *Full Surrogacy Now: Feminist against Family* (Manchester, UK: Manchester University Press, 2019), esp. chap. 3.

74. See Stephen Wilkinson, "Exploitation in International Surrogacy Agreements."

75. See also Straehle, "Is There a Right to Surrogacy?"

76. Jacobson, *Labor of Love*, esp. chap. 1. I acknowledge that this suggestion may sound odd to many ears—yet it is not clear why it should. Think of what we can call the "celebration of pregnancy" in popular culture, with many celebrities posting pictures of their pregnancies on social media. Of course, this picture has been contrasted by a medicalization of pregnancy, and the idea that pregnant women suffer. The span here seems to simply show the span of how female bodies react and live through pregnancy. Normatively speaking, when philosophers take women's agency seriously, this span should be enabled rather than scrutinized.

77. David Archard, "Freedom Not to Be Free: The Case of the Slavery Contract in J. S. Mill's *On Liberty*," *Philosophical Quarterly* (October 1990): 453–65.

78. The volenti principle, which suggests that consent to being harmed is sufficient to prevent punishment for the person inflicting the harm, has been defended by Feinberg, *Harm to Self*. For a discussion, see Gerald Dworkin, "Harm and the Volenti Principle," *Social Philosophy and Policy* 29, no. 1 (2012): 309–21.

79. I have in mind here recent decisions in several liberal democratic countries concerning assisted suicide. Witness, for instance, the 2015 Supreme Court of Canada decision in *Carter vs. Canada* that mandates the federal government to address the discrepancy between what many terminally ill patients hope for and what their well-intentioned doctors are allowed to provide. In its ruling, the court explicitly argues that denying terminally ill patients assistance to die denies them "the right to make decisions

concerning their bodily integrity and medical care and thus trenches on their liberty." This, still according to the court, is "a matter critical to their dignity and autonomy." See *Carter vs Canada*, available at the Supreme Court of Canada website. http://scc-csc.lexum.com/scc-csc/scc-csc/en/item/14637/index.do, accessed March 3, 2015.

80. Cohen, *Self-Ownership, Freedom and Equality*, 237.

81. Carla Bagnoli, "The Mafioso Case: Autonomy and Self-Respect," *Ethical Theory and Moral Practice* 12, no. 5 (November 2009): 477–93. Some could argue, of course, that watching *The Sopranos*, one had a clear sense that the stylized Italian American culture it depicts does instill sources of self-respect. I would argue instead that Bagnoli's argument seems to be verified by Tony Soprano's frequent trips to his therapist, who is meant to help him with his panic attacks.

82. See, for example, Andrea Dworkin, "Prostitution and Male Supremacy," *Michigan Journal for Gender and Law* 1, no. 1 (January 1993).

83. Jeremy Snyder, "Exploitation and Sweatshop Labor: Perspectives and Issues," *Business Ethics Quarterly* 20, no. 2 (April 2010): 187–213.

84. Critically, T. M. Wilkinson, "The Ethics and Economics of Minimum Wage," *Economics and Philosophy* 20, no. 2 (2004): 351–74.

85. The discussion of equality, and the discussion what should be equalized, has, of course, a long pedigree in political philosophy. For a discussion of the moral argument for equality, see Thomas Nagel, *Mortal Questions* (Oxford: Oxford University Press, 1980); Frances Myrna Kamm, "Equal Treatment and Equal Chances," *Philosophy & Public Affairs* 14, no. 2 (Spring 1985): 177–94.

86. Anita L. Allen, "Surrogacy, Slavery, and the Ownership of Life," *Harvard Journal of Law and Public Policy* 139 (1990): 141–46. Allen furthermore argues that the comparison between surrogacy and slavery diminishes the fundamental harm that slavery committed, and I would agree. I therefore also deny that surrogacy is "temporal slavery," and a comparison of the two doesn't hold; as I explained in section 2, surrogacy can be voluntarily chosen as an occupation, which cannot be said of slavery.

87. Pande, Wombs in Labour; Rudrappa, Discounted Life.

88. See Vida Panitch, "Global Surrogacy: Exploitation to Empowerment," *Journal of Global Ethics* 9, no. 3 (2013): 329–43.

89. Jacobson (2015), chap. 1.

90. See, for instance, the account of two surrogates in the United States who reported thinking of their surrogacy as a gift they can make to others.

Jenny Kleeman, "We Are Expected to Be OK with Not Having Children," *The Guardian*, October 1, 2022, Saturday Magazine section.

91. Kimberly D. Krawiec, "Price and Pretense in the Baby Market," *Baby Markets: Money, Morals and the Neopolitics of Choice*, ed. Michele Bratcher Goodwin (Cambridge: Cambridge University Press, 2009).

92. Humbyrd suggests a system she calls "fair trade surrogacy" in Casey Humbyrd, "Fair Trade International Surrogacy," *Developing World Bioethics* 9, no. 3 (2009): 111–18. See also section 4.

93. Debora Satz, *Why Some Things Should Not Be for Sale: The Moral Limits of Markets* (New York: Oxford University Press, 2012).

94. Christine Overall, "The Good of Parenting," in *Family-Making*, ed. Françoise Baylis and Carolyn McLeod (New York: Oxford University Press, 2014); Overall, *Why Have Children?* (Cambridge, MA: MIT Press, 2012).

95. See, e.g., Matthew Liao, *The Right to Be Loved* (New York: Oxford University Press, 2015), esp. chap. 6, in which Liao argues that to have children is a human right.

96. See Mary Warnock, *Report of the Committee of Inquiry into Human Fertilisation and Embryology* (London: Her Majesty's Stationery Office, 1994).

97. http://news.nationalpost.com/2014/04/09/ontario-to-fund-in-vitro-fertilization-with-a-caveat-one-embryo-at-a-time-to-cut-risky-multiple-births/, accessed April 10, 2014.

98. See https://www.nhs.uk/conditions/ivf/, accessed October 13, 2021.

99. The government of Ontario may in fact have been prompted to accept the funding of IVF after its lack of funding became the subject of a human rights complaint based on its lack of funding. See note 98.

100. See Harry Brighouse and Adam Swift, *Family Values: The Ethics of Parent-Child Relationships* (Princeton, NJ: Princeton University Press, 2014).

101. See "Gay Rights Advocates Fight to Lift Ban on Paying Surrogate Moms," *New York Daily News*, January 15, 2014, http://www.nydailynews.com/news/politics/push-nys-ban-paying-surrogate-moms-article-1.1581165, accessed April 10, 2014. See also Kleeman, "We Are Expected to Be OK."

102. See Overall, Why Have Children?

103. I am indebted to Colin MacLeod for pressing me on this issue.

104. See Straehle, "Is There a Right to Surrogacy?"

105. Weinstock and Wisperlaere argue that "access to adoption remains by and large too complex and burdensome for the time being to justify

significant restrictions on the availability of access to ART." See Daniel
Weinstock and Jurgen Wisperlaere, "State Regulation and Assisted
Reproduction: Balancing the Interests of Parents and Children," in Baylis
and McLeod, *Family-Making*, 131–50, at 143.

106. See Harry Brighouse and Adam Swift, "Parents' Rights and the Value of
the Family," *Ethics* 117 (2006): 80–108.

107. Warnock, *Report*, discusses this case and defends this motivation
against opponents who perceive here the instrumentalization of an un-
born child.

108. Thanks to Adam Swift for helping me clarify my position here.

109. Elizabeth S. Anderson, "Is Women's Labour a Commodity?" *Philosophy
and Public Affairs* 19, no. 1 (Winter 1990); and Anderson, "Why
Commercial Surrogate Motherhood Unethically Commodifies Women
and Children: Reply to McLachlan and Swales," *Health Care Analysis* 8
(2000): 19–26. See also Gheaus's contribution in Part I.

110. Anderson, "Why Commercial Surrogate Motherhood," 20.

111. Anderson, 26n.

112. The argument that a genetic link may be the best proxy to find the best
possible parent has some pedigree in the philosophy of childhood, as
Gheaus discusses.

113. See Charlotte Witt, "A Critique of the Bionormative Concept of the
Family," in Baylis and Mcleod, *Family-Making*.

114. See David Archard, "The Obligations and Responsibilities of
Parenthood," in *Procreation and Parenthood: The Ethics of Bearing and
Rearing Children*, ed. David Archard and David Benatar (Oxford: Oxford
University Press, 2010), 103–28.

115. I will discuss the role of intending parents further in my reply to Gheaus
in Part II.

116. In the UK, the surrogate mother is always considered the parent of the
child, regardless of genetic link. See https://www.gov.uk/rights-for-
surrogate-mothers, accessed October 2, 2021.

117. Anderson, "Why Commercial Surrogate Motherhood," 87, n.

118. Satz, Why Some Things Should Not Be for Sale.

119. Satz, 129. An instance of Satz's intuition about this was reported in the
media after India passed legislation stipulating that only heterosexual
couples can enter into surrogate contracts, excluding non-traditional
nuclear families. This left some women serving as surrogates for homosexual couples before the law came into effect, for example, in a state
of uncertainty about the future of the foetus in their womb. Here, Satz

could say that this is a typical instance of a society that neglects women's interest to the benefit of men. See "India Bans Gay Foreign Couples from Surrogacy," *The Telegraph* (UK) online, January 18, 2013, http://www.telegraph.co.uk/news/worldnews/asia/india/9811222/India-bans-gay-foreign-couples-from-surrogacy.html, accessed April 1, 2021.

120. Satz, *Why Some Things Should Not Be for Sale*, 46.

121. Pande, "Transnational Commercial Surrogacy in India," 618–25.

122. See Jacobson (2015). See also Karen Busby and Delaney Vun, "Revisiting the Handmaid's Tale," *Canadian Journal of Family Law* 26, no. 13 (2010).

123. Amrita Pande, "Gestational Surrogacy in India: New Dynamics in Reproductive Labour," in *Critical Perspective on Work and Employment in Globalizing India*, ed. Ernesto Noronha and Premilla D'Cruz (New York: Springer, 2017), 267–82, at 271.

124. Pande, "Gestational Surrogacy in India," 267–82.

125. Rayna Rapp, "Gender, Body, Biomedicine: How Some Feminist Concerns Dragged Reproduction to the Centre of Social Theory," *Medical Anthropology Quarterly* 15, no. 4 (December 2001): 466–77.

126. Pateman, quoted in Satz, *Why Some Things Should Not Be for Sale*, 119.

127. Archard, "Freedom Not to Be Free," 453–65.

128. Anderson, "Is Women's Labour a Commodity?," 91.

129. Anderson, 86.

130. See Pande, "Transnational Commercial Surrogacy in India."

131. See Bonnie Steinbock, "Surrogate Motherhood as Prenatal Adoption," *Law, Medicine & Health Care* 16 (1988): 44–50.

132. Teresa Baron, "Nobody Puts Baby in the Container: The Foetal Container Model at Work in Medicine and Commercial Surrogacy," *Journal of Applied Philosophy* 36, no. 3 (2019): 491–505. See also Gheaus, Part I.

133. To add, then, to Anderson's baking analogy—it isn't that we pay the baker for the service only, but also for the ingredients. If, on the other hand, we were to bring our formed loaves to be baked, as used to be the custom in many villages across Europe, then we *would* be paying the baker for her services, and for the use of her oven.

134. See also the direct response to Anderson in Hugh V. McLachlan and J. K. Swales, "Babies, Child Bearers and Commodification: Anderson, Brazier et al., and the Political Economy of Commercial Surrogate Motherhood," *Health Care Analysis* 8 (2000).

135. Canonically, see Susan Moller-Okin, *Justice, Gender and the Family* (New York: Basic Books, 1991).

136. See, e.g., Inhorn, *Cosmopolitan Conceptions*.

137. To see this, one only needs to read the newspaper stories that highlight the many ways women now have children. See E. Malan, "Baby, It's You," *The Observer Magazine*, October 31, 2021, 17–20.

138. Titmuss, Gift Relationship.

139. Satz, *Why Some Things Should Not Be for Sale*, 3.

140. Wilkinson, "Exploitation in International Surrogacy Agreements."

141. Casey Humbyrd, "Fair Trade International Surrogacy," *Developing World Bioethics* 9 (2009): 111–18.

142. Ruth Walker and Liezlvan Zyl, *Towards a Professional Model of Surrogacy* (London: Palgrave Macmillan, 2017).

143. https://www.canada.ca/en/health-canada/services/drugs-health-produ cts/biologics-radiopharmaceuticals-genetic-therapies/legislation-gui delines/assisted-human-reproduction/prohibitions-related-surrogacy. html,accessed, accessed January 5, 2022.

144. https://www.gov.uk/legal-rights-when-using-surrogates-and-donors, accessed January 5, 2022. It will be important to see what the revisions of the new UK Human Fertilization and Embryology Act will be—but at the time of writing, we cannot know whether the UK government will decide to allow remuneration for surrogacy.

145. The Indian government has since changed course again; it has introduced the Surrogacy (Regulation) Bill 2020, which seems to take a page from the Israeli system I describe just below in that the latest bill prohibits commercial surrogacy entirely; henceforth, only altruistic surrogacy with heterosexual Indian couples will be allowed. See https://www.firstp ost.com/india/mansukh-mandaviya-to-introduce-surrogacy-regulat ion-bill-2020-in-rajya-sabha-all-you-need-to-know-about-the-legislat ion-10191581.html, accessed January 3, 2022.

146. The United States is an exception here, where the intending parents must shoulder the costs of the surrogacy. Indeed, this has led to a series of scams in which surrogacy agencies and women would ask for funds for medical treatments without the woman's being pregnant or in need of medical attention, but with the sole purpose of defrauding hopeful commissioning parents. See https://www.fbi.gov/news/stories/surrog acy-scam-played-on-victims-emotions, accessed December 28, 2021.

147. For the history of surrogacy in Israel, see Weisberg, *Birth of Surrogacy in Israel*.

148. See State of Israel, Ministry of Health website at https://www.health. gov.il/English/Topics/fertility/Surrogacy/Pages/default.aspx, accessed January 2, 2022.

149. State of Israel, Ministry of Health website at https://www.health.gov.il/
English/Topics/fertility/Surrogacy/Pages/default.aspx, accessed January
2, 2022.

150. See Weisberg, *Birth of Surrogacy in Israel*.

151. See also Jacobson (2015) for statements from surrogates and their partners about how implantation affected their intimate life, for fear of
endangering the pregnancy

152. For an interesting and pertinent analysis of the role of social work in in-
ternational surrogacy contracts, see Karen Smith Rotbai, Nicole Footen
Bromfield, and Patricia Fronek, "International Private Law to Regulate
Commercial Global Surrogacy Practices: Just What Are Social Work's
Practical Policy Recommendations?," *International Social Work* 58, no. 4
(2015): 575–81.

153. Courtenay M. Holscher et al., "Anxiety, Depression and Regret of
Donation in living Kidney Donors," *BMV Nephrology* 19, no. 218 (2018).
https://doi.org/10.1186/s12882-018-1024-0.

154. The critic is indeed Colin MacLeod, to whose careful comment I try to
respond here.

155. Cecile Fabre, *Whose Body Is It Anyway? Justice and the Integrity of the
Person* (Oxford: Oxford University Press, 2006).

156. Cohen, *Self-Ownership, Freedom and Equality*, 237.

157. An analogy that may illustrate what I have in mind is the living will: these
are official documents that individuals sign, stipulating what kind of
treatment they want to receive at the end of their lives—to what extent
they want to be resuscitated, and so on. The argument for such patient
statements is based on autonomy concerns—as are statements about
seeking assistance in realizing such end-of-life decisions, as I illustrated with the Canadian Supreme Court decision allowing assisted
suicide. What living wills do, however, is prioritize the will of a self at
an earlier time over possible wills at a later time. This is why they are
often considered problematic for individuals with degenerative mental
illnesses such as Alzheimer's disease and dementia: should we heed
their earlier wish to die if they become other than what they now are? Or
should we accept the quality-of-life argument that even though a person
is unrecognizable to her earlier self, and might not wish to live like that,
she can still enjoy the chocolate pudding a nurse feeds her? What I wish
to illustrate with this example is that when deciding which expression of
will we should heed, I suggest that we should consider the original consent to have some weight, and not only the later refusal to consent.

158. Archard, "Autonomy and Self-Ownership," 19–33.
159. Walker and Zyl, *Towards a Professional Model of Surrogacy*, 35.
160. See Straehle, "Is There a Right to Surrogacy?"
161. In making this argument, I agree with Leroux and colleagues that the truly unfortunate are those who are unwillingly childless. So while states support those who can fulfil their wish for biological children, through childcare allowances etc., the truly unfortunate—that is, those who wish to have children but can't—are left behind. In this view, surrogacy should be not only state regulated but also state sponsored. See Marie-Louise Leroux, Pierre Pestieau, and Gregory Ponthiere, "Childlessness, Childfreeness and Compensation," *Social Choice and Welfare* https://doi.org/10.1007/s00355-021-01379-y.

Against Private Surrogacy: A Child-Centred View

1. As well as other powerful interests. For the rest of this chapter, I leave aside considerations about third parties' interest in childrearing.
2. I provide a defence of this child-centred understanding of the right to parent in Anca Gheaus, "The Best Available Parent," *Ethics* 131, no. 3 (2021): 431–59. The argument of this chapter relies on a child-centred view of the right to parent; but some dual-interests accounts, such as that developed by Liam Shields, support the same conclusion that surrogacy is illegitimate because individuals lack a moral power to transfer custody at will. Shields, "Parental Rights and the Importance of Being Parents," *Critical Review of International Social and Political Philosophy* 22, no. 2 (2019): 119–33.
3. Mary Warnock is a prominent critic, in *A Question of Life: Warnock Report on Human Fertilisation and Embryology* (Oxford: Oxford University Press, 1984). Another is Elizabeth Anderson, in "Is Women's Labor a Commodity?," *Philosophy and Public Affairs* 19 (1990): 71–92. Advocates include Richard Arneson, "Commodification and Commercial Surrogacy," *Philosophy and Public Affairs* 21 (1992): 132–64; and Cecile Fabre, *Whose Body Is It Anyway? Justice and the Integrity of the Person* (Oxford: Oxford University Press, 2006).
4. Anderson, "Is Women's Labor a Commodity?"; Kajsa Ekis Ekman, *Being and Being Bought—Prostitution, Surrogacy and the Split Self* (Melbourne, AUS: Spinifex Press, 2013).
5. Warnock, *Question of Life*; Bonnie Steinbock, "Surrogate Motherhood as Prenatal Adoption," *Law, Medicine & Health Care* 16, no. 1 (1988): 44–50; Arneson, "Commodification and Commercial Surrogacy"; Fabre, *Whose Body Is It Anyway?*

6. These are elements of surrogacy which have been proposed by Christine Overall, "Reproductive 'Surrogacy' and Parental Licensing," *Bioethics* 29, no. 5 (2015): 353–61; and Andrew Botterell and Carolyn McLeod, "Licensing Parents in International Contract Pregnancies," *Journal of Applied Philosophy* 33, no. 2 (2016): 178–96.

7. Norvin Richards, *The Ethics of Parenthood* (Oxford: Oxford University Press, 2010).

8. Andrew Botterell and Carolyn McLeod, "Can a Right to Reproduce Justify the Status Quo on Parental Licensing?," in *Permissible Progeny*, ed. Sarah Hannan, Samantha Brennan, and Richard Vernon (Oxford: Oxford University Press, 2015), 184–207.

9. For this view, see Matthew Clayton, *Justice and Legitimacy in Upbringing* (Oxford: Oxford University Press, 2006); and Harry Brighouse and Adam Swift, *Family Values* (Princeton, NJ: Princeton University Press, 2014).

10. I am grateful to David O'Brien for encouraging me to clarify this.

11. Warnock, *Question of Life*.

12. One possibility is that when the intention antedates the pregnancy, the child typically wouldn't have existed but for the intention; this line of reasoning is addressed in section 5, where I discuss the challenge from the non-identity problem.

13. Which doesn't go without saying. See, for instance, David Benatar and David Wasserman, *Debating Procreation: Is It Wrong to Reproduce?* (Oxford: Oxford University Press, 2015). I say more about the moral challenges raised by procreation in section 5.

14. For a brief explanation of the will and interest accounts of rights, and of the Hohfeldian system of rights, see Leif Wenar, "Rights," ed. Edward N. Zalta and Uri Nodelman, *Stanford Encyclopedia of Philosophy* (Spring 2020): https://plato.stanford.edu/entries/rights/.

15. Clayton, *Justice and Legitimacy in Upbringing*; Sarah Hannan and Richard Vernon, "Parental Rights: A Role-based Approach," *Theory and Research in Education* 6, no. 2 (2008): 173–89; Colin Macleod, "Parental Responsibilities in an Unjust World," in *Procreation and Parenthood*, ed. David Archard and David Benatar (Oxford: Oxford University Press, 2010), 128–50, at 142; Richards, *Ethics of Parenthood*; Brighouse and Swift, *Family Values*; Matthew Liao, *The Right to Be Loved* (Oxford: Oxford University Press, 2015); Joseph Millum, *The Moral Foundations of Parenthood* (Oxford: Oxford University Press, 2018); Serena Olsaretti, "Liberal Equality and the Moral Status of Parent-Child Relationships," in *Oxford Studies in Political Philosophy*, ed. David Sobel, Peter Vallentyne,

and Steven Wall, 3:58–83 (New York: Oxford University Press, 2017); Shields, "Parental Rights and the Importance of Being Parents"; Tim Fowler, *Liberalism, Childhood and Justice: Ethical Issues in Upbringing* (Bristol, UK: Bristol University Press, 2020).

16. In Gheaus, "Best Available Parent"; and Gheaus, *Child-Centred Childrearing*, in progress. Other philosophers who hold a child-centred account of the right to parent include James Dwyer, *Religious Schools v. Children's Rights* (Ithaca, NY: Cornell University Press, 1998); David Archard, *Children: Rights and Childhood*, 3rd ed. (London: Routledge, 2015); and Peter Vallentyne, "The Rights and Duties of Childrearing," *William & Mary Bill of Rights Journal* 11, no. 3 (2003): 991–1009.

17. Some may worry that children's lack of (full) autonomy is incompatible with their having the same moral status as adults. If having the same moral status means having the same rights, this is correct. Here, however, I go with the more common assumption that adults and children are moral equals in the sense that they are right-holders, and that their equally powerful interests are equally protected by rights. For defences of the view that children are rights-holders, see David Archard, "Wrongful Life," *Philosophy* 79 (2004): 403–20; and Samantha Brennan and Robert Noggle, "The Moral Status of Children: Children's Rights, Parents' Rights, and Family Justice," *Social Theory and Practice* 23, no. 1 (1997): 1–26.

18. For an extended version of this argument, see Gheaus, "Best Available Parent." Hugh LaFollette makes very similar points in defence of a scheme for licensing biological parents. See LaFollette, "Licensing Parents," *Philosophy & Public Affairs* 9, no. 2 (1980): 182–86.

19. I try to dispel obvious worries that a child-centred view is implausibly friendly to changes of custody, in Anca Gheaus, "Sufficientarian Parenting Must Be Child-Centered," *Law Ethics and Philosophy* 5 (2017): 189–97.

20. Gheaus, "Best Available Parent."

21. Millum, *Moral Foundations of Parenthood.*

22. For defences of the view that the parental role is fiduciary, see Dwyer, *Religious Schools v. Children's Rights*, and Brighouse and Swift, *Family Values.*

23. For a very helpful treatment of children's interests, see chapter 3 in Brighouse and Swift, *Family Values.*

24. Gheaus, "Best Available Parent."

25. Brighouse and Swift, *Family Values.*

26. I argued for this view in Anca Gheaus, "Is There a Right to Parent?," *Law Ethics and Philosophy* 3 (2015): 193–204; Gheaus, "Children's Vulnerability

and Legitimate Authority over Children," *Journal of Applied Philosophy* 35, no. S1 (2018): 60–75; Gheaus, "Child-Rearing with Minimal Domination," *Political Studies* 69, no. 3 (2021): 748–66; and Gheaus, "Best Available Parent."

27. Richards, *Ethics of Parenthood*.

28. Clayton, *Justice and Legitimacy in Upbringing*; Hannan and Vernon, "Parental Rights: A Role-based Approach"; Brighouse and Swift, *Family Values*; Samantha Brennan and Colin Macleod, "Fundamentally Incompetent: Homophobia, Religion, and the Right to Parent," in *Procreation, Parenthood, and Educational Rights Ethical and Philosophical Issues*, ed. Jaime Ahlberg and Michael Cholbi (New York: Routledge, 2017), 230–45.

29. Warnock, *Question of Life*, 45.

30. A worry raised by others—see Margaret Brazier, Alastair Campbell, and Susan Golombok, eds., *Surrogacy: Review for Health Ministers of Current Arrangements of Payments and Regulation* (London: Her Majesty's Stationery Office, 1998).

31. Cecile Fabre flags this possibility, which she neither rejects nor endorses, in "Surrogacy," in *The International Encyclopedia of Ethics*, ed. Hugh LaFollette (New York: Wiley & Sons, 2013), 5086–92.

32. See Catherine Lynch, "Putting Children First: What Adoption Can Teach Us about Surrogacy," in *Towards the Abolition of Surrogate Motherhood*, ed. Marie Josephe Devillers and Ana-Luana Stoicea-Deram (Melbourne, AUS: Spinifex Press, 2021), 141–55.

33. Anderson, "Is Women's Labor a Commodity?"

34. Warnock, *Question of Life*, 45.

35. For the same claim that child selling amounts to child slavery, see Overall, "Reproductive "Surrogacy" and "Parental Licensing."

36. Stephen Wilkinson, *Bodies for Sale: Ethics and Exploitation in the Human Body Trade* (London: Routledge, 2003), 147.

37. Arneson, "Commodification and Commercial Surrogacy," 149.

38. Not everybody finds them convincing, though: Fabre denies the claim that one cannot legitimately sell something over which one cannot have property, in *Whose Body Is It Anyway* (190). She points to the case of animals, which can be sold yet not treated as property. I find this unpersuasive; I suspect that people who believe that it is impermissible to treat animals as property should also object to the permissibility of selling them. In any case, this disagreement is irrelevant to the normative point I make in the current section.

39. Steinbock, "Surrogate Motherhood as Prenatal Adoption."

40. Philip Pettit, *Republicanism: A Theory of Freedom and Government* (Oxford: Clarendon Press, 1997).

41. For the current purposes, it doesn't matter whether the objection is one that liberals see as an objection to an insufficiently secure right to non-interference in the case of the slave (as suggested by Robert Goodin, in "Folie Républicaine," *Annual Review of Political Science* 6 [2003]: 55–76) or to wellbeing in the case of the child (as Gheaus does in "Child-Rearing with Minimal Domination"), or, as the more *sui generis* wrong of domination that exercises republicans.

42. Frederick Douglass, *My Bondage and My Freedom* (1855; repr. New York: Dover, 1969), 161.

43. Interestingly, some child liberationists see children's subjugation as the last stronghold of slavery. See John Holt, *Escape from Childhood: The Needs and Rights of Children* (New York: E. P. Dutton, 1974). Others, too, have compared children's dependence on the will of parents to the situation of slaves owned by (benevolent) masters. See Daniela Cutas, "Sex Is Over-Rated: On the Right to Reproduce," *Human Fertility* 12, no. 1 (2009): 45–52.

44. Arneson, "Commodification and Commercial Surrogacy," 149.

45. Fabre, *Whose Body Is It Anyway?*

46. Clayton, *Justice and Legitimacy in Upbringing*; Brighouse and Swift, *Family Values*.

47. In David Boudreaux, "A Modest Proposal to Deregulate Infant Adoptions," *Cato Journal* 15, no. 1 (1995): 117–35.

48. According to Fabre, a feature that renders both some cases of surrogacy and some cases of child selling impermissible is the wrongful attitude of parents, who may treat their foetuses or children as commodities by gestating, or raising, them with a view to sell them. This, of course, rules out as impermissible only some cases of child selling and those cases of surrogacy that are entirely motivated by financial gain. See *Whose Body Is It Anyway?*, 191.

49. As Fabre, who defends a view similar to the one I advance here, also notes in *Whose Body Is It Anyway?*

50. In Gheaus, "Child-Rearing with Minimal Domination," I argue that the second condition cannot be met—at least, not in good childrearing. Children's interest in protected intimacy with their parents means that states have, all things considered, reasons to always allow some domination in the child-parent relationship—that is, some degree of arbitrary

parental power. I think that Republicans should conclude that even the most justified form of childrearing doesn't fully eliminate domination, i.e., the normative similarity between being a child and being a slave.

51. Even though it may be wrong to enforce this ideal in ways that strip parents of any arbitrary power, for the reasons explained in Gheaus, "Child-Rearing with Minimal Domination." See also Brighouse and Swift, *Family Values*, 141–42.

52. Iwan Davies, "Contracts to Bear Children," *Journal of Medical Ethics* 11, no. 2 (1985): 61–65.

53. I discuss this in Anca Gheaus, "Biological Parenthood: Gestational, Not Genetic," *Australasian Journal of Philosophy* 96, no. 2 (2018): 225–40.

54. Boudreaux, "Modest Proposal."

55. I am grateful to Connor Kianpour for pressing me to make this explicit.

56. Page uses "genetic surrogacy" for what I call "partial surrogacy." "Total surrogacy," in this quote, refers to cases in which the child evolves from the gametes of the surrogate mother and her husband. See Edgar Page, "Review Article: Warnock and Surrogacy," *Journal of Medical Ethics*, no. 12 (1986): 45–52.

57. See R. J. Kornegay, "Is Commercial Surrogacy Baby-Selling?," *Journal of Applied Philosophy* 7, no. 1 (1990): 45–50; Steinbock, "Surrogate Motherhood as Prenatal Adoption"; Straehle, this volume.

58. In Edgar Page, "Donation, Surrogacy and Adoption," *Journal of Applied Philosophy* 2, no. 2 (1984): 167.

59. I make that assumption and so does Page. The belief that rights over gametes can be privately transferred is accepted even by proponents of the view that the gestational mother always has the right to parent, such as Warnock, *Question of Life*.

60. In Page, "Parental Rights" and "Donation, Surrogacy and Adoption."

61. Prominently, Anderson in "Is Women's Labor a Commodity?"

62. Warnock, *Question of Life*. Some believe this isn't a coherent position. According to John Harris, "The Warnock Committee set its face firmly against womb leasing or lending, but thought on balance that egg or embryo donation should be permitted provided that the woman giving birth should in all cases be regarded in law as the mother of the resulting child. It is not clear from the report how Warnock could justify the distinction between egg or embryo donation on the one hand, and womb leasing or lending on the other." In Harris, *The Value of Life* (London: Routledge, 1990), 141.

63. Ekman, *Being and Being Bought*, 145.

64. Steinbock, "Surrogate Motherhood as Prenatal Adoption," 48.

65. Fabre, *Whose Body Is It Anyway?*, 189.
66. In general, Page appears quite literal in his talk about parents having rights over their own children. He talks about "the rights and duties of ownership" over embryos, without any indication of how, if at all, the change in moral status between embryo and child bears on his views. For instance, he writes: "It is natural to take the donation of an egg or embryo to involve the surrender and transfer of all the rights and duties in respect of the child that would otherwise be the donor's as the child's genetic parents. A donation is a gift and if you give something away any rights and duties you have in respect of that thing are lost and transferred to the person to whom it has been given. If you give away a building you would normally expect to lose your right of access to it along with whatever liability you had to maintain it." In "Donation, Surrogacy and Adoption," 163.
67. This section is a development of the view I present in Gheaus, "Biological Parenthood: Gestational, Not Genetic."
68. Competitor accounts don't grant more than a presumptive right to biological parents, either, since they make custody conditional on being an adequate parent (in some versions) or, at the very least, on not being found guilty of child abuse or neglect (in the legal and scholarly status quo).
69. Barbara Hall, "The Origin of Parental Rights," *Public Affairs Quarterly* 13, no. 1 (1999): 73–82.
70. Page, "Donation, Surrogacy and Adoption"; Robert Nozick, *The Examined Life: Philosophical Meditations* (New York: Simon and Schuster, 1989); Jean Kazez, *The Philosophical Parent: Asking the Hard Questions about Having and Raising Children* (Oxford University Press, 2017).
71. For instance, Richards, *Ethics of Parenthood*; Fowler, *Liberalism, Childhood and Justice*; Erik Magnusson, "Can Gestation Ground Parental Rights?," *Social Theory and Practice* 46, no. 1 (2020): 111–42.
72. David Velleman, "Family History," *Philosophical Papers* 34 (2005): 362.
73. See David Archard, "What's Blood Got to Do with It? The Significance of Natural Parenthood," *Res Publica* 1, no. 1 (1995): 91–106; and Sally Haslanger, "Family, Ancestry and Self: What Is the Moral Significance of Biological Ties?," *Adoption and Culture* 2 (2009): 91–122.
74. In Melissa Moschella, *To Whom Do Children Belong? Parental Rights, Civic Education, and Children's Autonomy* (Cambridge: Cambridge University Press, 2016).
75. See Archard, *Children: Rights and Childhood*.
76. See Jeff McMahan, *The Ethics of Killing: Problems at the Margins of Life* (Oxford: Oxford University Press, 2002).

77. Susan Golombok, Lucy Blake, Polly Casey, Gabriela Roman, and Vasanti Jadva, "Children Born through Reproductive Donation: A Longitudinal Study of Psychological Adjustment," *Journal of Child Psychology and Psychiatry* 54, no. 6 (2013): 653–60.

78. Mark Vopat, "Parent Licensing and the Protecting of Children," in *Taking Responsibility for Children*, ed. Samantha Brennan and Robert Noggle (Waterloo, ON: Wilfrid Laurier University Press, 2007), 73–96.

79. LaFollette, "Licensing Parents."

80. Archard, "What's Blood Got to Do with It?," 91–106.

81. Archard, *Children: Rights and Childhood*.

82. In Anca Gheaus, "The Right to Parent One's Biological Baby," *Journal of Political Philosophy* 20, no. 4 (2012): 432–55; and Gheaus, "Biological Parenthood: Gestational, Not Genetic."

83. Alternative gestationalist accounts rely exclusively on the costs of pregnancy. See Uma Narayan, "Family Ties: Rethinking Parental Claims in the Light of Surrogacy and Custody," in *Having and Raising Children: Unconventional Families, Hard Choices, and the Social Good*, ed. Uma Narayan and Julia J. Bartkowiak (University Park: Pennsylvania State University Press, 1999), 65–86; and Millum, *Moral Foundations of Parenthood*. Thus, they advance a parent-centred version of gestationalism. Susan Feldman, by contrast, defends a child-centred form of gestationalism based on the fact that gestational mothers can, during pregnancy, greatly influence the development of the foetus and, therefore, the future child's wellbeing. In Feldman, "Multiple Biological Mothers: The Case for Gestation," *Journal of Social Philosophy* 23, no. 1 (1992), 98–104. Making sure that gestational mothers have a secure right to the custody of the children they bear is, the argument goes, the best means to motivate gestational mothers to take proper care of the developing baby. Feldman's account falls short of establishing that gestational mothers have a *moral* right to custody.

84. Antonella Sansone, *Mothers, Babies and Their Body Language* (London: Karnac, 2004).

85. A very important question is: Relative to what is the relevant setback of interests: to the level of wellbeing that the party who cannot consent would have if the relationship continued, or to the level of wellbeing she would enjoy if, due to the discontinuation of the first relationship, she would become available to enter an even better relationship? Here I assume the first answer; in my monograph I discuss at length this important point.

86. Brighouse and Swift, *Family Values*; Lindsey Porter, "Gestation and Parental Rights: Why Is Good Enough Good Enough?," *Feminist*

Philosophy Quarterly 1, no. 1 (2015), 1–27; Magnusson, "Can Gestation Ground Parental Rights?"

87. Magnusson, "Can Gestation Ground Parental Rights?," 122.

88. Caroline Whitbeck, "The Maternal Instinct," in *Mothering: Essays in Feminist Theory*, ed. J. Trebilcot (Totowa, NJ: Rowman & Allanheld, 1984), 185–98.

89. Amy Mullin, "Early Pregnancy Losses: Multiple Meanings and Moral Considerations," *Journal of Social Philosophy* 46, no. 1 (2015): 27–43.

90. This formulation belongs to Archard and Benatar, in *Procreation and Parenthood*, 26. Tim Bayne and Avery Kolers, who coined the principle, put it more vaguely, saying that "being a mother doesn't make a person more of a parent than being a father, or vice versa." Kolers and Bayne, '"Are You My Mommy?': On the Genetic Basis of Parenthood," *Journal of Applied Philosophy* 18 (2001): 273–85, at 280.

91. Porter, "Gestation and Parental Rights," 14–15; Magnusson, "Can Gestation Ground Parental Rights?," 123–26; Fowler, *Liberalism, Childhood and Justice*, 104.

92. There is some longitudinal research comparing children of surrogacy to children born through gamete donation who were not separated from their gestational mothers. The latter showed no developmental difference from children born and raised by traditional families, whereas the former showed higher levels of adjustment difficulties at age seven. The study concludes: "The absence of a gestational connection to the mother may be more problematic for children than the absence of a genetic link." See Golombok et al. "Children Born through Reproductive Donation," 653–60.

93. Steinbock, "Surrogate Motherhood as Prenatal Adoption," 46.

94. An interesting child-centred argument against (genuinely loving) kidnappers keeping custody is that, even if they are the best custodian with respect to the child's wellbeing interests, the child has a respect interest in not being raised by someone who kidnapped her. I am grateful to David O'Brian for flagging this possibility, which, if correct, does not bear on the permissibility of bonding during gestation.

95. Ekman, *Being and Being Bought*.

96. Anderson, "Is Women's Labor a Commodity?," 82.

97. Seana Shiffrin offers one such account in "Wrongful Life, Procreative Responsibility, and the Significance of Harm," *Legal Theory* 5 (1999): 117–48.

98. On Shiffrin's non-comparative view, harm entails being in a state the badness of which prevents the agent from being in control of her life, in "Wrongful Life, Procreative Responsibility, and the Significance of Harm," 123–24.

99. Golombok et al., "Children Born through Reproductive Donation," 653–60.

100. Amongst those who think this challenge indicates the permissibility of surrogacy are Harris, *Value of Life*; Steinbock, "Surrogate Motherhood as Prenatal Adoption"; Arneson, "Commodification and Commercial Surrogacy"; Wilkinson, *Bodies for Sale*; and Fabre, *Whose Body Is It Anyway?* For an attempt to resist, see Archard "Wrongful Life."

101. Gregory Kavka, "The Paradox of Future Individuals," *Philosophy and Public Affairs* 11 (1982): 93–112.

102. Or, perhaps, even non-comparative harms, understood as setbacks to one's agency, in the spirit of Shiffrin's proposal. First, a sufficiently benevolent master will not interfere with their slave's agency. (This kind of slavery seems significantly less objectionable; but is it not objectionable at all?) Second, wouldn't it be wrong to enslave accomplished stoics?

103. Perhaps procreation with the mere *intention* to violate the moral claims of the child is itself wrongful, in which case the child has complaints, not only against the enforcement, but also against the drafting of the surrogacy contract. I do not take a stand on this issue.

104. Derek Parfitt, *Reasons and Persons* (Oxford: Oxford University Press, 1984).

105. For instance, John Broome thinks that "a person's good consists partly in how fairly she is treated; unfairness is bad for a person, whatever she may feel about it." In Broome, *Weighting Goods: Equality, Uncertainty and Time* (Oxford: Blackwell, 1991), 128.

106. Mianna Lotz, "Rethinking Procreation: Why It Matters Why We Have Children," *Journal of Applied Philosophy* 28, no. 2 (2011): 105–21; and David Wasserman, "The Nonidentity Problem, Disability, and the Role Morality of Prospective Parents," *Ethics* 116, no. 1 (2015): 132–52.

107. This is a snappy summary of Shiffrin's view, which I find correct. David Benatar's anti-natalist work contains a detailed discussion of the risks and actual harms of life. In Benatar, *Better Never to Have Been: The Harm of Coming into Existence* (Oxford: Oxford University Press, 2006). The fact that I am not ultimately convinced by anti-natalism is not to say that Benatar's challenge can be easily dismissed.

108. Gheaus, *Could There Ever Be a Duty to Have Children?*

109. This may be (dis)value to persons—think, for instance, of how disturbing it is to suspect that one is part of the last generation—for which see Samuel Scheffler, "The Afterlife. Part I," in *Death and the Afterlife*, ed. Niko Kolodny (New York: Oxford University Press, 2013)—or impersonal (dis)value.

110. At least if procreation were to continue in the absence of surrogacy; indeed, this empirical assumption can hardly be doubted given the long-term trend of population growth.

111. Just as, in many societies today, they become the charge of the state when birth parents relinquish custody.

112. Archard, introduction to *Procreation and Parenthood*.

113. Lindsay Porter, "Why and How to Prefer a Causal Account of Parenthood," *Journal of Social Philosophy* 45, no. 2 (2014): 182–202.

114. Olsaretti, "Liberal Equality."

What's in It for the Baby? Weighing Children's and Parents' Interests in Commercial Surrogacy Agreements. A Reply to Gheaus

1. Critics in this vein motivate their worries with scenarios of child selling, child slavery, or both: "[A] surrogacy agreement is degrading to the child who is to be the outcome of it, since, for all practical purposes, the child will have been bought for money." See Mary Warnock, *Report of the Committee of Inquiry into Human Fertilisation and Embryology* (London: Her Majesty's Stationery Office, 1994), 45. See also Christine Overall, "Reproductive 'Surrogacy' and Parental Licensing," *Bioethics* 29, no. 5 (August 2015): 353–61. To be sure, the latest figures for 2017 suggest that child slavery is rampant: there are 4.4 child victims of slavery for every 1,000 children worldwide. https://www.alliance87.org/global_estimates_of_modern_slavery-forced_labour_and_forced_m arriage-executive_summary.pdf, accessed January 30, 2022. However, the one in four slavery victims who are children, predominately girls, are often forced to work because of the debt bondage of their families. Philosophers who make the analogy between surrogacy and slavery object to the changing of money for an individual human—but it seems borderline obscene to otherwise compare slavery and surrogacy. As I suggested in Part I, applying the slavery charge to surrogates neglects the fundamental harm that slavery inflicts; the same is true for the analogy between children born through surrogacy and child slavery: Children are not acquired to solely serve the interests of adults; children don't suffer abuse because they belong to a stigmatized group. And, importantly, children have rights that are actively enforced by many states and by the international community. Indeed, Gheaus in Part I suggests a system of surrogacy in which states accept the obligation to

designate the best available custodian—as an expression of the role of the state in protecting children's interests. No such state protection was ever available to slaves.

2. Christine Straehle, "Vulnerability, Autonomy and Self Respect," in *Vulnerability, Autonomy, and Applied Ethics*, ed. Christine Straehle (New York: Routledge, 2019), 33–48.

3. Some believe that this is a problem—that, instead, parents should be licensed before becoming parents. See Hugh LaFollette, "Licensing Parents Revisited," *Journal of Applied Philosophy* 27, no. 5 (August 2010): 327–43.

4. The list of positive rights that the United Nations Declaration of the Rights of the Child stipulates includes the rights "to grow and develop in health" (principle 4), "to an atmosphere of affection and of moral and material security" (principle 6), and to "an education which will promote his general culture and enable him on a basis of equal opportunity to develop his abilities and his sense of moral and social responsibility" (principle 7).

None of these "rights" is well formed as an enforceable claim, but they can be seen as ideals that should inform public policymaking. https://www.ohchr.org/en/instruments-mechanisms/instruments/convention-rights-child, accessed May 3, 2019.

5. See Samantha Brennan, "The Goods of Childhood and Children's Rights," in *Family-Making*, ed. François Bayliss and Carolyn McLeod (New York: Oxford University Press, 2014), 29–46; Colin Macleod, "Agency, Authority and the Vulnerability of Children," in *The Nature of Children's Well-Being*, ed. Alexander Bagattini and Colin Macleod, Children's Well-Being: Indicators and Research 9 (Dordrecht: Springer, 2015), 53–64.

6. A *disposition*, the way I use it here, simply means that children are inclined to have certain mental states or a state of mind. See *Oxford English Dictionary* online, s.v. "disposition": "7a. The state or quality of being disposed, inclined, or 'in the mind' (*to* something, or *to do* something); inclination (sometimes = desire, intention, purpose); state of mind or feeling in respect to a thing or person; the condition of being (favourably or unfavourably) disposed *towards*. (In *plural* formerly sometimes = mental tendencies or qualities; hence nearly = sense 6." See also sense "6. Natural tendency or bent of the mind, *esp.* in relation to moral or social qualities; mental constitution or temperament; turn of mind."

7. See also Luara Ferrracioli, "Carefreeness and Children's Well-Being," *Journal of Applied Philosophy* 37, no. 1 (July 2019): 103–17.

8. For a helpful discussion and clarification, see David Archard, "Children, Adults, Autonomy and Well-Being," in Bagattini and Macleod, *Nature of Children's Well-Being*, 3–14.

9. See, for instance, Martha Albertson Fineman, "The Vulnerable Subject: Anchoring Equality in Law," *Yale Journal of Law and Feminism* 20 (May2008): 1–25.

10. David Archard, "Children," in *Oxford Handbook of Practical Ethics*, ed. Hugh LaFollette (New York: Oxford University Press, 2005), 91–111, at 96.

11. Archard, "Children," 97.

12. Richard Noggle has argued in a similar vein that parents have the responsibility to promote moral agency in children. See Noggle, "Special Agents: Children's Autonomy and Parental Authority," in *The Moral and Political Status of Children*, ed. Colin MacLeod and David Archard (Oxford: Oxford University Press, 2002), 97–117.

13. See, e.g., "Third, mature agents have a sophisticated array of affective and integrated psychological traits. This kind of psychological maturity is characterized, in part, by a reasonably stable sense of self, marked by an ongoing and self-aware commitment to values and projects that the agent recognizes as hers. To some degree, this involves a coherent integration of such commitments and a capacity to locate their current preferences and values in relation to their future selves." Colin Macleod, "Doctrinal Vulnerability and the Authority of Children's Voices," in Straehle, *Vulnerability, Autonomy and Applied Ethics*, 171–84.

14. Brennan, "Goods of Childhood and Children's Rights," 43.

15. As I reported, indeed, some surrogacy agencies had to lay down the law to prohibit some intending parents from being too intrusive in the lives of surrogates for fear for the welfare of the child. They are too much invested in the child.

16. Think here of other options that people have been given but that have turned out to put a burden of justification on their shoulders, such as the possibility of ending a life in the case of terminal illness or the possibility of having prenatal genetic testing. Both technologies have been criticized for possibly leading to social expectations that demand justifications for not adopting them. For the assisted suicide debate, see David Velleman, "Against the Right to Die," *Journal of Medicine and Philosophy* 17, no. 6 (1992): 665–81. For expectations accompanying genetic prenatal testing and constructions of responsible motherhood, see Ainsley Newson,

"Ethical Aspects Arising from Non-invasive Fetal Diagnosis," *Seminars in Fetal and Neonatal Medicine* 13, no. 2 (April 2008): 103–8.

17. P. Butler, "Vulnerable Children Are Being Failed by Social Care Firms—Report," *The Guardian*, March 11, 2022, 20.

18. For an important discussion of how the promotion of autonomy can determine our ideas about custodial rights and their defence, see Matthew Clayton, *Justice and Legitimacy in Upbringing* (Oxford: Oxford University Press, 2006).

19. Similarly, see Harry Brighouse and Adam Swift, "Advantage, Authority, Autonomy and Continuity: A Response to Ferracioli, Gheaus and Stroud," *Law, Ethics and Philosophy* 3 (2015): 220–40, in which they underline the importance of continuity of relationships for children.

Women and Children First. A Reply to Straehle

1. For instance, Melissa Moschella, whose view I detail in my main chapter.

2. In Porter, "Why and How to Prefer a Causal Account of Parenthood," *Journal of Social Philosophy* 45, no. 2 (2014): 182–202.

3. Elizabeth Anderson, "Is Women's Labor a Commodity?," *Philosophy and Public Affairs* 19 (1990): 71–92, at 82. A lot more seems to be going on in Anderson's reasoning, most importantly, a presumption that the surrogate is the moral parent of the child. One doesn't have to share this assumption in order to complain that a prudential injunction against bonding is not humane.

4. Anca Gheaus, "The Best Available Parent," *Ethics* 131, no. 3 (2021): 431–59.

5. Gheaus, "Best Available Parent," 431–59.

6. The scope of her argument extends to intending parents who provide one or both gametes that they have purchased from others. After all, surrogacy is often used by gay couples who cannot produce both gametes. I focus, in my analysis, on the case that is most amenable to Straehle's defence of surrogacy; if her defence is not successful for that case, neither will it be for more complicated cases when the intending parents are not, in fact, genetically related to the child.

7. She writes about surrogates that "the remuneration they receive is for their service of carrying the foetus to term; it is not for the product of their labour."

8. Such as Norvin Richards, *The Ethics of Parenthood* (Oxford: Oxford University Press, 2010); Tim Fowler, *Liberalism, Childhood and Justice* (Bristol, UK: Bristol University Press, 2020); and Eric Magnusson, "Can Gestation Ground Parental Rights?," *Social Theory and Practice* 46, no. 1 (2020): 111–42.

9. To be clear, I don't believe that it is appropriate to think about raising a child in terms of a project. Here I am merely trying to unpack the logic of the best case in favour of the intending parents' claim to custody.

10. See, for instance, Elizabeth Brake, "Willing Parents: A Voluntarist Account of Parental Role Obligations," in *Procreation and Parenthood: The Ethics of Bearing and Rearing Children*, ed. David Archard and David Benatar (Oxford: Oxford University Press, 2010), 151–77.

11. In "Best Available Parent" I explain why this line of reasoning is unpersuasive. A claim right to become the parent of a child cannot be derived from duties towards the child.

12. She writes that "for at least some surrogates working in the Global South, the alternatives to surrogacy are equally if not more wretched."

13. Such as that of Serena Olsaretti, in *Liberty, Desert and the Market: A Philosophical Study* (Cambridge: Cambridge University Press, 2004), the view of voluntariness on which Straehle herself relies.

14. In fact, I have doubts that one's self-respect, if robust enough, can depend on one's occupation. For a powerful defence of this, see Colin Bird, "Self-Respect and the Respect of Others," *European Journal of Philosophy* 18, no. 1 (2010): 17–40. But many philosophers today believe that one can have claims to occupational opportunities that are grounded in the value of self-respect, and so does Straehle.

15. This is how Hillel Steiner puts it: "[T]he right of self-ownership is bulwark against involuntary enslavement *and against paternalistic preventions of voluntary self-enslavement*, as well as against abrogations of freedom of contract" (my emphasis). In Steiner, *An Essay on Rights* (Oxford: Blackwell, 1994): 232–33, fn5. For an overview of arguments that seek to establish that contractual slavery is not possible (because it is incoherent) and their refutation, see Danny Frederick, "The Possibility of Contractual Slavery," *Philosophical Quarterly* 66, no. 262 (2016): 47–64.

16. Or, at least, to surrogacy that is not regulated against exploitation.

17. Andrew Botterell and Carolyn McLeod, "Can a Right to Reproduce Justify the Status Quo on Parental Licensing?," in *Permissible Progeny*, ed. Sarah Hannan, Samantha Brennan, and Richard Vernon (Oxford: Oxford University Press, 2015), 184–207; and Botterell and McLeod, "Licensing Parents in International Contract Pregnancies," *Journal of Applied Philosophy* 33, no. 2 (2016): 178–96.

18. In Gheaus, "Children's Vulnerability and Legitimate Authority over Children," *Journal of Applied Philosophy* 35, no. S1 (2018): 60–75; and Gheaus, "Child-Rearing with Minimal Domination," *Political Studies* 69, no. 3 (2021): 748–66.

Bibliography

Allen, Anita L. "Surrogacy, Slavery, and the Ownership of Life." *Harvard Journal of Law and Public Policy* 139 (1990): 141–46.

Anderson, Elizabeth. "Is Women's Labor a Commodity?" *Philosophy and Public Affairs* 19 (1990): 71–92.

Anderson, Elizabeth. "Why Commercial Surrogate Motherhood Unethically Commodifies Women and Children: Reply to McLachlan and Swales." *Health Care Analysis* 8 (2000): 19–26.

Archard, David. "Autonomy and Self-Ownership." *Journal of Applied Philosophy* 25, no.1 (2008): 19–33.

Archard, David. "Children." In *The Oxford Handbook of Practical Ethics*, edited by Hugh LaFollette, 91–111. Oxford: Oxford University Press, 2005.

Archard, David. "Children, Adults, Autonomy and Well-Being." In *The Nature of Children's Well-Being*, edited by Alexander Bagattini and Colin Macleod, 3–14. Children's Well-Being: Indicators and Research 9. Dordrecht: Springer, 2015.

Archard, David. "Children, Multiculturalism, and Education." In *The Moral and Political Status of Children*, edited by David Archard and Colin Macleod, 142–59. Oxford: Oxford University Press, 2002.

Archard, David. *Children: Rights and Childhood*. 3rd ed. London: Routledge, 2015.

Archard, David. "Freedom Not to Be Free: The Case of the Slavery Contract in J. S. Mill's *On Liberty*." *Philosophical Quarterly* 40 (1990): 453–65.

Archard, David. "The Obligations and Responsibilities of Parenthood." In *Procreation and Parenthood: The Ethics of Bearing and Rearing Children*, edited by David Archard and David Benatar, 103–28. Oxford: Oxford University Press, 2010.

Archard, David. "What's Blood Got to Do with It? The Significance of Natural Parenthood." *Res Publica* 1, no. 1 (1995): 91–106.

Archard, David. "Wrongful Life." *Philosophy* 79 (2004): 403–20.

Archard, David, and David Benatar. Introduction to *Procreation and Parenthood: The Ethics of Bearing and Rearing Children*, edited by David Archard and David Benatar, 1–30. Oxford: Oxford University Press, 2010.

Archard, David, and David Benatar, eds. *Procreation and Parenthood: The Ethics of Bearing and Rearing Children*. Oxford: Oxford University Press, 2010.

Archard, David, and Colin Macleod, eds. *The Moral and Political Status of Children*. Oxford: Oxford University Press, 2002.

Arneson, Richard. "Commodification and Commercial Surrogacy." *Philosophy and Public Affairs* 21 (1992): 132–64.

Arvanitis, Alexios, and Konstantinos Kalliris. "A Self-Determination Theory Account of Self-Authorship: Implications for Law and Public Policy." *Philosophical Psychology* 30 (2017): 763–83.

Austin, Michael. *Conceptions of Parenthood: Ethics and the Family.* Aldershot, UK: Ashgate, 2007.

Bagnoli, Carla. "The Mafioso Case: Autonomy and Self-Respect." *Ethical Theory and Moral Practice* 12 (2009): 477–93.

Baron, Teresa. "Nobody Puts Baby in the Container: The Foetal Container Model at Work in Medicine and Commercial Surrogacy." *Journal of Applied Philosophy* 36 (2018): 491–505.

Baron, Teresa. *The Philosopher's Guide to Parenthood: Storks, Surrogates, and Stereotypes.* Cambridge: Cambridge University Press, forthcoming.

Bayne, Tim. "Gamete Donation and Parental Responsibility." *Journal of Applied Philosophy* 20 (2003): 77–87.

Bayne, Tim, and Avery Kolers. "Towards a Pluralist Account of Parenthood." *Bioethics* 17 (2003): 221–42.

Benatar, David. *Better Never to Have Been: The Harm of Coming into Existence.* Oxford: Oxford University Press, 2006.

Benatar, David, and David Wasserman. *Debating Procreation: Is It Wrong to Reproduce?* Oxford: Oxford University Press, 2015.

Berlin, Isaiah. "Two Concepts of Liberty." In Isaiah Berlin, *Four Essays on Liberty*, 118–72. Oxford: Oxford University Press, 1986.

Bird, Colin. "Self-Respect and the Respect of Others." *European Journal of Philosophy* 18 (2010): 17–40.

Blustein, Jeffrey. *Parents and Children: The Ethics of the Family.* New York: Oxford University Press, 1982.

Botterell, Andrew, and Carolyn McLeod. "Can a Right to Reproduce Justify the Status Quo on Parental Licensing?" In *Permissible Progeny*, edited by Sarah Hannan, Samantha Brennan, and Richard Vernon, 184–207. Oxford: Oxford University Press, 2015.

Botterell, Andrew, and Carolyn McLeod. "Licensing Parents in International Contract Pregnancies." *Journal of Applied Philosophy* 33 (2016): 178–96.

Boudreaux, David. "A Modest Proposal to Deregulate Infant Adoptions." *Cato Journal* 15 (1995): 117–35.

Brake, Elizabeth. "Willing Parents: A Voluntarist Account of Parental Role Obligations." In *Procreation and Parenthood: The Ethics of Bearing and Rearing Children*, edited by David Archard and David Benatar, 151–77. Oxford: Oxford University Press, 2010.

Brazier, Margaret, Alastair Campbell, and Susan Golombok, eds. *Surrogacy: Review for Health Ministers of Current Arrangements of Payments and Regulation.* London: Her Majesty's Stationery Office, 1998.

Brennan, Samantha. "The Goods of Childhood and Children's Rights." In *Family-Making*, edited by Françoise Baylis and Carolyn McLeod, 29–46. New York: Oxford University Press, 2014.

Brennan, Samantha, and Colin Macleod. "Fundamentally Incompetent: Homophobia, Religion, and the Right to Parent." In *Procreation, Parenthood, and Educational Rights Ethical and Philosophical Issues*, edited by Jaime Ahlberg and Michael Cholbi, 230–45. New York: Routledge, 2017.

Brennan, Samantha, and Robert Noggle. "The Moral Status of Children: Children's Rights, Parents' Rights, and Family Justice." *Social Theory and Practice* 23 (1997): 1–26.

Brighouse, Harry, and Adam Swift. "Advantage, Authority, Autonomy and Continuity: A Response to Ferracioli, Gheaus and Stroud." *Law, Ethics and Philosophy* 3 (2015): 220–40.

Brighouse, Harry, and Adam Swift. *Family Values: The Ethics of Parent-Child Relationships*. Princeton, NJ: Princeton University Press, 2014.

Brighouse, Harry, and Adam Swift, "Parents' Rights and the Value of the Family." *Ethics* 117 (2006): 80–108.

Broome, John. *Weighting Goods: Equality, Uncertainty and Time*. Oxford: Blackwell, 1991.

Busby, Karen, and Delaney Vun. "Revisiting the Handmaid's Tale." *Canadian Journal of Family Law* 26, no. 13 (2010).

Butler, Patrick. "Overhaul of Children's Social Care in England Urgent and Unavoidable, Review Finds." *The Guardian*, May 23, 2022.

Butler, Nick, Shiona Chillas, and Sara Louise Muhr. "Professions at the Margins." *Ephemera: Theory and Politics in Organization* 12 (2012): 259–71.

Carens, Joseph H. *Equality, Moral Incentives, and the Market: An Essay in Utopian Politico-Economic Theory*. Chicago: University of Chicago Press, 1981.

Casal, Paula. "Occupational Choice and the Egalitarian Ethos" *Economics and Philosophy* 29 (2013): 3–20.

Clayton, Matthew. *Justice and Legitimacy in Upbringing*. Oxford: Oxford University Press, 2006.

Cohen, Gerald Allan. *Rescuing Justice and Equality*. Cambridge, MA: Harvard University Press, 2008.

Cohen, Gerald Allan. *Self-Ownership, Freedom and Equality*. Cambridge: Cambridge University Press, 1995.

Cutas, Daniela. "Sex Is Over-rated: On the Right to Reproduce." *Human Fertility* 12 (2009): 45–52.

Davies, Iwan. "Contracts to Bear Children." *Journal of Medical Ethics* 11 (1985): 61–65.

Douglass, Frederick. *My Bondage and My Freedom*. New York: Dover Publications, 1969. First published in 1855.

Dworkin, Andrea. "Prostitution and Male Supremacy." *Michigan Journal for Gender and Law* 1 (1993): 1–12.

Dworkin, Gerald. "Harm and the Volenti Principle." *Social Philosophy and Policy* 29, no. 1 (2012): 309–21.

Dwyer, James G. *Religious Schools v. Children's Rights.* Ithaca, NY: Cornell University Press, 1998.

Ekman, Kajsa Ekis. *Being and Being Bought: Prostitution, Surrogacy and the Split Self.* Melbourne, AUS: Spinifex Press, 2013.

Ettinger, Derek J. "Genes, Gestations and Social Norm." *Bioethics* 31 (2012): 243–68.

Fabre, Cecile. "Surrogacy." In LaFollette, *International Encyclopedia of Ethics,* 5086–92.

Fabre, Cecile. *Whose Body Is It Anyway? Justice and the Integrity of the Person.* Oxford: Oxford University Press, 2006.

Feinberg, Joel. *Harm to Self.* Oxford: Oxford University Press, 1986.

Feldman, Susan. "Multiple Biological Mothers: The Case for Gestation." *Journal of Social Philosophy* 23 (1992): 98–104.

Ferrracioli, Luara. "Carefreeness and Children's Well-Being." *Journal of Applied Philosophy* 37 (2019): 103–17.

Fineman, Martha A. "The Vulnerable Subject: Anchoring Equality in Law." *Yale Journal of Law and Feminism* 20 (2008): 1–25.

Fowler, Tim. *Liberalism, Childhood and Justice: Ethical Issues in Upbringing.* Bristol, UK: Bristol University Press, 2020.

Frederick, Danny. "The Possibility of Contractual Slavery." *Philosophical Quarterly* 66 (2016): 47–64.

Gheaus, Anca. "The Best Available Parent." *Ethics* 131 (2021): 431–59.

Gheaus, Anca. "Biological Parenthood: Gestational, Not Genetic." *Australasian Journal of Philosophy* 96 (2018): 225–40.

Gheaus, Anca. "Child-Rearing with Minimal Domination." *Political Studies* 69 (2021): 748–66.

Gheaus, Anca. "Children's Vulnerability and Legitimate Authority over Children." *Journal of Applied Philosophy* 35 (2018): 60–75.

Gheaus, Anca. "Could There Ever Be a Duty to Have Children?" In *Permissible Progeny,* edited by Sarah Hannan, Samantha Brennan, and Richard Vernon, 87–106. Oxford: Oxford University Press, 2015.

Gheaus, Anca. "Is There a Right to Parent?" *Law Ethics and Philosophy* 3 (2015): 193–204.

Gheaus, Anca. "The Right to Parent One's Biological Baby." *Journal of Political Philosophy* 20 (2012): 432–55.

Gheaus, Anca. "Sufficientarian Parenting Must Be Child-Centered." *Law Ethics and Philosophy* 5 (2017): 189–97.

Golombok, Susan, Lucy Blake, Polly Casey, Gabriela Roman, and Vasanti Jadva. "Children Born through Reproductive Donation: A Longitudinal

Study of Psychological Adjustment." *Journal of Child Psychology and Psychiatry* 54 (2013): 653–60.

Goodin, Robert E. "Folie Républicaine." *Annual Review of Political Science* 6 (2003): 55–76.

Hall, Barbara. "The Origin of Parental Rights." *Public Affairs Quarterly* 13 (1999): 73–82.

Hannan, Sarah, and R. J. Leland. "Childhood Bads, Parenting Goods, and the Right to Procreate." *Critical Review of International Social and Political Philosophy* 21 (2018): 366–84.

Hannan, Sarah, and Richard Vernon. "Parental Rights: A Role-Based Approach." *Theory and Research in Education* 6 (2008): 173–89.

Harris, John. *The Value of Life.* London: Routledge, 1985.

Haslanger, Sally. "Family, Ancestry and Self: What Is the Moral Significance of Biological Ties?" *Adoption and Culture* 2 (2009): 91–122.

Hodgson, Louis-Philippe. "Kant on the Right to Freedom: A Defense." *Ethics* 120 (July 2010): 791–819.

Holscher, Courtenay M., Joseph Leanza et al. "Anxiety, Depression and Regret of Donation in Living Kidney Donors." *BMV Nephrology* 19, no. 218 (2018).

Holt, John. *Escape from Childhood: The Needs and Rights of Children.* New York: E. P. Dutton, 1974.

Humbyrd, Casey. "Fair Trade International Surrogacy." *Developing World Bioethics* 9 (2009): 111–18.

Inhorn, Maria C. *Cosmopolitan Conceptions: IVF Sojourns in Global Dubai.* Durham NC: Duke University Press, 2015.

Jacobsen, Heather. *Labor of Love: Gestational Surrogacy and the Work of Making Babies.* New Brunswick, NJ: Rutgers University Press, 2016.

Kamm, Frances Myrna. "Equal Treatment and Equal Chances." *Philosophy & Public Affairs* 14 (1985): 177–94.

Kavka, Gregory. "The Paradox of Future Individuals." *Philosophy and Public Affairs* 11 (1982): 93–112.

Kazez, Jean. *The Philosophical Parent: Asking the Hard Questions about Having and Raising Children.* New York: Oxford University Press, 2017.

Keep, Lennlee. "Surrogacy Facts and Myths: How Much Do You Know?" *Independent Lens* (blog), PBS, October 22, 2019. https://www.pbs.org/inde pendentlens/blog/surrogacy-facts-and-myths-how-much-do-you-know/. Accessed July 10, 2022.

Klein, Renate. *Surrogacy: A Human Rights Violation.* Melbourne, AUS: Spinifex Press, 2017.

Kolers, Avery, and Tim Banye. '"Are You My Mommy?': On the Genetic Basis of Parenthood." *Journal of Applied Philosophy* 18 (2001): 273–85.

Kornegay, R. J. "Is Commercial Surrogacy Baby-Selling?" *Journal of Applied Philosophy* 7 (1990): 45–50.

Korsgaard, Christine. *Self-Constitution.* Oxford: Oxford University Press, 2009.

Krawiec, Kimberly D. "Price and Pretense in the Baby Market." In *Baby Markets: Money, Morals and the Neopolitics of Choice*, edited by Michele Bratcher Goodwin, 41–55. Cambridge: Cambridge University Press, 2009.

LaFollette, Hugh. "Licensing Parents." *Philosophy & Public Affairs* 9 (1980): 182–86.

LaFollette, Hugh. "Licensing Parents Revisited." *Journal of Applied Philosophy* 27 (2010): 327–43.

LaFollette, Hugh, ed. *The International Encyclopedia of Ethics*. Malden, MA: Wiley-Blackwell, 2013.

Lee, Eric. "Our Flawed Approach to Undue Inducement in Medical Research." *Bioethics* 33 (2019): 13–18.

Leroux, Marie-Louise, Pierre Pestieau, and Gregory Ponthiere. "Childlessness, Childfreeness and Compensation." *Social Choice and Welfare* 59 (2022): 1–35.

Lewis, Sophie. *Full Surrogacy Now: Feminist against Family*. Manchester: Manchester University Press, 2019.

Liao, Matthew. *The Right to Be Loved*. Oxford: Oxford University Press, 2015.

Locke, John. *Two Treatises of Government*. Rev. ed. Edited by Peter Laslett. Cambridge: Cambridge University Press, 1988.

Lotz, Mianna. "Rethinking Procreation: Why It Matters Why We Have Children." *Journal of Applied Philosophy* 28 (2011): 105–21.

Lynch, Catherine. "Putting Children First: What Adoption Can Teach Us about Surrogacy." In *Towards the Abolition of Surrogate Motherhood*, edited by Marie Josephe Devillers and Ana-Luana Stoicea-Deram. Melbourne, AUS: Spinifex Press, 2021.

MacCallum, Gerald. "Negative and Positive Freedom." *Philosophical Review* 76, no. 3 (1967): 312–34.

Macleod, Colin. "Agency, Authority and the Vulnerability of Children." In *The Nature of Children's Well-Being*, edited by Alexander Bagattini and Colin Macleod. New York: Springer, 2015.

Macleod, Colin. "Doctrinal Authority and the Authority of Children's Voices." In *Vulnerability, Autonomy and Applied Ethics*, edited by Christine Straehle. New York: Routledge, 2015.

Macleod, Colin. "Liberal Equality and the Affective Family." In Archard and Macleod, *Moral and Political Status of Children*, 212–30.

Macleod, Colin. "Parental Responsibilities in an Unjust World." In Archard and Benatar, *Procreation and Parenthood*, 128–50.

MacLeod, Mark. "Reimbursement of Expenditures and Possible Sub-delegation of the Assisted Human Reproduction Regulations." In *Surrogacy in Canada*, edited by V. Gruben, A. Cattapan, and A. Cameron, 113–54. Toronto: Irwin Law, 2018.

Magnusson, Erik. "Can Gestation Ground Parental Rights?" *Social Theory and Practice* 46 (2020): 111–42.

de Marneffe, Peter. *Liberalism and Prostitution*. Oxford: Oxford University Press, 2009.

McDonald, Christie. "Changing the Facts of Life: The Case of Baby M." *SubStance* 64 (1991): 31–48.

McLachlan, Hugh V., and J. K. Swales. "Babies, Child Bearers and Commodification: Anderson, Brazier et al., and the Political Economy of Commercial Surrogate Motherhood." *Health Care Analysis* 8 (2000): 1–18.

McMahan, Jeff. *The Ethics of Killing: Problems at the Margins of Life*. Oxford: Oxford University Press, 2002.

Mills, Catherine. "Nuclear Families: Mitochondrial Replacement Techniques and the Regulation of Parenthood." *Science, Technology, and Human Values* 46 (2021): 507–27.

Millum, Joseph. *The Moral Foundations of Parenthood*. Oxford: Oxford University Press, 2018.

Moody-Adams, Michelle. "On Surrogacy: Morality, Markets, and Motherhood." *Public Affairs Quarterly* 5 (1991): 175–90.

Moschella, Melissa. *To Whom Do Children Belong? Parental Rights, Civic Education, and Children's Autonomy*. Cambridge: Cambridge University Press, 2016.

Mullin, Amy. "Early Pregnancy Losses: Multiple Meanings and Moral Considerations." *Journal of Social Philosophy* 46 (2015): 27–43.

Nagel, Thomas. *Mortal Questions*. Oxford: Oxford University Press, 1980.

Narayan, Uma. "Family Ties: Rethinking Parental Claims in the Light of Surrogacy and Custody." In *Having and Raising Children: Unconventional Families, Hard Choices, and the Social Good*, edited by Uma Narayan and Julia J. Bartkowiak, 65–86. University Park: Pennsylvania State University Press, 1999.

Newson, Ainsley. "Ethical Aspects Arising from Non-invasive Fetal Diagnosis." *Seminars in Fetal and Neonatal Medicine* 13, no. 2 (April 2008): 103–8.

Noggle, Richard. "Special Agents: Children's Autonomy and Parental Authority." In Archard and Macleod, *Moral and Political Status of Children*, 97–117.

Nozick, Robert. *The Examined Life: Philosophical Meditations*. New York: Simon and Schuster, 1989.

Nozick, Robert. *Utopia, Anarchy, and the State*. New York: Basic Books, 1974.

Okin, Susan Moller. *Justice, Gender and the Family*. New York: Basic Books, 1989.

Olsaretti, Serena. "Liberal Equality and the Moral Status of Parent-Child Relationships." In *Oxford Studies in Political Philosophy*, vol. 3, edited by David Sobel, Peter Vallentyne, and Steven Wall, 58–83. New York: Oxford University Press, 2017.

Olsaretti, Serena. *Liberty, Desert and the Market: A Philosophical Study*. Cambridge: Cambridge University Press, 2004.

Overall, Christine. "The Good of Parenting." In Baylis and Mcleod, *Family Making*, 89–108.

Overall, Christine. "Reproductive 'Surrogacy' and Parental Licensing." *Bioethics* 29 (2015): 353–61.

Overall, Christine. *Why Have Children?* Cambridge, MA: MIT Press, 2012.

Page, Edgar. "Donation, Surrogacy and Adoption." *Journal of Applied Philosophy* 2 (1985): 161–72.

Page, Edgar. "Parental Rights." *Journal of Applied Philosophy* 1 (1984): 187–203.

Page, Edgar. "Review Article: Warnock and Surrogacy." *Journal of Medical Ethics* 12 (1986): 45–52.

Pande, Amrita. "'At Least I Am Not Sleeping with Anyone': Resisting the Stigma of Commercial Surrogacy in India." *Feminist Studies* 36 (2010): 292–314.

Pande, Amrita. "Gestational Surrogacy in India: New Dynamics in Reproductive Labour." In *Critical Perspective on Work and Employment in Globalizing India*, edited by Ernesto Noronha and Premilla D'Cruz, 267–82. New York: Springer, 2017.

Pande, Amrita. "Transnational Commercial Surrogacy in India: Gifts for Global Sisters?" *Reproductive BioMedicine* 23 (2011): 618–25.

Pande, Amrita. *Wombs in Labour: Transnational Surrogacy in India.* New York: Columbia University Press, 2014.

Panitch, Vida. "Global Surrogacy: Exploitation to Empowerment." *Journal of Global Ethics* 9 (2013): 329–43.

Panitch, Vida. "Surrogate Tourism and Reproductive Rights." *Hypatia* 28 (2013): 274–89.

Parfit, Derek. *Reasons and Persons.* Oxford. Oxford University Press, 1984.

Patel, Nayana Hitesh, and Yuvraj Digvijaysingh Jadeja. "Insight into Different Aspects of Surrogacy Practices." *Journal of Human Reproductive Sciences* 11 (2018): 212–18.

Perkins, Karin M., Sheree L. Boulet, Denise J. Jamieson, and Dmitry M. Kissin. "Trends and Outcomes of Gestational Surrogacy in the United States." Report for the National Assisted Reproductive Technology Surveillance System (NASS) Group. *Fertility and Sterility* 106 (2016): 435–42. http://www.ncbi.nlm.nih.gov/pubmed/27087401. Accessed July 10, 2022.

Pettit, Philip. *Republicanism: A Theory of Freedom and Government.* Oxford: Clarendon Press, 1997.

Porter, Lindsey. "Gestation and Parental Rights: Why Is Good Enough Good Enough?" *Feminist Philosophy Quarterly* 1 (2015): 1–27.

Porter, Lindsey. "Why and How to Prefer a Causal Account of Parenthood." *Journal of Social Philosophy* 45 (2014): 182–202.

Radcliffe-Richards, Janet. *The Ethics of Transplants.* Oxford: Oxford University Press, 2012.

Rapp, Rayna. "Gender, Body, Biomedicine: How Some Feminist Concerns Dragged Reproduction to the Centre of Social Theory." *Medical Anthropology Quarterly* 15 (2001): 466–77.

Rawls, John. *A Theory of Justice*. Cambridge, MA: Harvard University Press, 1999.

Raz, Joseph. *The Morality of Freedom*. Oxford: Oxford University Press, 1986.

Richards, Norvin. *The Ethics of Parenthood*. Oxford: Oxford University Press, 2010.

Rotbai, Karen Smith, Niocle Footen Bromfield, and Patricia Fronek. "International Private Law to Regulate Commercial Global Surrogacy Practices: Just What Are Social Work's Practical Policy Recommendations?" *International Social Work* 58 (2015): 575–81.

Rudrappa, Sharmila. *Discounted Life: The Price of Global Surrogacy in India*. New York: New York University Press, 2015.

Sansone, Antonella. *Mothers, Babies and Their Body Language*. London: Karnac, 2004.

Satz, Debra. *Why Some Things Should Not Be for Sale: The Moral Limits of Markets*. Oxford: Oxford University Press, 2010.

Scheffler, Samuel. "The Afterlife. Part I." In *Death and the Afterlife*, edited by Niko Kolodny. New York: Oxford University Press, 2013.

Shaffer, Michael J. "The Publicity of Belief, Epistemic Wrongs and Moral Wrongs." *Social Epistemology* 20, no. 1 (2006): 41–54.

Shalev, Camel. *Birth Power: Case for Surrogacy*. New Haven, CT: Yale University Press, 1989.

Shields, Liam. "Parental Rights and the Importance of Being Parents." *Critical Review of International Social and Political Philosophy* 22 (2019): 119–33.

Shiffrin, Seana. "Wrongful Life, Procreative Responsibility, and the Significance of Harm." *Legal Theory* 5 (1999):117–48.

Shklar, Judith. *American Citizenship*. Cambridge MA: Harvard University Books, 1998.

Snow, David. "Measuring Parentage Policy in the Canadian Provinces: A Comparative Framework." *Canadian Public Administration*, 59, no. 1 (March 2016): 5–25.

Snyder, Jeremy. "Exploitation and Sweatshop Labor: Perspectives and Issues." *Business Ethics Quarterly* 20 (2010): 187–213.

Srinivasan, Amia. *The Right to Sex*. Bloomsbury: London, 2021.

Stanzyk, Lucas. "Productive Justice." *Philosophy and Public Affairs* 40 (2012): 144–64.

Steinbock, Bonnie. "Surrogate Motherhood as Prenatal Adoption." *Law, Medicine & Health Care* 16 (1988): 44–50.

Steiner, Hillel. *An Essay on Rights*. Oxford: Blackwell. 1994.

Straehle, Christine. "Is There a Right to Surrogacy?" *Journal of Applied Philosophy* 33 (2016): 146–59.

Straehle, Christine. "Solidarity, Social Deprivation and Refugee Agency: What Does It Mean to Stand in Solidarity with Refugees?" *Journal of Social Philosophy* 51 (2020): 526–41.

Straehle, Christine. "Vulnerability, Autonomy and Self Respect." In Straehle, *Vulnerability, Autonomy and Applied Ethics*.

Taylor, Charles. "What's Wrong with Negative Liberty." In *Philosophy and the Human Sciences*, 187–210. Cambridge: Cambridge University Press, 1985.

Titmuss, Robert M. *The Gift Relationship*. London: Georg Allen, 1970.

United Nations. Convention on the Rights of the Child. Adopted and opened for signature, ratification and accession by General Assembly resolution 44/25 of 20 November 1989, Entry into force: 2 September 1990, in accordance with article 49. Office of the High Commissioner of Human Rights. https://www.ohchr.org/en/professionalinterest/pages/crc.aspx.

Vallentyne, Peter. "The Rights and Duties of Childrearing." *William & Mary Bill of Rights Journal* 11 (2003): 991–1009.

van der Vossen, Bas. "Libertarianism." *The Stanford Encyclopedia of Philosophy* (Fall 2023 edition).

Velleman, David. "Against the Right to Die." *Journal of Medicine and Philosophy* 17, no. 6 (1992): 665–81.

Velleman, David. "Family History." *Philosophical Papers* 34 (2005): 357–78.

Verrier, Nancy Newton. *The Primal Wound: Understanding the Adopted Child*. Baltimore, MD: Gateway Press, 1993.

Vopat, Mark. "Parent Licensing and the Protecting of Children." In *Taking Responsibility for Children*, edited by Samantha Brennan and Robert Noggle, 73–96. Waterloo, CAN: Wilfrid Laurier University Press, 2007.

Waldron, Jeremy. "Property and Ownership." *The Stanford Encyclopedia of Philosophy* (2016).

Walker, Ruth, and Liezl van Zyl. *Towards a Professional Model of Surrogacy*. London: Palgrave Macmillan, 2017.

Warnock, Mary. *A Question of Life: Warnock Report on Human Fertilisation and Embryology*. Oxford: Oxford University Press, 1984.

Warnock, Mary. *Report of the Committee of Inquiry into Human Fertilisation and Embryology*. London: Her Majesty's Stationery Office, 1984.

Wasserman, David. "The Nonidentity Problem, Disability, and the Role Morality of Prospective Parents." *Ethics* 116 (2015): 132–52.

Weinstock, Daniel, and Jurgen De Wisperlaere. "State Regulation and Assisted Reproduction: Balancing the Interests of Parents and Children." In Baylis and Mcleod, *Family-Making*, 131–50.

Weisberg, Kelly. *The Birth of Surrogacy in Israel*. Tampa: University of Florida Press, 2005.

Wenar, Leif. "Rights." *Stanford Encyclopedia of Philosophy*, edited by Edward N. Zalta and Uri Nodelman (Spring 2020). https://plato.stanford.edu/entries/rights/.

Whitbeck, Caroline. "The Maternal Instinct." In *Mothering: Essays in Feminist Theory*, edited by Joyce Trebilcot, 185–98. Totowa, NJ: Rowman & Allanheld, 1984.

Wilkinson, Stephen. *Bodies for Sale: Ethics and Exploitation in the Human Body Trade*. London: Routledge, 2003.

Wilkinson, Stephen. "The Ethics and Economics of Minimum Wage." *Economics and Philosophy* 20 (2004): 351–74.

Wilkinson, Stephen. "Exploitation in International Surrogacy Agreements." *Journal of Applied Philosophy* 33 (2016): 125–45.

Williams, Bernard. "Voluntary Acts and Responsible Agents." *Oxford Journal of Legal Studies* 10 (1990): 1–10.

Witt, Charlotte. "A Critique of the Bionormative Concept of the Family." In Baylis and Mcleod, *Family-Making*, 49–63.

Index

For the benefit of digital users, indexed terms that span two pages (e.g., 52–53) may, on occasion, appear on only one of those pages.